A Path Prepared

A Path Prepared

*The Story of Isa A. Northage,
with accounts of her
mediumship including
Healing and Materialisation*

Written and Compiled
by

Allan MacDonald M.S.F.

© Saturday Night Press Publications

All rights of the owners reserved. Except for brief quotations
in critical articles or reviews, no part of
this book may be reproduced in any manner
without prior written permission
of the owners, authors or publisher.

First printed privately circa 1960
This Edition printed 2012

Published by
Saturday Night Press Publications
England
snppbooks@gmail.com
www.snppbooks.com

ISBN 978 1 908 421 04 3

Printed by Lightning Source
www.lightningsource.com

Dedication

To all those dedicated people in both worlds who worked together to make the 'miracles' recorded in this book possible, showing us just what can be achieved by love and dedication.

Ann Harrison

Acknowledgements

My gratitude goes to Lew Sutton and Freddie Giddings for the time they have taken in scanning the text and illustrations from copies of the original book when I was unable to obtain a copy myself.

My thanks go to Violet Eccles who told me of the mediumship of Isa Northage and the existence of the book; to Nicky Bone, Vice-President of the London Spiritual Mission who found the book for me in their library; and to Christine Carlin for responding to a request for help.

I send an extra special thank you to her mother, Hannah Carlin for writng the Foreword to this edition and for supplying the photograph of the completed church.

The extracts from the Two Worlds are again reprinted by kind permission of the present Editor, Mr Tony Ortzen.

Ann Harrison
Saturday Night Press Publications

Acknowledgements
in the First Edition

The extracts from the Two Worlds are reprinted by kind permission of the Editor, Mr Maurice Barbanell (1960)

Contents

		Page
Foreword	by Hannah A. Carlin	9
Introduction by Allan Macdonald		11
Chapter 1	Pinewoods Healing Church	15
Chapter 2	Early Days	19
Chapter 3	Church Work, Travels and Phenomena	44
Chapter 4	Healing	101
Chapter 5	Experiments	130
Chapter 6	Dr Reynolds Operates	185
Chapter 7	Apports – with Illustrations	201
Chapter 8	'Towards the Light'	215
Glossary of terms		242
Some examples of spiritual gifts		245

List of Illustrations

Portrait of Dr Reynolds	14
Pinewoods altar and chancel	14
Preparing the site (4 pictures)	17
Isa Northage outside the completed church	18
Isa A. Northage	21
Flask containing tumour	187
Malignant growth from the pancreas	200
Silver case and ring	202
Ivory cross	202
Nun's cross and chain	203
Scrap of paper from scribe's inkpot	204
Large bronze vases from China (apported 1936)	205
Apports received in 1937 (4 pictures)	206
Religious apports received 1940 & 48 (4 pictures)	207
Apports received in 1941 (4 pictures)	208
Apported message from prisoners of war	209
Production of ectoplasm by Isa A. Northage	210
Principle spirit helpers of Isa A. Northage	211
Sailors' (materialised) cap bands	212
Photograph with spirit extras	214

Foreword

As the youngest child of Isa Northage, growing up I participated in some of the experiments in this book, *A Path Prepared*. It seemed perfectly natural in our home to see objects move, to see the table we ate at rise and we would say, "Put the table down, Sambo, we know you are with us." The information in the séances and experiments are all true. I was a witness to the apports arriving and the Christmas tree with the spirit children materializing to share the gifts their parents put on the tree.

As a schoolgirl I helped mother to take the bread to the sanctuary to go to our military prisoners captured by the enemy in World War II. Sometimes, if we were late, as soon as the Sanctuary door closed the bread would dematerialize from our arms. Other times we would leave it and it would be gone when we went back.

From the beginning, through experiments with ectoplasm from which materializations built, I was there.

Before I close I would like to mention my brother's son John Northage. He passed into spirit January 29, 2012. John was the one in our family who inherited my mother's gifts. As a healer John was gifted and amazing like his grandmother. John was clairaudient, clairvoyant but very humble about his gifts.

I would like to thank Ann Harrison for the reprinting of this book for future generations as a continuing story of my mother's work.

Hannah A. Carlin (nee Nina Northage)
March 18, 2012

Introduction

It is indeed very difficult to try and comply with so many requests from all walks of life for a story covering the varied and outstanding life of such a personality as Isa A. Northage whose mediumistic abilities in every phase of phenomena to which her life has been devoted have also been given to helping those less fortunate souls who were in need of help. Her manifold gifts of clairaudience, clairvoyance, direct voice, telekinesis, materialisation, apports, etc., are now carried on in church and sanctuary, both of which she built to give her time to those in need.

In very early childhood she first heard 'voices' which, to the young mind were similar to the experience of many children, so often called 'playing with fairies', but so persistent were these and of such compelling beauty and command that she eventually sort a dear friend, Canon Jackson, of Delaval Hall Church, and as a child will chatter to such an understanding soul, she told him all her troubles. After listening to her story the Canon very wisely replied: "You are another Samuel. Treasure your gifts from God, my child. Some day you will make good use of them." I can well understand, in that bleak north-east coast town, among simple, kindly, hardworking folk, that no time could be spared to cultivate any gifts while life was so hard and rough. Yet, this rugged coast town, with its solitude and the child's loneliness, seemed to lend itself to the spirit world which must have seemed very close to her, and who better to contact spirit than a child in all its trusting simplicity; more so, an unspoilt child?

I have often met the parents of this lady, kind, honest, outspoken, and full of plain common sense, with little time for wishful thinking. Only the hard facts of everyday life mattered in the struggle to bring up a family fifty years ago. Today, Mr and

Mrs Phillips, the parents of Isa A. Northage, still, whenever able, visit their daughter and attend the church.

Those, who, like myself have shared for many years the company and friendship of this medium, esteem it an honour and privilege to share in her work and experiments, and we realise the tremendous task we undertake to try to bring before a material world something that is everyone's birthright.

Yet, so forsaken or ridiculed is such, that to ask one to try to study or understand, finds little sympathy, indeed none at all, in those who will not trouble, either to investigate or accept this evidence. Yet the very book they profess to believe in, the Holy Bible, contains the greatest collection of spiritual and psychic phenomena ever written.

To us and those who have sat with us, have returned from spirit, people of all creeds and colours, of all nations, both highly progressed souls and undeveloped, to help and to receive help.

Among those who have returned are doctors, scientists, clergy and writers, bringing evidence of the continuity of life and ever ready to serve mankind.

Many people accuse us of subjecting ourselves to wrong influences and all the wickedness of sin is laid at our door. Is this the way wrong influences would speak with you?

"Seek truth with pure motives, and although you may be in darkness, yet surely you will be guided into light."

Or again: "There is naught in life more solemn than the waiting hush that falls before the coming of the great change men call death – to watch, as it were, for the gate of death to open and the great revelation to flash for one blinding moment upon the dazzled eyes that may not grasp the meaning of what they see ; this is to stand, for a space, within the very sanctuary of God."– (Direct Voice – Doctor Reynolds).

We do not publish this book with any desire for publicity; we have always refrained from such, even to the extent that on more than one occasion we have prepared for an operation, only to find it has not taken place because publicity-seeking people were present for sensation purposes and the publication of such an operation which the public were not ready to understand would have started controversy and built up hopes in suffering souls, whilst we were, as yet, far from ready to deal with large numbers of people. The disappointments would have been tremendous to those who could not receive treatment.

We therefore now feel we can disclose some of the experiments we are doing, whilst still in the experimental stage, because, in the not too distant future, we trust we shall have reached that point when we are able to receive large numbers of people and heal them.

This then is our purpose, briefly, in making our work known and in publishing our experiments, and to show the gradual development of our leader in her mediumship, who, of her own free will has given so much of her life to be of service to God and man.

The many material disappointments, setbacks and difficulties encountered were, to say the least, discouraging. The loss of 'friends' and the personal problems met with so often in this work, was sorrowful, yet with such a goal in view, nothing could be allowed to stand in the way.

Throughout life, under the guidance and companionship of ministering angels, difficulties gradually smoothed out and our work has now reached a point where we see the fruits of sacrifice.

It is hoped the events here recorded will cause people to think more deeply of God's love at all times, and also of life's continuity. It may perhaps encourage them to re-read their Bible in a new light and understanding, and know that so-called miracles and ministering angels are as close and intimate today as they have been since the beginning of time.

Perhaps also, these events may help mankind to prepare himself for his new life, when God calls him.

None among us who has been privileged to share in this work claims praise; all praise belongs to God and His angel messengers and to our leader Isa A. Northage.

The author would like to express his grateful thanks to all who have contributed in any way to the experiences recorded in this book and especially to the one whose efforts have done so much for humanity.

Allan Macdonald.

Top: Portrait of Doctor Reynolds – painting taken from sketch of Doctor whilst he materialised in white electric light.

The glass containers also shown were 'apported'. When used for ceremonial purposes such as Baptism, Marriages, Ordination, etc., they are filled with liquid, also 'apported'.

Below: Altar and Chancel.

The Church's motto is "Action not Words".

Chapter One

Pinewoods

"Know ye not, that ye are the temple of God and that the Spirit of God dwelleth within you?"

It was in the summer of 1949 that a group of friends from Northumberland were staying at Pinewoods, in the grounds of Newstead Abbey, a lovely woodland setting in the heart of Nottinghamshire. Most of them were convalescing after being cured by 'Doctor' Isa, and to occupy their time were amusing and busying themselves by putting up boundary fences round about Pinewoods, when two airmen arrived for further treatment from 'Dr' Isa. There was in the garden at that time a small wooden sanctuary where experiments in direct voice and materialisations were held. 'Dr' Isa being engaged at that moment, the two airmen walked quietly into the sanctuary and kneeling before the altar offered their prayers and thanks to God that they were being cured after the plane crashes in which they were injured.

A little later, 'Dr' Isa being ready, the friends went to seek them and found them kneeling in front of the altar. it was the sight of this simple act of reverence and thanks to God which inspired them to build a brick church, a permanent edifice which they could beautify for people who were sick, a place in which to thank God for being made well again.

Plans and specifications were drawn up for the councils and other authorities, and on approval being given, the actual building commenced. It can be truly said that all sorts and conditions of men applied themselves to the task, and the enthusiasm was such that they lived on the job, giving up their holidays and all the available time they could. A small canteen was in daily operation, and so the church took shape, built by the voluntary labour of love under skilled technical guidance.

Among those who so willingly helped, felling trees, levelling ground, and clearing the site were the daughter and granddaughter of 'Dr' Isa, and to see men who had been recently cured of heart, cancer, ulcer troubles, etc., using pick and shovel with such gusto was indeed evidence of the healing work accomplished in the Sanctuary.

When the church was completed the dedication service was conducted by one of the ministers, Mr D. Liveridge. After the address, Dr Reynolds controlling 'Dr' Isa, gave his blessing and a short talk in which he spoke of the future work and thanked all who had helped in any way.

It became necessary to ordain ministers, and certain people who had worked to produce the church were chosen. For the purpose of ordination, wine and water were required, the water to be used for the blessing. A vessel was placed upon the altar and Dr Reynolds apported the liquid to be used. The liquid has a slightly heavier density than normal water and has a beautiful fragrance. This is apported straight into the glass container. After due preparation the ordinands are assembled before the altar and kneeling during the ceremony, partake of a little wine as in the Confirmation Service, and the sign of the Cross is made on each breast with the apported water. During this part of the service Dr Reynolds is ready to control 'Dr' Isa and give his blessing after he had given a short address.

It is perhaps interesting to know that Dr Reynolds is fully aware of all our individual activities in daily life and conduct, and furthermore when necessary will inform each minister if his way of life is not compatible with his position.

All with whom we have had the pleasure of working have expressed gratitude, and have contributed in many ways towards the furnishing of the church. Those who could afford to bought a chair and had the name of a loved one who had passed on placed upon the back of the chair.

The members of the church, from the funds they provided, bought carpet curtain and linen. The altar, pulpit and rostrum were

Top Left: Site for Church   *Top Right:* Removing trees
Lower: Clearing the site

erected by the ministers. The floor design in front of the altar is for experiments and future work. The altar Cross and memorial Cross were made by a minister of the church. The Cross on the beam before the altar is a mark of gratitude from the Belgian Underground Movement – 1940-45. The figure of Jesus and the lamb was apported as detailed in this book. The organ was given in gratitude to Dr Reynolds. The members contribute towards the upkeep and maintenance and any further costs are borne by

'Dr' Isa, as there is no standing fund or outside financial aid the burden is not light but the reward is great.

This is the short and simple story of the erection of Pinewoods Healing Church where services are conducted each Sunday by men and women who have been cured of many and various ailments by Dr Reynolds through 'Dr' Isa Northage, and in the seven years life of the church many miracles of healing have been performed.

Isa Northage(right) and friend outside the completed Pinewoods Healing Church.

Chapter Two

Early Days

'Dr' Northage tells of her first experiences.

On 16th April, 1916, feeling lonely as my fiancé Kit Dixon was overseas serving his country; I walked to the woods as we usually did when together. Being a fine day I sat for a while in the quiet, my thoughts naturally on Kit.

Quite unexpectedly the whole scene changed around me and I seemed to be looking onto a battlefield of torn buildings and shell-potted roads. Mounted soldiers were returning along the roadway and suddenly I heard a rifle shot and saw Kit fall from his horse: another of the troop rode forward, aimed his rifle at the tree and fired, bringing down a German sniper. I saw this soldier then return and kneel by Kit whom I knew had been fatally wounded. When the vision faded I was dreadfully shaken and returned home. From previous experiences I knew what this vision meant. Mother, seeing my distress, made some tea, and as we sat, she waited for me to explain. Having told her, she tried to comfort me and suggested I dismiss the whole thing. I could only reply: "It came and I believe." We did not refer to this matter again.

Some letters arrived from France requesting me to make arrangements for our wedding as my fiancé had been granted leave. Retiring one evening and regarding his photo by my bedside I furtively hoped my vision was not real. I was soon asleep, but shortly afterwards awoke, feeling someone was in my room and then the vision again appeared, so real and life-like that I could not restrain my feelings and in despair cried : "Oh, Kit!" My whole world had collapsed. Time passed until 9th July, 1916, when I received the usual sad letter informing me that Kit had been killed.

Hoping to be of service myself I joined the W.R.A.F. New surroundings and people helped me a little and I tried my best to find forgetfulness in the service, soon, in 1917, becoming a Section Leader. I became great friends with a Nurse Brown who was serving with me. She was suffering from nervous trouble, having had some very frightening war experiences. We often walked together and on this particular day had set out for a quiet country stroll.

Soon we heard the droning of a Zeppelin and bombs began to fall. Already suffering from nervous tension, Nurse became hysterical and I could not control her. In my dilemma I cried: "If there is a God who can hear me, please help me." At once a man's voice replied: "Take off your coat and put it over her head." This was repeated three times and there was not a soul in sight. I obeyed the voice, and as Nurse became quieter I tried to half carry and half drag her to the camp. Nurse Brown was eventually discharged on medical grounds.

About six months later, still serving in the W.R.A.F. I was collecting my mail which included a letter from France. This was from Kit's soldier friend, Jack Northage who was with Kit in France. He stated that he had a message for me and some personal belongings of Kit which he would like to deliver personally. We agreed to meet when we had leave about the same time and eventually did so and after delivering his message from Kit, Jack told me this story.

They were riding along the road to return to base and leave when Kit was shot through the heart by a German sniper; he at once fell to the ground. Jack saw the sniper and shot him and then, returning to Kit, he at once knew the shot was fatal. After uttering a few words Kit died in his arms. This distressing event so absorbed his attention that he forgot his own danger until he was himself shot in the shoulder. On his way to the dressing station he was caught in a gas attack with the result that he spent six months in hospital, and this was his first leave; my vision was true in every detail.

It was always in times of imminent danger that the Voice spoke to me and advised me. We married, after a long correspondence, in the New Year following the Armistice.

Isa A. Northage

In the difficult times that followed I formed a small orchestra for entertaining people wherever we were required. For a time everything went quite well. Then I began to see faces, and people standing before me and in front of the music stand. They indicated a desire to speak to me and gave me tunes they knew and messages for their own folks who believed them dead. These requests and visions grew to such proportions that I gave up the orchestra and devoted my time to the needs of these 'visitors'.

One evening when alone, I played *Sanctuary of the Heart* and from out of the air a tenor voice sang the whole song through. I knew that Kit was the singer; it was his favourite song.

People began to hear of my gifts and requests to show my work in public rapidly poured in.

At this time a well-known psychic paper described a meeting I attended at Matlock, Derbyshire. 'It was held in a small and well-lighted hall. I stood beside a small table on which was a vase of flowers. While I was addressing the audience the flowers left the vase and floated above the heads of the people and, following this, when the table with the vase still on it rose several inches above the floor I was as surprised as the audience. This was in April 1937, and from then on the phenomena increased in many different ways.

I decided to continue with whatever work I was requested to do. I felt that this was the desire of those who had given me these gifts and I started to experiment and have continued to do so ever since.

Although quite a number of spirit entities have attached themselves to me throughout the years and still return on occasions, there are three ever present who guide and control the séances, these being Dr Reynolds, who practised on earth about 150 years ago, Chedioack (affectionately known as Sambo) a West African negro, and Ellen Dawes, a Yorkshire girl.

The spirit voice that spoke to me in 1917, the voice which spoke to me on many subsequent occasions I later came to know as that of Dr Reynolds. It was through his influence that I gave up the ordinary way of life and concentrated on ascertaining more about the great gifts which God had bestowed upon me.

Sambo first made his presence known in the early days of my experimenting with a trumpet which is a miniature kind of megaphone made of aluminium for lightness and with a luminous band around the broad end to enable it to be visible as it levitates in the darkened séance room. On the occasion in question, the trumpet which was standing on a table, rose a few inches and from it there came a gurgling sound. Obviously someone was trying to communicate with the sitters, but it was not until the voice became stronger during subsequent sittings that it revealed itself in broken English to be that of the West African Negro previously mentioned. He had passed into spirit many years ago at the age of nineteen following a bout of fever. He has endeared himself to all and is a most lovable and loyal entity who has attached himself to me as my bodyguard, watching over me whenever I am in trance, It was also at one of these early experimental sittings that a sweet voice whispered through the trumpet:

"Mother, speak to me, it is Ellen." The feelings of that mother upon hearing her daughter's voice again cannot be expressed in words. It was the voice of Ellen Dawes, who was also aged only nineteen when she passed into spirit and said she was helping the Negro (Sambo) and would be with him all the time he was attached to me in my work.

In the early years of my mediumship I travelled a great deal to give talks and demonstrations on psychic matters, but eventually, through Dr Reynolds, I was brought to realise there was a greater work for me to do and from then onwards in my Sanctuary and in my surgery I have in my humble way ministered to many people of various races and creeds who have come to me for spiritual help and healing. Through Dr Reynolds' guidance and with the help of Sambo and Ellen, rapid and startling progress has been made during later years.

The early sittings were mainly devoted to experiments with different powers and colours of light in order to establish the most suitable combinations for voices, materialisations, apports, etc., and to establish other links or circles in different parts of the country. These links always sat at the same time on the same day of the week so that Dr Reynolds could draw upon an accumulated source of power for his experiments. It was during these early sittings that much valuable knowledge was gained concerning the different types of ectoplasm, the substance which emanates from various points of the medium's body when in trance and through which spirit entities are able to materialise and become visible to the sitters.

In this was built up a power which enabled me not only to bring home to so many the truths and comforts of spirit return and communication, but greatest of all to enable Dr Reynolds and his band of helpers from the spirit world to perform operations on mortal beings in cases such as cancer, tumour, duodenal ulcer, etc. in some instances where they had been given up by medical men as being incurable. Some of these people are still helping me in my work of healing, and once again enjoy a normal and healthy life. I shall have more to say about spirit operations and healing later on.

From these early experimental meetings and through the dominating and driving force of Dr Reynolds has been established The Sanctuary, a centre to which many come daily, seeking spiritual healing and up-liftment. Here I have gathered around me a circle of friends who have sought and found much knowledge about the higher side of life, and how, with the help of those from the spirit world so much can be done to aid and alleviate the mental and physical conditions to which we earth people are subject. They give their time and labour freely in service to those in need of assistance, irrespective of social standing, colour or creed. They try to carry into effect some words spoken by Ellen Dawes: "He who lifteth his brother, who giveth the helping hand, and who sustaineth in love, buildeth for himself the elements of spirituality. Whatever the nature; he who giveth in love, receiveth in proportion to that which he giveth."

Now let me pass on to you some messages of wisdom and truth given by Dr Reynolds from the spirit world, messages which I hope will further uplift those of you who already believe and may sow a seed of thought among those who do not. I once asked Dr Reynolds if there was anything worthwhile for us earth children in psychic phenomena, to which he replied : "Of course there is – it is a religion, a science, and a philosophy, and a genuine psychic is a very learned man or woman. But remember to seek truth with pure motives and although you may be in darkness, yet surely you will be guided into light."

Speaking of the experiments he would carry out Dr Reynolds said they were a challenge to the unbeliever and a support to every person who believed. "The mass of evidence I am going to present," he said, "is from my own experiences and from those of many of the greatest thinkers who have made the change called death. We know that we can materialise out of something less than air and go back into the same 'nothingness'. There is a supernatural and spiritual world in which human spirits, good and bad, live in a state of consciousness. These spirits may, according to the order of God's laws in their places of habitation, have intercourse with your earth world and become visible mortals. Death is only the beginning of a new and infinitely better life. Possessing this certainty, while we feel a deep regret and a poignant sense of loss on the passing of a loved one, we should not grieve because of their promotion.

"As well grieve because a worm has broken through its cocoon and become a winged thing of beauty shining in the sunlight. When the earth world accepts these facts as truths, then you shall know that death should leave small occasion for grief. You shall realise that the seed of life is encased only for a time in the flesh and that when it has completed the particular cycle of growth it will blossom into the fruition of being, evoluting for eternity in the spiral of ever-growing consciousness.

"There is naught in life so solemn as the waiting hush that falls before the coming of that great change which men call death, and it is to the watchers rather than to the passing soul itself that the wonder seems to draw closest. To stand before the veil, to know that very soon it must be lifted for the loved one to pass beyond; to wait for a glimpse of the spirit world, from which only the frail wall of mortality divides even the least spiritual; to watch, as it were, for the gate of death to open and the great revelation to flash for one blinding moment upon the dazzled eyes that may not grasp the meaning of what they see; this is to stand for a space within the very sanctuary of God."

It is perhaps only natural that you will be wondering if the search for spiritual knowledge gives any information regarding, conditions in the higher life and in what ways, if any, you can so order your life here on earth as to prepare yourselves for it: whether it will be possible for you, having passed through the veil called death to return and contact those loved ones you have left behind on the earth. Once again let me quote Dr Reynolds, and I would ask you to note how in his opening words he infers that spirit life is only a continuation of life here on earth.

"There may be some who would like to know whether all their faculties will be retained when they reach this side of life. To such I would answer, yes – all faculties are retained in spirit life. Not one of them is dropped or lost at transition, but gradually the functions are so changed as to subserve the uses and needs of the spirit as advanced conditions allow and demand. So whatever legitimate and natural desires you may have will still be susceptible of complete fulfilment in the life eternal.

"In my investigations of conditions in the spirit world I find there are those who do not realise that there is a possibility and a way of spirit return to those yet inhabiting the mortal form. I find others who do not care to return. On the other hand I meet some whose highest heaven is hunting up the darkened ones and teaching them the way of light and life. I meet those who do not realise they are out of the mortal body and whom it takes guides a long time to lead to a consciousness of their true condition.

"Again, I meet some who are absolutely lost and in total darkness because of false theological training whilst on earth. Such go in search of a personal God seated on a great white throne, and their Saviour, the only begotten Son of God, sitting at the right hand of God with great convoys of angels flying in the midst of the heavens and round the Throne with golden harps in their hands. From birth until they reached the hour of death these souls never knew, heard or dreamed of any possibly different conditions to meet them in the great Beyond. These are the hardest of all to lead to the real and saving truth and light. They only knew what the priests told them and were greatly disappointed to find these things they had been promised were not there. But, my friends, words cannot express the trouble and awful retribution awaiting those teachers of false doctrine who did not themselves believe their own teachings. When they pass to this side of life they hear those who were once their disciples asking them, 'Where is our Saviour you told us about? Where shall we find the great city of paved streets, the golden throne, and the harps of gold?' All clouds of false teaching must be rolled away and those lost ones must be redeemed from darkened conditions by being filled with knowledge and truth instead of the false and darkened theology of ignorant priests and people. This is the sad result of false teachings by those who themselves were utterly ignorant of the actual conditions of those who pass on and whose blind followers find themselves in a very uncomfortable condition."

Those speaking from the spirit world frequently stress that conditions on earth which bring about untold misery and distress are the result of the misuse by man, for his own selfishness and power, of that great gift of free will, given by God to every one of us. Particularly is this referred to in reference to the world conflicts which we have unfortunately seen so much of in our time. If only there was a much wider knowledge of spiritual matters, and especially of the retribution exacted on the other side for our failings here on earth, a tremendous improvement in all conditions of earth life would ensue.

Speaking on this theme, Dr Reynolds said: "When man fully realises that his every action is being recorded for and against him; when he is convinced that it is not what he professes to do, but what he does of good that matters, and is quite certain that he is his brother's keeper; when he knows the truth that he is not on earth solely for his own pleasure and comfort, and can realise that the earth life is but a testing, qualifying span for the development of character and spiritual senses in a world which man has made more difficult than need be; when it is recognized that all men, good or bad, of whatever race, colour or belief are children of the great Creator, then and only then will peace and happiness reign on earth, and cruelty, suffering, dread, and worry be banished."

Such a state of perfection as represented in these words of Dr Reynolds would be bringing about what our Lord endeavoured to make mankind understand many years ago. We may or may not be nearer to it than were the people of His day, but there is something each of us can do and that is to govern our every action in life towards our fellow men with love and tolerance; to let our every thought, word, and deed be actuated by unselfish motives and in service to God, the great Creator of all earth children.

If you have attended séances you may know something about the organisation which takes place in connection with them, especially the arrangement of the séance room and what is expected of the sitters. You will know that spirit entities speak both in the direct voice and through trumpets; that some of them, when powerful enough to do so, manifest themselves or materialise in various light formations, and often speak to those they wish to contact. But what do you know concerning the organisation taking place on the spirit side, and which is more important than what you have witnessed in the séance room? For without it there would not be any communication at all between their world and ours. They do in fact from the other side work to law and order, and the smoothness of the whole proceedings of a séance is a perfect example of intelligent organisation on their part. What we will term the Band of Friends in spirit all play their special parts. There are the Bodyguards whose business it is to protect the medium's physical body while in trance, not only against possible interference from evil spirit entities which might attempt to take possession of the body during that state, but also to guard against physical shock through the foolishness, or mischievous curiosity of any of the sitters. For any action on their part interfering with the ectoplasm emanating from the medium's body, which during trance is still an integral part of the physical body, could cause very serious bodily harm through shock, and bring about haemorrhage, and even death. Then there is the Controlling Spirit who determines which of the many entities attracted to the séance shall be allowed to speak or manifest, and who also decides when the medium's body has been used sufficiently for the one occasion, and frees him or her from the trance state. There are also those appointed to prepare entities for materialisation: to those making a first return since their passing this is quite an ordeal. Again, there are those who have the important duty of guarding and watching the 'manifestors' during the time they are in contact with the physical or material plane. Indeed these beings who carry out the duties of watching and guarding have been long trained to them, as it requires much experience of earth return to enable a spirit to remain in materialised form for any length of time. For there have been instances in my own psychic experience where spirit entities could have become earth bound through their unwillingness to obey the control of the guardians. I have also suffered severe physical shock, being temporarily blinded through the lack of understanding and foolish curiosity of a sitter flashing a bright light on me whilst I was in a state of trance. On another occasion, thanks to the vigilance of my bodyguard Sambo, I was saved from much more serious harm, when he locked the hands of a sitter who foolishly tried to take a sample of ectoplasm with a pair of scissors.

To appreciate these dangers, one has to witness ectoplasm being drawn from the medium's body, through the mouth, nose, ears, or the solar plexus, to see how it moves and vibrates gently all the time in tune with the heart-beats of the medium. It is this living ectoplasm which enables spirit friends to move and speak. Under good conditions the flow of ectoplasm may broaden into a wide ribbon of such length as to circle completely a sitting of twelve or more persons. Again it may be in the form of a block of ectoplasm from which the spirit clothes itself in order to materialise. This block will first move slightly from the floor, a hand will protrude, and then the ectoplasm slowly expand both upwards and downwards, a face will build up in the upper portion, a body in the lower, and in this way a fully materialised form appears before the sitters. So you will see from the foregoing that a séance is not merely a getting together with a set purpose of a few people on this side, but that it requires contacts with the spirit world, and much organisation from their side also.

At this point it will not come amiss to say something about mediumship, and I cannot do better than quote the words spoken by a spirit friend who, during his earth life was a well-known Parliamentarian and much interested in the rights of mediums: "I am afraid that mediumship is gravely misunderstood not only by the public, but by those who profess to understand the return of spirit. The 'nature' of the medium is one of peculiar psychic impressibility or extreme sensitiveness to certain vibrations and forces. The average person cannot appreciate the acute sensations to which a medium is susceptible. Imagine one whose nerves are exposed to the elements, and some idea may be formed of the sensitive or psychic condition of the medium in a trance state. How essential it is therefore to prepare a calm and harmonious atmosphere in the séance room. A discordant influence such as antagonism, prejudice, grief, or jest, may easily prove a source of pain to a sensitive medium, and may distort any psychic phenomena or even inhibit it altogether. A genuine medium is simply a channel through which spirit forces function; a passive agent, and therefore largely irresponsible."

Earlier, I made mention of the wonderful powers of healing possessed by some of the spirit entities and even of operations being performed on mortal beings. To the uninitiated this statement will doubtless sound very much like a flight of fancy, but I can assure you that the incidents I am about to relate did actually take place and there are many to bear witness to them besides those on whom the operations were actually performed. In all cases I was the medium through whom Dr Reynolds worked and in several instances he had other doctors present from the spirit world. Dr Reynolds has in fact gathered around him a number of friends who, like himself, were of the medical profession during their earth lives and who on the other side are still interested in such work. These doctors still possess in spirit the faculties they had on earth as you and I will retain whatever powers we now have and which will be susceptible of complete fulfilment in the spirit life providing our desires are legitimate and natural.

First, let me tell you about an operation for tumour on the brain, this account being given from notes taken at the time by one of the helpers during the time I was in trance, being the medium through whom Dr Reynolds worked. The patient in this case was a boy aged fourteen who had been operated upon a few years previously in hospital. The doctors had told the mother that a cure was impossible and nothing further could be done. As it had been impossible to remove the tumour completely, the roots would remain, only to grow again and each succeeding operation would be worse than the previous one. Since the operation, the boy David had gradually got worse, his eyesight was seriously affected, and blindness feared. It had been arranged for him to learn Braille. The tumour had also retarded his growth. The mother, having given her consent brought David to the Sanctuary on the date fixed, but preferred to stay in another room leaving the boy in the care of a friend who was present throughout and witnessed everything that took place. Present also in the flesh were myself (the medium) one female and three male assistants. The operation was performed by the light of a 25watt ruby lamp, in addition to which Dr Reynolds used a red flash-lamp. Dr Reynolds materialised throughout the entire operation and continually drew the attention of the assisting healers to his actions, giving the reasons for them. His hands were clearly seen during the whole period, except for those moments when they sank into the patient's head.

As he completed the operation Dr Reynolds turned to those present and said: "I have been assisted this evening by Dr Bernard Hollander. Before taking the case we decided, as the roots of the tumour were deep-seated, to kill the tumour, leaving it to shrivel and in so doing destroy the roots as well. It will not grow again or adversely affect the boy. We will watch it closely and in a few months' time, when all signs of life have gone from it, will dematerialise it and take it completely away. The tumour is of long-standing; we are glad to have got it away now; in another two years it would have been too late. From now on the boy will gradually begin to grow, his eyesight will be better and you will find him improving in every way. Now Hollander is coming to have a few words with you."

A trumpet standing on the floor was seen to rise and a voice from it said: "This is Hollander and I thank you for your assistance to Reynolds and myself. This is my first operation of such a type. I was a brain specialist on earth. I discussed this case with Reynolds and we decided to operate by killing the tumour and then, when the life had gone out, to de-materialise it and take it away. Everything will be all right now and so will the eyes."

The sequel took place seven months later when the dead and shrivelled tumour was removed from David's head. All was ready, with swabs, towels, etc., on the trolley, when Dr Reynolds gave us greeting and began to talk to David whilst his hands moved over the boy's head. Then as on the previous occasion Dr Reynolds drew the attention of the helpers to what he was doing and in a short time the dead matter was withdrawn from David's head and placed on swabs, Dr Reynolds remarking that it could be inspected more closely later but must be burned immediately afterwards. The matter had a most obnoxious smell and we were warned by the doctor to keep our noses well away from it.

On these occasions he (Dr Reynolds) usually brought some sort of disinfectant, but owing to remarks he had heard at a previous operation had decided that the helpers should be permitted to know that *something had been done* this time.

David and Dr Reynolds then conversed together the doctor showing himself in the strong red light of a torch and David was able to shake hands with him; the boy was then taken from the room full of excitement and pleasure. Again Dr Hollander spoke with those present, saying it was the first case in which he had been permitted to take part since his passing.

After this second operation on David, Dr Reynolds attended to several other patients who had come for advice about their ailments, viz., deafness, kidney trouble, nervous debility, etc., after which he and Dr Hollander gave one of their usual talks on matters relating to Spiritual Healing.

Spiritual operations like those just described are typical of very many carried out by Dr Reynolds through my mediumship. Most of the cases have been considered difficult; in fact, as mentioned previously, some have been declared incurable by the medical profession, such as a cancer case of long standing. Another was one of pregnancy, quite an abnormal case which had baffled the doctors. Dr Reynolds visited the lady concerned, performed a spiritual operation and then told those interested that the hospital authorities would wonder why she had been sent to them as everything would be found normal, this being exactly what did happen.

Another interesting incident I recall was Dr Reynolds' treatment of a case of chronic asthma when he remained fully materialised to the helpers and sitters and proceeded to remove the mucus from the chest by inserting his de-materialised hand

and taking away the matter in long strands. This he repeated several times, the filth being deposited in a kidney tray held by one of the helpers, the patient remarking upon the pungent and offensive smell which came from it.

Another instance was that of relieving acute frontal sinus pains in which the de-materialised hand had been inserted into the head thus easing bone pressure on the brain.

Then there was the young man, badly injured in a mining accident near Doncaster, who had been treated in hospital for a fractured skull, injured pelvis, severed nerve tissue and was unable to move arms or legs. He had been sent home as nothing further could be done for him, and was not given long to live. As a last resort he was brought to my surgery in an ambulance by his father and an uncle to see if anything could be done for him. After two spirit operations he was able to get on his feet again. For these operations Dr Reynolds again fully materialised and was assisted by Dr Hollander whom I have mentioned previously. One operation was performed on the skull and another on the pelvis. Within a year this young man was again able to walk and play games.

At other times much valuable work has been done by the band of helpers who assist Dr Reynolds, and by the power of prayer and concentration in cases which he is treating away from the Sanctuary and which he attends upon receiving thought messages for help from people who have the knowledge of what is possible in healing through spiritual contact. Even blood transfusions have been supplied by helpers in cases of emergency.

To conclude this account of only a few of Dr Reynolds' cases and maybe to help clear away some scepticism about the possibility of such things, I should like to emphasise that on innumerable occasions doctors attached to hospitals and institutions, and others in private practice have contacted me for help and through me have been able to discuss difficult cases and medical matters with Dr Reynolds and a number of other spirit doctors who have attached themselves to him and often assist in his wonderful work of healing. For, strange as it may appear to many people, these spirit doctors still keep watch on what takes place in our hospitals and operating theatres and are remarkably conversant with modern methods; when called upon by their earth colleagues they impress them as to what to do, for they are able to see for themselves as much as and often more than what is revealed by an X-ray examination.

Finally, as a further matter of interest, Dr Reynolds gives frequent reports and diagnoses upon surgery cases and those on absent healing; prescribes remedies in prescription form and in some cases apports for the patient's use such things as tablets, liquid medicines and ointments with precise instructions as to their use.

Impossible you say? Nothing is impossible with God, who is the Source of all power – "O God in the Silence, let me feel that which I cannot hope to understand – Thy Greatness."

Most of the messages received at sittings are of a personal nature, communicated by relatives and friends of the sitters, from the spirit world and are of little interest except to those for whom they are intended and who find that such messages often contain interesting and valuable information relating to family affairs, etc. But, not infrequently, other spirit entities are attracted to the séance room, whose presence and messages are of unusual interest, giving as they so often do, an insight into conditions on the other side and what has been revealed to them since their passing; showing also, that although passed over so long ago, such spirits are frequently still concerned with earthly matters which were of interest to them during their lives here. I have previously quoted words of truth and wisdom spoken by Dr Reynolds and stated how those who were of the medical profession are still interested in healing, as practised from the spirit world.

And so it is with others. Times without number and especially round about Armistice-tide, people of various nationalities frequently visit the Circle. Sometimes they come for family reasons, but so often to emphasise the futility of war and to tell how from the spirit world they watch over ships and aircraft and combatants with the Forces, and assist to the other side those unfortunate ones like themselves who become the victims of man's inhumanity to man. In their messages and talks they make it abundantly clear that wars are the outcome of man's misuse of that freedom of will which is God's gift to all and which instead of being directed into channels of love towards their, fellow men is with so many turned into a lust for power and the brutality which follows in its path. In this such people are influenced by evil spirits – oh yes, there are evil as well as good spirits – who despite the efforts of the latter refuse to be rescued from the earth plane, brought to the light and a progression to higher spheres. Instead, they choose to remain in close contact with earth conditions and exercise their malign influence upon their counterparts in life. I shall give an example of this later relating to an incident which took place in my Circle during the war years.

I now give a few of many instances when the Circle was visited by unusual spirit people and have chosen these specially as their remarks were fully recorded at the time which unfortunately has so often not been done. In stating what was said by these spirits I should mention that on some of the occasions when they spoke in language different from our own, Ellen, or some other guide, acted as interpreter. But in other cases interpretation was unnecessary, the entities having gained a knowledge of different tongues during their time in the spirit world.

A description of the conditions and lighting arrangements under which these messages were given would take up too much space and I shall therefore merely introduce the spirits by name and state what they said.

Ali Hymed: An Egyptian professor, spoke in the direct voice, of experiments of hundreds of years ago and said the Ancient Phenomena was known as the Inner Mystery. He had returned to help Dr Reynolds in the great experiment of healing he was carrying out. Ali Hymed referred to those chosen as – "a fortunate band of people in being able to experience such wonders from the spirit world."

Mai Feng Shang: The beautiful form of this Chinese girl emerged from mists which seemed to rise from the floor, and spoke as follows: "Survival is no new revelation as you people of the West seem to think. We Chinese have known and practised communion with spirits for thousands of years. I passed over to the world of spirit six hundred years ago and it was practised thousands of years before my time. This religion is only a repetition of what occurred four thousand years ago in Asia. It is well known to many of you white people that in the East the Mandarin class and educated Chinese, Confucians, Taoists and Buddhists all believed in spirits, which they called ancestral worship. Trance utterances and materialisations of spirit forms are all known to the Chinese. Gifted psychics were carefully selected and trained for demonstrations in Halls of Revelation. The Taoist priests have always been experts in these spiritistic affairs. These ceremonies involve the use of incense and chants to ensure right conditions for the spirit friends to have communion with their mortal brethren. As I return tonight in your temple the conditions are very beautiful." With these words Mai Feng Shang dematerialised, leaving behind a lovely perfume of incense.

Huai-Nan-Tzu: (A Taoist philosopher who materialised with Mai Feng Shang on another of her visits to the Circle). In a mellow voice he referred to the original Taoism as a philosophy which, he said, was based on nature in her abstract and concrete phases. The old Taoists were devout worshippers of nature and considered it far more important to investigate natural phenomena than to study ancient beliefs. They had no theology; man on earth was a wanderer and death was simply 'going home'. To fear death was a mistake. What should be most feared was the indulgence of appetites and of passions which clouded the mind and shortened life. Many Taoists lived to extreme old age and frequently attained a century or more. Some found the elixir of life and lived on earth for more than two hundred years. "I will tell you about the perfect Tao," he continued, "its essence is surrounded by the deepest obscurity; its highest reach is in silence and darkness; there is nothing to be seen, nothing to be heard. You must be still, you must be pure; not subjecting your body to toil, not agitating your vital force, then you may live for long. Watch over what is vital within you; shut up the avenues which connect you with what is external. Much knowledge is pernicious. Watch over and keep your body in good state and all things will of themselves give it vigour. I maintained the unity of these elements and in this way I cultivated myself for two hundred and fifty years and my bodily form knew no decay. This was in the year 2,700 B.C., so I return tonight with Mai Feng Shang to help Dr Reynolds in his experiment with the peoples of the West."

With these words he dematerialised. Then Mai Feng Shang spoke in a cultivated voice, saying she would also help towards the success of this work.

Chandra Lila: A voice said: "I must speak with white sister, one of the chosen ones." To which I replied: "You are welcome, my sister in spirit; speak to me tell me who you are." She continued: "I am an Indian girl and woman; for I was young in age but old in years. I was born in Nepal and was married when only seven years of age. My husband died soon after and, like other widows I was thought to be the cause of his death through some sin committed before birth, so I had to make a pilgrimage for seven years. With other girl widows I travelled from one sacred place to another, from the north of India to the east, then down to the extreme southerly point on to the west and back to the far north among the Himalayan mountains until I reached the source of the Ganges amid the snow and ice of those heights where some of my sisters died from cold. I and a few who were left were taken from the sacred place to a temple where I performed the office of a priestess for seven years. But I found no peace and no atonement for my sin although I suffered physical tortures, one of which was to sit amidst five fires, with the hot sun overhead and four fires built around me. I was afraid of the Brahmin priests.

"One day I learned how they deceived my poor people by going over to an island in a boat, where stood one god whom my people were afraid to anger. If the eye of the god was lit up they were afraid of evil spirits taking away their hovels or bringing disease and famine. They would bring all their savings and all they could to the priests. One night I saw the Brahmin priest cross over to the island and light a lamp inside the god. I could bear it no longer, so escaped, and after wandering many miles came to the home of a white woman, ill and weary with my sufferings; she nursed me and taught me about your God. But I was a hopeless cripple and soon died, and your white sister found peace for me. I come now to bring you peace and to help you to give peace and knowledge to all who suffer. Goodnight, chosen one. I may return as God wills." To her I said: "Goodnight, my friend. I should like you to return and speak with me again, and bring some of those widows you mentioned, and they too will find a welcome in my little home. God bless you, and goodnight."

Rhumar: Message received late one evening when I was writing letters in my study. A strange voice spoke through the trumpet in a foreign tongue, but finding that I did not understand it, then spoke in broken English. "I am Rhumar, of Bombay, India. I watch you much for many years; I bring you image of God of Shiva. I do not see my God among your treasures in your room – why? Do you not like him?"

I tried to think what I had done with this image which had been apported into my study about 1938, but I do remember a huge thing coming through with a lot of small images attached. Around the neck of the image was twisted a deadly cobra, and a necklace of human skulls. In one hand he held the noose of thugs, in another a bleeding head, and in the third hand he held the Gada, a mace of war; in the fourth hand was the Trisul, or pitchfork with which he rakes, makes or mends the petty affairs of the human race. I had it taken to pieces and each image made into ash-trays, etc., as gifts for my friends. So I told Rhumar what I had done and how sorry I was. Patiently, Rhumar continued in his broken English: "Behold, chosen one, I was set apart by Shiva's seal, thou art ordained to work for thy God; I return to help thee in and through thy precepts and sacrifices, but would I could see one little part of my image among your treasures; look in the bottom drawer of thy desk and you will find one such left. I will come again."

I found the image which now stands on my desk among my treasured apports.

Madame Blavatsky (a noted medium): "My child, you are very worried. I have watched you studying your book on reincarnation and I so wanted to come to you. This evening I am very pleased and I believe in the work you are doing. I wish there were more to help us to meet on a half-way basis to understand that there is no death. I do wish that I had taught this truth more and had tried to look further into it. Truth is always hidden; we have to search to find it; theories and dogmas seem to have more chance in the world than truth. Everyone has some manifestations of truth but hides instead of acknowledging them. I wanted to be a leader in some way or other. Now I want to bring the truth to the world. I knew of spirit manifestations and experienced them myself. I did much in my early days along this line, then began to investigate Theosophy and Philosophy. To me came Reincarnation; it appealed to me for a time but I could not see the truth clearly. It seemed unjust that some should be rich and have such good times, while others should be so poor and have much trouble. Others did not get enough earthly experience, at least so I felt. I thought there was truth and justice in the theory that we come back to learn and have more experiences. I taught it and wanted to bring it out to all peoples. I was mistaken in supposing I could remember far back into my past. Memories of past lives are revived by spirits bringing such thoughts that represent the lives they had lived and their experiences are impressed on your mind as your own. You then think you remember your past. When you study Theosophy you develop your mind and live in an atmosphere of mind; you remove yourself as much as possible from the physical, becoming sensitive and aware of spirits around you. They speak to you by impressions and their past will be like a panorama; you feel it and live their past over again. This you mistake for the memory of former incarnations.

"I did not know this when I lived on earth. I took it for granted that these memories were true, but on reaching the spirit side I learned differently and studied a great deal. Theosophy is the best and highest philosophy of life intrinsically, but let us study and live up to the truth, forgetting theories and developing the highest within us, to find ourselves. Do not let us look far into the past or future, finding ourselves in our present state, and be true to ourselves. Let us forget all theories and dogmas and know the nearness of God.

"Reincarnation is not true; I do not want to believe that. They told me here in spirit that I could not reincarnate. I have tried and tried to come back to be somebody else but could not. We cannot reincarnate; we progress, we do not come back. Some may say this is not Madame Blavatsky, but do not doubt it; it is. If you have any questions I will answer them."

So I asked her: "What are Masters?" She replied: "We speak of Masters. We are all Masters when we study higher things, but a Master as we understand it in Theosophy is some great mind, one who can conquer matter, live a good and pure life, and overcome all adverse conditions. What did I do that was really good for humanity? I only gave them a theory. I could have done so much more had I continued with my mediumship and worked to bring the two worlds together. Goodnight, my child; maybe you will allow me to visit you again."

Sir Arthur Conan Doyle has visited the Circle on several occasions. One of his messages was: "Take heed of a brother who speaketh unto you. He who liveth with the spirit knoweth no fear." Another time, speaking of Dr Reynolds' work he said: "This is an experiment after my own heart and were I in the body I should have been delighted to have joined you and given all the help and time I could command. However, I am eager to help Dr Reynolds from the spirit side, so you people will hear and see more of me in the future."

At another sitting a tapping or beating was heard on the trumpet which then floated to one of the sitters. A voice was then heard, but the words could not be understood. However, a second trumpet arose alongside the other and a voice addressed the sitter: "This is Conan Doyle and I have brought along Nicoolai who took my party through the jungle when I travelled through Africa. He was a most faithful negro who saved me many times from wild animals. He was the only one who could take the boat to the island and whenever you hear the beat of the drums which he has just demonstrated to you, you can be sure you are among friends. Wherever you are and you hear the roll of the drums, he will be with you. He ultimately gave his life for me and since I passed into spirit life I have sought him out and he has been a good pal. His name is Nicoolai, please remember that; but you can just call him 'Sack,' as I used to do and he will understand." Other matters were discussed by Conan Doyle and the sitter mentioned, then with a sound like a drum-beat, and "goodnight" from Conan Doyle, both trumpets sank to the floor.

John Edgar (Physician and Surgeon, of Glasgow): "By faith we are justified; have faith with God." These words were spoken to the Circle by John Edgar, who then continued: "I used to be convinced that spiritism where it was not fraud or trickery was a manifestation of evil spirits or fallen angels and that we must look to God Himself and expect to get our answer. I did not believe in visions or peculiar manifestations, but looked to the Bible, being sure that no man could be wise above the Bible. Although a doctor, I never saw a soul leave a body at death. Now, since my passing-over or death, I understand, and tonight have returned to help undo all the harm my lack of knowledge has done during my earth life, for now I know of a greater truth: life after death."

David Livingstone: (At a sitting when, among those present was a Crown representative who had served for many years on the Gold Coast (Ghana)). A good many natives made their presence known to him, one being his head boy who had disappeared and was neither seen nor heard of afterwards. Questioning this boy in his native tongue, the sitter learned that he had been shot by French frontier guards while attempting to cross the border to reach his native village. It was following these talks that the trumpet rose again and a voice said: "I am David Livingstone. I know about the work you have done to help those black people who were my friends as they were yours. It was a work after my own heart and I thank you, for all you did for them. I am still working for them from the spirit world. There is much misunderstanding between the black and the white peoples and before long there will be serious strife in Africa." This message was given in September 1951.

Two Airmen tell a story and give advice:

Two trumpets levitated simultaneously and a voice from one said: "Sing something." On being asked what they would like, one of them said: "Sing *I'll Walk Beside You.*" and on the sitters responding, he whistled it with them. Then a tapping came from the other trumpet but no one understood what was happening, for the voice then said: "Well, there's a soldier and a sailor present and neither of them understood what I tapped out in Morse. I thought they would have got the message, but they do not appear to know it." The voice then continued:

"We are two airmen, John Patterson and Billy Gray and are happy to meet you. It seems like starting again, but I wish you people would try and help the hundreds of lads who are over here and do not know where they are. I was fortunate, for I knew a little about it before coming over. It was Jack here who told me something about this. He was always a rum chap and used to seem queer to the rest of us, but that was because we didn't know. I understand it better now," (then in an aside as if speaking to the other trumpet), "you don't mind, chum, if I tell them?" and apparently receiving assent he went on: "Well it was this way. Jack had a ring of which he was very proud and would never go up without it. We used to chaff him about this but he always said that money could not buy it. One day we all wanted a bit of enjoyment but were broke, so we got a jeweller to look at Jack's ring so that we could raise something on it, but though he offered a good price, Jack would not part. We others had raised a bit in other ways and enjoyed ourselves as much as we could, but though we tried Jack again he would not part with his ring. So one day I asked him why it was so precious to him, and when he had explained I began to be interested in spiritual matters, for I was privileged and no longer looked upon him as queer like the others did. He told me that eight times the ring and the contact he had with the spirit world through it had brought him safely back home when all seemed lost, having been picked up each time. So you can see how I became interested. Then came the last flight. Jack had met a dame and in a month they were married. Well, he had promised to take her to a dance but at the last minute could not go as he had received sudden orders and could not tell her exactly why. In retaliation she hid his things and he had to go without some of them, among which was the ring. And from that flight we did not return. Now you can tell them the rest of the story, Jack."

Then John Patterson spoke through the other trumpet: "We ran into a blizzard and I tried all I knew to keep the machine going. Suddenly I saw Aunty's face in the windscreen – then I knew I was coming down and that it was the end. The contact that I'd had to bring me back before was not with me. I would like you folks always to help a person who has a duty to perform; that is why I came here tonight. We have come on behalf of a lot of our pals who are with us now and we try to keep them away from planes. Pray for them and that God will send someone from the higher realms to assist them. Think of the lads who have gone over; pray for them." The trumpets then sank to the floor.

John Patterson again: On another occasion, after discoursing on various matters for about ten minutes, he promised to return and play for us some records of music on a portable gramophone of which he was very fond when on the earth plane. He asked that it should be placed on the top landing in his old home, with records on a table near by. He also said he would experiment on the radiogram and play any records purchased at his request. These things were done and the gramophone was played many times day and night when the family were in other parts of the house. The music was heard at varying times and, on several occasions, records were seen to change – even the needle – though no human hands were near or touching them.

Spirit Choirs: (The occasion was the final night on one of our sessions of experimental sittings when Dr Reynolds permitted us to listen to singing from the world of spirit.)

At first there was only the sound of a child's voice and then others joined in. One lovely-toned voice sang *Abide with Me* with such feeling that it brought tears to the eyes of many present. Then from time to time we heard many voices singing as if great choirs were joined in harmony. This experience prompted one of the sitters to say: "Who are they who say that God will not allow us to peep into heaven and see the beauty thereof before we make the change called death? If we seek we shall find; but we must seek."

Chapter Three

Church Work, Travels and Phenomena

*Reports written to the **Two Worlds** magazine and other accounts.*

The Two Worlds – 4th March, 1938.

Doncaster Activities

Mrs Northage, of Nottingham, paid a special visit to the Doncaster Society last week and attracted a large congregation. Madame Marian Sykes, of Huddersfield, rendered two solos, which were warmly applauded. Mrs T. Khan, of Stockport, paid her first visit to this Society on Tuesday, February 22nd, and gave a convincing demonstration. At the evening service the partition separating the Church from the Schoolroom had to be removed in order to accommodate the congregation

The Two Worlds – 2nd December, 1938.

Doncaster

Mrs Isa Northage of Nottingham gave an interesting trance address at the Baker Street Church, Doncaster. The control was a young man who had been a sailor and eventually joined the army in the Great War, where he was killed. He described to an interested audience his recovery in spirit life, his visits to his home, his distress at seeing the people mourning over his death, his effort to make his loved ones understand that he was with them and his joy when he found his sweetheart and she became aware of his presence. He concluded by imploring the people to work for peace and universal brotherhood. The clairvoyance which followed was delivered to the music of a concertina. A number of evidential descriptions were given, with their names, the places to which they belonged, messages to their friends, and other evidential details. In one case, five spirit people were described to one lady, with their names, and all were recognised, and we feel sure that the country will hear more of this versatile medium.

The Two Worlds – 23rd September, 1938.

Round the Churches

Mrs Northage, of Nottingham, conducted successful services last week at the Coventry 'Broadgate' N.S. Church, attracting large congregations and demonstrating evidential clairvoyance of a high order. This was the medium's first visit to the Society and a return visit is eagerly awaited by all who witnessed her work.

The Two Worlds – 20th January, 1939.

Clairvoyance

Sir – A platform worker seldom gets the opportunity of attending services as a member of the congregation.

This weekend, however, I have attended services at a Skegness church, which have been conducted by Mrs Northage, of Bulwell, and would like to take this opportunity of commenting on the excellent clairvoyant powers of this medium.

Mrs Northage appears to have an extremely 'selective' type of mediumship, which enables her to give amazingly accurate details, especially regarding the exact relationship of the communicating spirits to the sitters. In every case, wives, husbands, sisters and brothers were unhesitatingly acknowledged, together with names and intimate details that would have convinced the most sceptical investigator.

Mrs Northage is already well known in the provinces, and I venture to prophesy that this gifted medium will soon rank among our most prominent workers.

John L. Jackaman.

The Two Worlds – 9th December, 1938.

Rare Phenomenon

The Spiritualist Brotherhood Church, Pontypridd, reports very successful meetings and transfiguration séances with Mrs Northage, of Nottingham, which were remarkable for an unusual phenomenon. Mr J. C. Flye says: "A young soldier who passed over in the war took control of Mrs Northage, spoke to me, related a number of incidents pertaining to his earthly life, told me the cause of his passing over, and gave a resume of his experiences in the Great Beyond. One of the peculiarities of his passing was that he was wounded by a bullet in the hand. On the medium recovering consciousness, we were astonished to find that the bullet wounds had produced clear marks on the hand of the medium in the exact place where my friend was struck. This was demonstrated before a large company. The phenomena of stigmata has, of course, historical sanction, but this is the first case we have heard of where a deceased person controlling a medium has reproduced physical evidence of his wounds."

The Two Worlds – 28th July, 1939.

I recently attended a materialisation and direct voice séance at the home of Mrs Northage, of Bulwell, at which some remarkable phenomena took place. First we had the materialised form of a parrot, which flew freely round the circle, finally resting upon my shoulder, flapping its wings against my cheek. Mrs Northage's child control stated that she would pull feathers from the parrot's tail, and after the séance we found a number of these feathers upon the floor.

Many spirit voices came through the trumpet, and each sitter received convincing evidence of the identity of the communicators.

The wife of one of the sitters materialised in full form, and was clearly seen, the voice being loud and clear. She kissed her husband upon the forehead; the sound of the kiss being audible to all. After raising her robe to the knee she lifted her left foot, and this was clearly seen by all the sitters.

After the spirit had retired into the cabinet, we were told that each sitter would be allowed for a moment to handle the spirit robe, and the material floated from one sitter to the other. It was moderately heavy, but very beautiful and soft to the touch. A Chinese lady then materialised, speaking in what was claimed to be her own tongue. This control frequently helps with apports.

Then another voice came through the trumpet, this time the voice of a highly trained soprano, who sang *Love's Old Sweet*

*Son*g without the use of the trumpet. Two of the sitters were able to recognize this spirit.

We were then told that an attempt was to be made to levitate the medium above the sitters' heads, and we certainly felt her feet touch our heads as she seemed to float above us. A large drum was levitated, the rattle of which was terrific. A number of articles, bells, a mouth organ, tambourines, toys, dolls, cigarettes, etc., were levitated, and carried round the circle. After we had joined in singing *The Rosary*; my own guide, Sister Agnes, materialised, walked from sitter to sitter and showed the cross attached to her rosary. She placed this upon my knee, whispering words of encouragement I clearly saw her lips moving; the movement of her eyes and I could feel her breath as she caressed me.

Messages came for friends of mine who were not present at the séance. I gladly bear my testimony to the evidential nature of the phenomena I witnessed at this séance.

D. M. Antliff,
Secretary, Matlock Spiritualist Church.

The Two Worlds – 25th August, 1939.

Sir – Evidence of the continuity of life is always forthcoming, as witnessed by eighty people at a service held in Darnall (Sheffield) N.S. Church on Sunday, July 30th the medium being Mrs Northage, of Bulwell, Notts.

After giving a series of Christian names and descriptions, which were readily acknowledged, the medium said there was a boy there who was looking for his mother. He was built up at the top end of the church, and gave his name as Billie Hudson. He said his mother was on the front row of the church, but his grandma was at the top end. His mother had done nothing but grieve for this boy of sixteen since he passed on, and his assurance to her that he was happy in a lovely world has made this lady pull herself together.

At the supper table, Mrs Northage's guide (Sambo) started moving the table round the room; they had a lively time.

My friend and I had the privilege of sitting at a séance held for a few friends at her home, where we witnessed remarkable phenomena – beating of a drum, mouth organ playing, tin whistle playing, also liquid perfume coming from the medium's hands, which her doctor guide, who gave his name as Dr Reynolds, told me to use for my deafness, etc., as it contained healing properties.

Then I had the greatest privilege of all, my mother built up for me, told me to feel at her robe, and discussed with my wife and me intimate family matters (who cannot recognise his own mother?), spoke of my sisters and brothers. My brother also spoke to me through the trumpet. My friend's little daughter spoke to him (she passed over six years ago at seven-weeks-old), gave her name, and promised to manifest (materialise) next time if her mummy comes along (she was wanting her mummy).

A little boy came through; his name was Kenneth Probert. He was killed on a fairy cycle. His father was vicar of a church in Seaton Sluice, Northumberland. He asked the medium's son to write to his mother and said she would come down on the next train.

Great credit must go to Mrs Northage for her wonderful patience in development. May she be with us for many more long years to come.

W. Gillett.

The Two Worlds – 8th September, 1939.

Articles have already appeared in *The Two World*s in reference to the excellent mediumship of Mrs Northage, of Bulwell, which is making steady progress. I had the pleasure of attending a remarkable séance in her home on August 17th, at which we had apports, voices through the trumpet, and materialisation. Mrs Northage's guide, Sambo first spoke to us, and then produced through the trumpet a small ivory pig. It was handed to a gentleman sitter, who was requested to keep it. This sitter was then able to speak to his mother and father, two trumpets being used simultaneously.

Following this a remarkable materialisation took place. In a previous report on this medium, I alluded to a lady who had materialised, kissed her husband, and allowed each sitter to handle her spirit drapery. That gentleman had expressed the hope that some day he might be permitted to hold his wife's wedding ring. At this séance she appeared, held out her left hand, showed the ring, and tapped it upon a plaque that all might hear. She promised that next time she would allow him to take off the ring as a present for her daughter. Another materialised form was that of an Egyptian, who gave his name and spoke in his own Egyptian tongue. Next came a foreign lady who was unable to speak English, but both her form and robe were visible to all sitters. Another gentleman had the remarkable experience of seeing his guide (a monk calling himself 'Brother Bernard') fully materialise. He handed to the sitter his own black, bone-like Cross and chain, explaining that this was buried with him, but he would like the sitter to cherish it as a personal gift. At a subsequent séance, on the 22nd, at which the same gentleman was present, the Cross was dematerialised before our eyes, the chain only remaining. The chain was carefully examined by everyone – the Cross was not there. Immediately the control left, however, the Cross reappeared on the chain.

Then came a Chinese lady bringing apports. She first materialised herself, then presented us with a valuable incense burner (a rare specimen), which we were instructed not to part with. Then a bangle was produced which she claimed had been brought from her own tomb.

On the following Sunday night, while some of my friends and I were having supper, the table, loaded with eatables, crockery etc., was clearly levitated and moved freely about the room and answered questions put to the guides. Mrs Northage's mediumship is certainly very remarkable.

D. Antliff.

The Two Worlds – 1st December, 1939.

A remarkable materialisation séance was held on Remembrance Day, November 11th, at the home of Mr and Mrs Crowcroft, at Doncaster, the medium being Mrs Northage.

There were nineteen materialised forms in all, one of which appeared twice. The ten sitters sat in horse-shoe fashion, the medium taking up her place to complete the circle. Three trumpets were placed on the floor in the centre of the circle, and on a table at the side of the medium were two luminous plaques, a mouth organ, mandolin, tambourine, bells and some flowers.

Immediately following a short prayer by Mrs Venables, one of the trumpets rose almost to the ceiling and then slowly came down and floated around the circle with the large end toward the sitters, before alighting on the floor. This was said to be a test of the power.

Sambo, who seems to act as director, asked us to sing to keep up the power. Then the trumpet rose again and a voice spoke to Mr Venables, saying, "I was a railwayman – but the engines you are driving are much better now. I am often with you on the footplate." (Mr Venables is an engine-driver, and commented that he could do with all the help he could get under present difficult conditions.)

Again came a voice through the trumpet saying, "Guess who I am, guess." One of the sitters replied: "It is Marklew," and the voice replied "Yes. That is right." Mrs Marklew asked: "Is that really you, Ernest ?" and the voice replied "Yes. Who do you think I have brought with me? Charlie White." (an old friend of the family). He then said: "I will materialise later. What are you worrying about?" Mrs Marklew said: "I am worrying about the boys." "Don't worry. I will look after them, and they will be all right. My word what a fine medium you have here." Mr Marklew then retired to allow Charlie White to speak to Mrs Marklew. He conversed with her and gave her a message to pass onto his son. The trumpet then came to rest on the floor.

Then Sambo spoke again, and announced that "the Egyptian guide of Mr Frank Ward is here." Immediately there came from the cabinet the striking figure of an Oriental, with a curious headgear, and robed in an Oriental style. He made a number of low bows and salutations before dematerialising. Next, a Sister of Mercy came from the cabinet. She gave her name as Sister Nora, held a materialised Cross over the luminous plaque, went towards Mrs Farrell, and for a time they conversed together until the form slowly faded away.

After a little singing, Mr Marklew came out of the cabinet, drawing the curtains with him so that only those near Mrs Marklew could see him. He carried in his hand one of the luminous plaques upon which was placed a rose that had been plucked out of his own garden that day and brought to the séance by his wife. He tucked the rose on Mrs Marklew's breast, saying "Don't worry any more; all is well. You will know me better when the roses bloom again." He then stroked and pulled Mrs Marklew's hair in a very characteristic way, which she thought very evidential. He then said: "Your mother is here, and is going to speak to you. Give my love to Edith when you go to Chesterfield," Mrs Marklew said: "Don't go yet, Ernest." He replied: "I must go, dear; you understand. Good-night and God bless you."

Then Mrs Marklew's mother materialised, and held a short conversation with her daughter, and before leaving the form kissed her. Next came Dorothy, a school friend of Mrs Marklew. She advanced from the cabinet, saying: "I am glad to meet you again. I have noticed your interest in the children." She then deliberately turned to Miss Bacon and said: "Nurse, when you have finished with the children on your side, my work commences – I am in the hospital in the spirit world." (Miss Bacon is a nurse.) Dorothy then walked round the circle, patting several of the sitters on the cheek, and before disappearing crossed over to Mrs Marklew and said goodbye. She was a beautifully developed form.

The next spirit form was announced by Sambo as Mr Ward's grandmother. She came out of the cabinet showing a clear face, and both Messrs J. and F. Ward leaned forward and pressed their heads against the forehead of the spirit form. It was solid and had natural warmth, and was clearly recognisable. She patted them both on the back and said: "Look after your mother!"

The trumpet then crossed to Mr Venables, and a voice spoke to him saying that he was a German, named Muller, who had changed his name to Miller. He had had a business in Doncaster when on earth, and had three sons, two of whom were killed in the British Army during the Great War. He said he was very fond of the British people.

The present international conditions of Germany were very bad, and there would be internal upheaval. He believed that the German people 'would arrange things for themselves'.

The trumpet next floated round the circle, and the voice of a child was heard crying: "I want my mummy. Where is my mummy?" and then said, "She is not here."

The trumpet continued to float round the circle, touching various sitters in a caressing manner, and finally floated over to Miss Bacon, and the spirit announced himself as John Burnett, of Cleethorpes.

Miss Bacon then asked: "Where did you see me?" and he replied, "In a large hospital." The scene was rather distressing, as the nurse could not remember him. He was probably one of her many patients.

'Helen'*(Ellen)*, one of the controls of Mrs Northage, passed materialised drapery round the circle for the sitters to handle. She played the mandolin and the mouth organ and taking an electric torch off the table showed herself fully in a red light.

Signed: Ivy Bacon.
F. and J. B. Ward.
Clara A. Marklew.

The Two Worlds – 15th December, 1939.

Through the mediumship of Mrs Northage, of Bulwell, a number of sitters at Matlock Bath, were privileged to witness a most remarkable and evidential demonstration of direct voice and materialisation. Most of the sitters had had previous experience of her mediumship.

Two trumpets floated about the room, sometimes at a great pace and at varying heights. One of the trumpets usually tapped the friend for whom the communication was intended, and immediately a voice spoke, giving the name of the communicator. Identity being established, many spirited conversations of considerable importance to the sitters took place.

In one case the trumpet went to a sitter and began stamping round his feet, reminiscent of a man with a peg leg stamping round. The incident caused considerable amusement, but its importance was realised by the grandson of the manifesting spirit. The voice which followed explained who he was, his occupation when on earth, and cited a considerable number of incidents, all of which were recalled by the sitter, whose grandfather certainly had a peg leg.

Another materialised form tendered advice to one lady concerning the physical defects of her granddaughter, and was promised relief from Dr Reynolds' health circle.

Another sitter was addressed by a friend who had terminated his own life some seven years before. He was very sad and deeply contrite for his act, for which he said he had suffered severely. Quite a number of sitters recalled the sad affair one or two were conversant with certain incidents mentioned by the spirit, and the reference to his relatives by name, some of whom have now passed over.

The most unusual manifestation occurred towards the end of the séance. The spirit guide Sambo asked one of the sitters to place her hands on the medium's knees. While she was still holding them, a spirit person materialised, left the cabinet, and walked across the circle to speak to and embrace her mother. We thereby had definite evidence that the medium was in her chair, obviously in a deep trance.

One amusing incident was when a number of 'Negro children', who seemed to be working under the direction of Sambo, could not resist the temptation to disarrange the writer's carefully groomed hair, pull out his tie, and tickle his legs, with yelps of delight at attracting attention.

One sitter asked if it would be possible to have a message written on a postcard and left on the table. Sambo agreed, and we saw a materialised hand float to the floor, pick up a luminous tray, and then proceed to write under the very nose of the writer, who, I can assure you, was regarded as sceptical and not above honest doubt.

I am glad to have witnessed and to testify to this remarkable evidence.

J. Julian Ward.

(Note: Our contributor has enclosed the post-card, which seems to be written in some foreign language. It consists of six words. – *Editor*)

The Peterborough Citizen – 16th April, 1940.

Mediums reputed to possess remarkable gifts have often visited Peterborough Spiritualist Church, but the lady who conducted the services and meetings last weekend, Mrs Northage, of Bulwell, Nottingham, is one of extraordinary versatility. In an interview with an *Advertiser* representative after she had addressed a large congregation on Sunday evening she recounted some truly astounding phenomena which have occurred through her mediumship.

After each service at the Cromwell Road Church during the weekend, Mrs Northage gave clairvoyance with music – she is popularly known as the 'concertina medium'. She uses a concertina which she has had for many years, and said that while giving clairvoyance she picks music up which is passed over from the spirit world on a vibration. "If a loved one who has passed over was particularly fond of a certain song or hymn, even a march tune," she said, "they give that and I play it, at the same time giving a description of the spirit friend who is bringing the music, and what they did in life, also their names. I go direct to a person in the congregation saying, 'So-and-so is with you. I have to play so-and-so,' and then I give them the message from the other side." Many such messages were given on Saturday evening and on Sunday.

But even more remarkable than her musical mediumship are the 'apports' which have been received at séances held in the sanctuary which she has had erected at her Bulwell home. An apport is described by the Universal English Dictionary as 'a material object appearing at a séance without visible agency'. That the apports are 'material' will be realised when it is stated that they include a pair of vases which are solid bronze and weigh about 30 lb. each. Mrs Northage received her first apport at Easter last year, when a necklace of Chinese gold, in exquisite mosaic work was received.

Asked: "How do they come?" Mrs Northage replied: "There is no simple explanation. I am in a trance at the time, securely tied in a chair, and in the presence of about twelve persons as a rule. My guide directs attention to a particular side of the sanctuary and sitters see something resembling a smoke cloud at the place indicated. When it clears away the solid articles are left." Truly a remarkable phenomena, but Mrs Northage has many photographs of the various objects which have been apported, and the curator of Nottingham Museum has inspected them all with much interest and has secured Mrs Northage's consent to their being placed on loan exhibition at the Museum.

One photograph shows a 'devil head' from the Gold Coast and other African figures which have been apported. A box also shown, is an exquisite example of, Chinese workmanship, being carved on each side with eighty-six diminutive figures in great detail.

The Two Worlds – 26th July, 1940.

Sir – With reference to the letter signed 'I. A. Northage' in your issue for June 21st, the remark, "One of the difficulties of the investigation is the dark séance which prevents accurate observation," is scarcely understood in this particular case, because I witnessed materialisation of one of Mrs Northage's guides, named Ellen, at the end of a sitting in Doncaster last February, where the white light from a hand torch showed the spirit form in full.

Why is it now necessary for experiments with infra-red ray or special blue light, when a white light has been already used?

F. H. Ireland.

(We suggest that exceptions do not prove a rule, and it would be wise to find a procedure which could be regularly employed: – *Editor.*)

The Two Worlds – 14th February, 1941.

Mrs Northage, of Nottingham, paid a very successful visit to Ashington, Northern Counties, where her fine mediumship was much appreciated.

Two séances were held and brought conviction to many. My wife and daughter materialised, and both of them talked to me, kissed me, and caressed me. They brought a flower from the cabinet and handed it to me. Then my brother came and spoke to us through the trumpet. I suggested that it was a pity we had not a violin with us, as he was a skilled violinist. He said: "Bring one tomorrow night and I will play it for you." We borrowed one, and on the following evening he picked up the violin from outside the cabinet and asked us to sing *Auld Lang Syne* while he played for us. Every member of the circle had some communication from a loved one. Several of these materialised, whilst others spoke through the trumpet.

One member of the circle, Mr Ball, had communications from two of his brothers; they each raised a trumpet and were speaking simultaneously. Then his little girl came out of the cabinet, climbed on his knee, pulled his tie and exclaimed: "Hello, Daddy."

Mr Finlayson received a visit from his father, who exclaimed: "Hello Tom." The son asked him who he was, and he instantly answered: "I am your father, Tom Finlayson." Then a spirit came to Mr Whillis and said she was Aunt Lissie. Mr Whillis could not place her, and she told him that her name was written in the back of a certain book belonging to his father who would be able to tell him who she was. These facts were subsequently verified. Mr Whillis also had a visit from his brother, who, when asked if he would like to come back to earth replied: "Not for £100." Mr Hulme, one of the sitters, has attended more than fifty séances. His daughter materialised and spoke to him and he claims that it is the most clear and distinct spirit voice he has ever heard. At the close of the séance Dr Reynolds (Mrs Northage's guide) addressed us and gave useful advice to various members of the circle concerning the state of their health while Sambo, another of the guides, kept moving the table backwards and forwards all the time we were at supper.

The Two Worlds – 9th May, 1941.

Mrs Northage, of Bulwell, recently paid a couple of visits to Skegness. My youngest son and I had attended a sitting with her in February last and were so satisfied that I arranged for all my family to attend a séance at the Skegness Church with the same medium on April 3rd. I can never forget it.

After a brief opening, Mrs Northage passed into trance, and her guide Sambo welcomed us all and jokingly spoke of the black man and his place in the world. In a few minutes a mass of ectoplasm emerged from under the curtain of the cabinet. Sambo pulled the curtain aside and, by the light of a luminous plaque, we saw it emerging from the medium in a stream and flowing into the circle. Then from the cabinet came the North American Indian guide of Mr Jackaman, in full headdress. We saw his profile and features clearly. (At the previous séance in February he asked us to examine his muscles, like huge balls in his arms.) Mr and Mrs J's little son, Gerald, next spoke through the trumpet and talked to his parents, his grandmother and myself – but chiefly to his mother. He did not like her A.T.S. uniform – but said that she wouldn't wear it long.

Flowers which I had brought and put in a vase were distributed to each sitter and perfumes were produced which were quite different to that borne by the flowers. Sam then asked Mr J if he could feel the weight of the ectoplasm on his knees. He had noticed it, but the question called the attention of the rest of us. It flowed from under the curtain over Mr J's knees and out into the room, where it formed a white mass about a foot high and some three feet in circumference. It seemed alive and self-luminous, from an inner light, like phosphorous. It bubbled like living water rising from a spring. None of us had seen anything like it. My two sons, each with seven years' service in the Royal Navy, and my A.T.S. daughter, were deeply impressed.

Slowly the stuff was drawn back into the cabinet, and immediately out stepped the form of a nun, 'Sister Julia'. This spirit I have known for some years. She had appeared when I sat with Mrs Duncan last year, and the two forms were identical. She said she had brought my sailor son, who went down in the Royal Oak, and begged me not to grieve for him.

Now my hopes were realised. First came another bubbling mass of ectoplasm in the centre of the circle on the floor. Then a hand formed in the mass. I knew my son's hand, but we only said: "Come on, boy! You're doing fine." Like a flash my boy stood before us, smiling and full of life.

Sambo urged him to show all he could, and his response was immediate. Saying, "Jack, Jack," he ran to his brother, and for several minutes they engaged in conversation. (These two boys were inseparable when on earth and always spent their leave together.) The hand grip was so strong that Jack's hand was sore for some hours. Next he went to his sister, ran his hand through her hair, just as he used to do, teasingly pulled her tie from her uniform coat, shook her hand and kissed her. Then across to his grandmother, "Granny, good old Gran," he said. He put both arms around her, rubbed her face with his hand and stroked her hair. Next across to his father. "Hello, Dad you're not frightened of me?" (His father showed signs of emotion.) Next he spoke to his two brothers, Jim and Leonard, and to his mother-in-law, expressing his disappointment that his bride was not present. (She's in the A.T.S., but is detained in hospital.) "Kath is a little better today," he said. "I'm looking after her and spend most of my time with her – she'll soon be right." He next went to his 'Aunt Ciss', and, patting her back, told her that he was present with her when she gathered daffodils recently in Gloucestershire on his birthday. (Quite right.)

To me – his mother – he came at last. I can't remember what he said, but his arms were around me and I had 'my boy' again. He spoke to his brother Jack, assuring him of his interest in his work. Then he stood in the middle of the circle and melted slowly away. He did not go to the cabinet, but dissolved before our eyes.

Sambo next said he had brought a sailor named Maurice, who knew Jack Burrows. Jack knew only one lad by this name, Maurice Slade, who went down in the Royal Oak. They had been shipmates in the Mediterranean four years ago. This young man was apparently quite ignorant of the possibility of communication, but after some coaxing raised the trumpet and called, "Jack, Jack." My son said, "Hello, Maurice, how are you?" He replied, "I'm not dead, am I? Tell me I'm not dead, Jack." He seemed quite alarmed. We reassured him, and Sambo told us we had helped to liberate a spirit who was earthbound and who would now be able to progress. He thanked us for our handling of the case. Sambo spoke of the great benefit my own boy had received by being taught in his boyhood of the nature of spirit life it had enabled him to assist many of his pals.

The next to appear was my still-born daughter – now about ten years old. She first spoke to me at a séance with Louiza Bolt, when she was about eighteen-months old. She has grown into a beautiful girl. She came and kissed me, saying, "Mother, my little mother." My heart was overjoyed. She went to all her brothers and sisters and talked with each. Her brothers were astonished at her beauty, and jokingly remarked to Iris, "You don't hold the first place now – she's lovely." They remarked that her voice reminded them of the silver bells they had heard in the East. She did not like her sister's A.T.S. uniform, as she said: "It means war and hate, whilst only love is good." Then, crossing to her grandmother she said, "My lovely Granny, I'm waiting for you. I'll show you all the lovely flowers and gardens when you come. There's a beautiful home waiting for you." Going across to Jack, she said, "My big brother. I'm helping to look after you and I come to you on the big ship."

She kissed him, pulled his hair and stayed talking quite fifteen minutes. The texture of her robes was remarkable; they felt like satin or ring velvet.

The next visitor was my paternal grandmother, Granny Brett, who died before I was born and now proved her identity to me. Mr Jackaman's grandfather and Mr Jack Greaves – husband of the president of the church, came and spoke to us, and were followed by the grandfather of my daughter-in-law.

A female French spirit manifested and thanked my son Jack for his kindness to her brother – a French sailor whom she named – a casual incident almost forgotten.

Ernest Marklew, late M.P. came next and urged Mr Jackaman to continue his work for Spiritualism. He said that he had died a disappointed man, for he had not accomplished all he desired. Much of his conversation was highly evidential concerning his Parliamentary life. He told of having apologised to Mr Chamberlain since the latter's arrival in spirit, for names he had applied to him in life. He spoke of his early life and struggles, and urged my boys to heed the lessons and evidences they were getting that night.

This is a very incomplete record of a family séance, but I pledge my honour to its truth. May it encourage others and bring hope and courage to the bereaved. It illustrates the results which can be obtained in a family circle when all the sitters are harmoniously related. My sons and daughter were deeply impressed and for a long time their thoughts will be directed to the sacredness and continuity of life. They know their brother and sister still live.

S. Burrows.

The Two Worlds – 30th May, 1941.

Quite recently I visited Nottingham and, having a few hours to spare I remembered an invitation from that well-known medium, Mrs Northage, to call whenever I should be in the district, and therefore enquired my way to her residence.

On arrival I found that a Healing Service was in progress in the Sanctuary, or place set apart for that purpose, so I decided to wait, and spent the time chatting with people who had accompanied patients for treatment. One gentleman in particular informed me that he had been completely cured of a cancerous growth, and there was no sign of any recurrence.

In due course this Healing Service was over. Helpers and patients alike came up to the house for tea, and I had an opportunity of speaking to Mrs Northage. She was surprised to see me, but expressed her delight that I had called and gave me an invitation to attend her developing class that evening, after which, time permitting, she would hold a séance as a special favour for me. Needless to say I was delighted and agreed to stay.

Although the hour was then late, Mrs Northage redeemed her promise and went into the cabinet. Immediately the voice of Sambo – one of her guides – was heard speaking, and in a few seconds the trumpets were floating round the room, accompanied by the voice saying: "Sambo him test the Power and it good."

A 'form' then materialised which was clearly seen by all, and, after giving us a greeting went on to speak with her mother who was one of the sitters.

I felt something rather like rain-drops on my hands and face and immediately the whole room was permeated with a rare and refreshing perfume. (My clothing during the next day seemed impregnated with this perfume), and I also had a number of flowers placed on my hands and on my lap. Each of the sitters had some communication from loved ones; some spoke through the trumpet, several materialised, whilst others contented themselves by playing a drum and moving it up to the ceiling where it was plainly seen by all. One 'voice' who gave his name and said he was a choirboy asked us to sing something with him and chose *Oh for the Wings of a Dove*. We all started to sing this song, but gradually 'faded out' as we listened entranced to the boyish 'trilling' which made the song vibrate with love, and it will live long in my memory.

The loved ones that materialised and showed themselves to me left no room for doubt. As I gazed on features I well remembered, looked intently into their eyes, watched their lips as I talked with them and they replied; studied their mannerisms as of old, the years faded away and they were with me just as emphatically as ever they were. I asked if they would write me something so that I could compare this with previous handwriting, and a promise was made. (This promise was redeemed a few evenings afterwards and a message written by the 'materialised loved one' in view of several other people). To feel their arms around me, their fingers stroking my face and caressing me, disarranging my hair and pulling at my tie were all reminders of 'what once used to be'.

One rather excited voice addressed me through the trumpet and called me by a name used only in my boyhood days. He subsequently gave his full name and our associations in school and sport; all of which I recognised and remembered. And so it went on for nearly two hours, this reunion of family and friends, until Dr Reynolds – another guide of Mrs Northage's, and to whom I was introduced – decided to call a halt as 'the instrument' needed rest after such a busy day.

So ended a pleasant and memorable evening and we were all very grateful to Mrs Northage and her guides for such a fine display of evidential mediumship. May her health be maintained to enable her to carry on such good work in these strenuous and critical times.

R.P.N.

The Advertiser, Grimsby – 16th August, 1941.

I had the most astounding experience of my life on Tuesday evening when I attended a materialisation séance held in connection with the Louth Spiritualist Church. I went as an entirely independent observer and have tried to write about and describe what I saw and heard and my reactions to the same, though no one could ever express in words what they experienced. It was the first séance I have ever attended, and I went as a freshman to Spiritualism, not knowing the first thing about it, and frankly, rather sceptical. But after what I saw and heard the fact was thrust upon me that sceptical though I was, I am bound to admit that there must be something in Spiritualism. What I witnessed was not the result of trickery. In the light of this there was nothing to do but accept the explanation given to me and say that what I saw was a materialisation of persons who have passed on from this earth and who were able to speak and appear through the marvellous powers of the medium, Mrs Northage, of Nottingham.

The séance took place in a room of the house occupied by Mr A. F. Cutforth, who is vice-president of the Louth Spiritualist Church. Both before and after the ceremony I was allowed to make a free search of the room, and at neither time did I find anything which could be associated with any of the manifestations witnessed.

We were seated in a circle round the room, one corner of which was partitioned off by a thin curtain so as to make a kind of cabinet for the medium. I was third from the cabinet. Before the medium entered the room the lights were turned off, leaving it in darkness except for a very faint red light which was turned off once the medium had taken her place in the cabinet. The room was now in complete darkness, and for the next few minutes my feelings were very mixed. I was not frightened, for my nerves are good, but I was assailed by a feeling of uncertainty, it being the first séance I had attended. We all linked hands forming a continuous chain, and during the singing of a hymn the medium passed into a kind of trance. I did not know the particular hymn that was sung, and, listening intently, I could just hear the heavy breathing of the medium above the sound of the singing.

As the hymn was nearly finished there was a slight noise and I could see a faint luminous glow about three inches long and an inch wide floating through mid-air round the room. At first I thought it was the darkness playing tricks with my eyes, but no, it was there true enough, and I suddenly realised that it was a trumpet used at these séances which was being levitated. The hymn finished and then quite distinctly I could hear the voice of Sambo, a Negro who died many years ago, talking in the dialect which is peculiar to natives when speaking the English language.

I learned later that Sambo is the spirit guide. Many spirits, some of them relations or friends of those present, spoke through the trumpet, and although all I could see was a faint light which I presumed to be coming from the end of the trumpet, I could hear the voices quite distinctly. By this time the feeling of strangeness which I had experienced at the commencement was beginning to wear off. Those present spoke to the spirits quite naturally and in fact carried on a normal conversation with them. But this feeling of equanimity was shattered when a spirit stronger than those who had been before it commenced to materialise. At first all I could see was a faint blur, slightly lighter than the blackness of the room and then the luminous plaque, which the spirits use to illuminate their features, apparently picked itself up from the floor.

This the spirit shone on itself, and in the faint greenish glow I could see distinct features forming out of the shapeless mass. Soon they were stable and easily recognisable, while the rest of the body below the shoulders seemed to merge into the blackness of the room. This form was recognised, and bearing the plaque so that its light could be clearly seen, moved across the room to the person who had recognised it as a relation who had died some time ago. To reach this person, who was on the other side of the room, the spirit had to pass right in front of me, and as it passed I could feel the swish of drapery past my knees and became aware of a subtle perfume, unlike anything I had ever smelt before. It was only a faint rather pleasing smell, but it seemed to pervade the atmosphere all round. I was told later, when the séance was over, that this perfume is brought by the spirits from their sphere.

When the shape reached the person it knew, greetings were exchanged and a normal conversation was carried on, the spirit saying how happy it was on the other side. It probably stayed in the material form for about half a minute and then the plaque fell slowly to the floor and the shape whispered good-bye as it dematerialised in a greenish glow of light which spread on the floor, to be followed by complete darkness.

For two and three quarter hours this continued; spirits speaking through the trumpet; the stronger ones materialising so that they could be seen. In fact some of these materialised forms were so strong that one man present kissed his grandmother again, although she had been dead for some years. All of those present spoke to at least one of their departed loved ones.

At the close of the séance the medium came out of her trance and about a quarter of an hour later I was talking to her. She told me about her Sanctuary at her home in Nottingham, and explained that the intelligence of the spirit shapes, in a materialised form is Ectoplasm, which is drawn from the medium's body.

I, who had gone as an entirely uninterested and independent observer, could not help but be impressed by what I had seen, and I shall never forget that experience as long as I live.

G. W. Marshall, *Advertiser* Reporter.

By A. F. Cutforth – 22nd August, 1941.

It was appropriate that Mrs Bessie Burrows, of Skegness, should conduct the first services at the Louth Spiritualist Church after its affiliation to the S.N.U. Her address and clairvoyance gave pleasure and evidence to a full church.

Another visitor was Mrs Northage, of Nottingham, who was fulfilling a promise to give a séance at my home to celebrate our affiliation. With two mediums in the house we had an excellent blending of the two worlds, which illustrated the value of good mediums. Mrs Northage gave two sittings to carefully chosen sitters, amongst whom were Mrs Ernest Marklew, Messrs. I and F. Ward, Grimsby, and Mr and Mrs Marshall, president and secretary at Louth. The conduct of the séances was in the capable hands of Mrs Burrows.

Prior to the séance, Sambo, Mrs Northage's guide, had distinguished himself by the levitation of a very heavy table in full light. The table rested an inch from the floor and was as firm as if it had been supported. It delighted the children.

The phenomena witnessed in our Sanctuary was remarkable. My grandmother, who passed in 1901, materialised, and I was able to kiss her, and my son, who passed over five years ago and would have celebrated his birthday on the 12th, was clearly seen carrying a cross. He kissed his mother and asked for his birthday present.

At the first sitting on Monday, August 11th, we were all sprayed with scent as soon as the séance had opened. White drapery was floating all over the circle it was firm and beautifully scented, and its delicate texture would be difficult to imitate. Two trumpets were levitated at the same time. While one spirit was holding a conversation through the trumpet at one side of the room, a fully materialised form was conversing with friends and relations on the other side. Mothers, sons, husbands, wives, brothers, sisters, children and guides appeared as solid forms, and able to shake hands with us and exchange kisses.

At the second séance a reporter from the local paper was present and gave us an excellent column report in the *Advertiser*, which he concluded by saying: "I who had gone as an entirely independent observer, could not help but be impressed by what I had seen, and I shall never forget that experience as long as I live." He had examined the room very thoroughly before the séance.

Amongst the spirits who appeared was Ernest Marklew, M.P. who held a long conversation with his wife, and was strong enough to kiss her and shake hands. He expressed his opinion that at the end of the war Mr Churchill would resign owing to the state of his health. We also had a visit from two air-raid victims who were known to a number of sitters. Cyril, the sailor son of Mrs Burrows, told us of the work he was doing amongst the sailors who pass over. These forms came from the cabinet and walked around amongst the sitters, most of them dematerialised 'through the floor' in front of us, often talking until they were only an inch or two above the floor. We were much impressed by Dr Reynolds, the spirit guide of Mrs Northage's healing circle. Sambo chose two cacti plants in pots and asked us to arrange simultaneous séances at Louth and Nottingham in order that he might try to apport them. I hope this may be possible.

During the two séances there must have been nearly one hundred materialised forms and many voices. We thank Mrs Northage and her guides for this privilege.

The Two Worlds – September 26th, 1941.

A very enjoyable evening was spent with Mrs I. A. Northage of Bulwell, Nottingham, at the Psychic Research Fellowship, Swindon, on Monday, 15th inst. There were fourteen sitters. The séance was opened with a hymn and prayer and immediately we felt scent sprinkled on our hands.

The 'control' of the cabinet spoke and introduced himself as Sambo. The two trumpets rose well above the heads of the sitters and Sambo said they were testing the power of the circle and found it very good. About thirty-six spirit visitors manifested, some sitters having as many as five and six loved ones to visit them. The materializations were particularly good and were instantly recognised.

There was a very impressive meeting with one sitter. A little girl called for her daddy; she said her name was June. Having made contact with her daddy she asked if he would like to see 'Mummy', being assured he would she went back to the cabinet to fetch her. It was very impressive to hear the grateful joy in their voices for the privilege of coming back and being able to contact the loved one again.

Then Sambo said: "A lady wants to speak to White Lady by the cabinet; she come from your and my country, Africa." The niece of the sitter expressed her great joy at being able to speak to her Auntie and proved she was aware of what goes on this side of the veil by saying: "I am so glad daddy got the young driver off. It was a terrible accident, Auntie, but I was so proud daddy did all he could for him. Please, Auntie, I want to speak to my daddy very much, will you try to bring him to me, and I want to speak to Don." (meaning her husband). This was very evidential to another sitter, who knew the circumstances. Then a brother of the same sitter came and spoke through the trumpet in Dutch.

The séance lasted two hours and at times there were three voices speaking at once. The voices were strong and clear, even when they whispered they could be distinctly heard by the rest of the circle. The firmness of the materialized hands, which were warm, could be felt as they caressed the faces of the sitters.

We felt very privileged indeed to have had Mrs Northage with us for the whole weekend. Just as her séance was a joy and comfort so were the public meetings which she took. Her address and musical clairvoyance will long be remembered for the comfort and upliftment we received.

The Two Worlds – 12th December, 1941. (E Oaten, *editor* writes:)

Mr J. Whittles, of Dewsbury, writes to me: "On a recent Sunday I visited Mrs Northage, of whose mediumship you have given many reports. She very kindly gave me a séance. I was invited to open with prayer, during which spirit hands touched mine. Subsequently the following dialogue took place.

Sambo: "Did you feel someone touch you while you were praying?"

"Yes, Sambo."

Sambo: "It was a spirit helper who wishes to speak to you. I will let him come now."

Then through the trumpet came the words: "I am Armitage."

"Yes, friend – Armitage who?"

Trumpet: "I am Armitage from Hanging Soothill. I was a member of the Soothill Board of Education. I was a Unitarian preacher before I was a Spiritualist."

"You mean Hanging Heaton, Friend? Not Hanging Soothill. But I am afraid I don't know you."

Trumpet: "But you do know me, I am Armitage." He then repeated the above particulars.

My wife: "I think I know him." I added: "Oh, you don't mean old Joe Armitage from Hanging Heaton."

Trumpet: "Yes, yes, I am helping you."

Self: "God bless you, Mr Armitage, and thank you."

The reason I am writing you, Mr Oaten, is to ask if he was a Unitarian preacher before becoming a Spiritualist. I have confirmed that he was a member of the Soothill Board of

Education. Mr Armitage passed over when I was very young, and I'd only just entered Spiritualism. – J. Whittles."

I have been familiar with the name Joseph Armitage for 40 years but had no knowledge of his connection with the Unitarian body. I accordingly wrote Mr Frank Hepworth, his son-in-law. (Mr Hepworth is married to Mr Armitage's eldest daughter). I have received the following reply.

"Dear Mr Oaten,

In confirmation of the communication received by Mr and Mrs Whittles through the mediumship of Mrs Northage, I may state that Mr Joseph Armitage, of Hanging Heaton, near Dewsbury, was for some years superintendent of the Unitarian Sunday School, Dewsbury, and frequently lectured at the school there. After he became a Spiritualist he sat on the Soothill School Board and was for some years its chairman. He was also for many years chairman of the local council. As you know, he served the Spiritualist movement as a speaker for forty years. He was presented with an oil painting of himself, and Mrs Armitage was presented with an inscribed tray and tea service by the Yorkshire Union in 1906. The tray is now in my wife's possession and the painting and tea service in the possession of other members of the family.

Frank Hepworth."

I wonder if it is a coincidence that I mentioned Mr Armitage in my 'Topics of the Week' last week? – (*Editor*)

The Two Worlds – July 1st, 1949. (by the Editor, Ernest Thompson).

Deep in the heart of the country, miles from any town, lives one of the world's greatest mediums, Mrs Isa Northage.

Her little bungalow lies hidden in a wood on the crest of a hill. Among the tall trees are three other small buildings. The first containing a waiting room and healing clinic, the second is an operating theatre, where Mrs Northage's spirit guide, Doctor Reynolds regularly materialises and performs operations, and the third is a Sanctuary where wonderful séances are held.

Mrs Northage does not now do public work, on the advice of her spirit guide, and only her well-known friends attend the séances and assist in healing the sick.

I was fortunate, through the offices of one of these friends, to be included amongst those who were privileged to sit with her at a recent séance. A party of about twelve people very informally entered the Sanctuary, and Isa sat in a large armchair in front of a beautiful stained glass window.

Settling herself, she closed her eyes and asked for the lights to be put out, and the proceedings commenced immediately.

The only forms of lighting used were luminous plaques and a red electric torch.

Without delay manifestations occurred, and two forms materialised and respectively engaged two people in conversation on opposite sides of the circle. For three hours and twenty-five minutes numerous spirit friends returned and either used the direct voice or else materialised in full form. These materialised figures were of different sizes, some quite small, others of normal height, and one quite tall.

I was most fortunate in receiving what was possibly the most outstanding evidence of the evening. A spirit visitor spoke to me in the direct voice, stating that he was Peter Lee (passed to the higher life in 1908), and that what he was going to tell me was solely for the purpose of evidence.

He stated that the following incidents in his life all occurred in the year 1894. "I was the first Socialist to be elected as a member of the Rochdale School Board. Secondly, I presided at the Annual Conference of Spiritualists. Thirdly I was vice-chairman of *The Two Worlds*. I am giving these facts to you, Thompson, as evidence – you will understand."

On my return to Manchester I spent a considerable time looking up old records to verify the above items and found the following – "An account of Peter Lee's passing in the Rochdale Observer of 1909 states: "About eighteen years ago he identified himself with the Socialists – the I.L.P. Section – who put him forward as their candidate at the memorable School Board election of 1894. He was one of the successful candidates, being fifth on the poll and receiving 9,346 votes; Colonel Fishwick who headed the poll, obtained 12,602. At the next triennial election there was no contest, and Mr Lee remained on the Board. Three years later, however, the Socialists nominated a second candidate, Mrs George Chew. Both were defeated." In regard to the second item, a report of the Fifth National Conference of the National Federation of Spiritualists, held at Darwen on July 1st, 1894 states: "Mr Peter Lee (the president), opened the conference with a few well chosen, considered and impressive remarks."

For the last item I referred to an old minutes book of *The Two Worlds Publishing Co.Ltd.*, which confirmed the fact that he was vice-chairman in 1894.

As a personal message he stated that he was very interested in my work for the movement and was helping me. "Whenever you want any help send out a thought and I will be with you," he said. (It is interesting to note, in view of my work as S.N.U. Education Secretary and my Editorship of *The Two Worlds*, that Mr Lee considered that the Education of Exponents was the 'greatest need of all' for the movement.) In an interview he had stated: "The future of the movement lies in this direction on account of the ever onward march of intelligence and education which will become more exacting in their scientific attitude. Old theology is fast passing away, and nothing but the revelations of Spiritualism can check the tendency of Scientific Materialism to take its place, hence the necessity for a Scientific Spiritualism, as well as its purely ethical or religious aspect." He also occupied the editorial chair of *The Two Worlds* when Mr E. W. Wallis was touring in the United States.

Whilst travelling to Mrs Northage's séance I had radiated, thoughts to my mother (she passed to the higher life November 23rd, 1939), hoping that she would come and be allowed the opportunity to materialise. My wife, who was with me, possesses one of my mother's rings which is set with three opal stones.

In the darkness at the beginning of the séance, my wife gave me this ring, and I slipped it on one of my fingers, with the stones concealed, according to an arrangement we had come to on the journey. To my intense joy my mother materialised and, obviously very excited, came very close to us calling, "Ernie, I want my boy."

An old lady, mother of a sitter, materialised and spoke in a very loud voice indeed. Her conversation was as normal as any living person's. (She had been before several times.)

My wife's nun guide came and gave her a blessing in Latin, and then translated it, stating she was always with her. She made the sign of the cross with a luminous trumpet before and after her manifestation.

Another materialised figure was that of the father of one of the sitters who was reunited with his daughter. His features were definitely masculine and complete with moustache. Many young men who had passed over on active service also returned.

A young boy from Ashington, Northumberland, amused everyone with his 'Geordie' dialect and sang *Blaydon Races*. A young girl, giving her name as Ivy Chaters, of Scott Terrace, Cramlington, said: "Next time yer up theer, gan and ca' on mi muther, she'll gie ye a cup a tea. It's only twenty-five minutes in the bus from Newcastle." She said that her body had been buried in Seghill cemetery.

Another visitor referred to a recent presentation, and said that Mr L. had been given an electric clock. (Correct). "Was there anything missing?" asked the recipient. "Yes, the name (inscription) is missing." (Correct.)

A Russian girl, who had died during the war, came to plead with the circle for a better understanding of her country. She had died for freedom and peace, and stated that her country also wanted peace but was greatly misunderstood in this.

Space does not permit me to go into greater detail or even to give a brief account of all the other spirit visitations. It is enough to state however that the spirit friends and loved ones came continuously for nearly three and a half hours.

"Are you folks staying here till tomorrow?" said the guide, but now the power was almost used up, and the séance came to a close.

May I pay tribute to the wonderful mediumship of Mrs Northage and to her most generous hospitality; a truly amazing person, yet humble and unaffected in her great service to mankind.

Account from Mr and Mrs Ventress,
Woodbury Salterton, Near Exeter:

"In the spring of 1951 we received a letter which was to change our lives completely. It was from a friend of my mother who died suddenly in 1943. She told us she had attended evening service at Pinewoods Healing Church on the previous Sunday, and had been given a message from 'Pixie' through a Mrs Edith Hill. She had been asked to give her love to her daughter (me), and to ask if my husband and I could visit Pinewoods at some time to enable her to talk to us. 'Pixie' had been my pet name for my mother, and to hear that she had given this on her first return from the spirit world was to me the most conclusive evidence.

On November 14th, 1951, my husband and I attended Mrs Northage's Armistice Séance at which over 30 people were present. Sambo greeted us all warmly, with a special welcome for my husband, who had spent over twenty years on the Gold Coast: "Brother Ventress, who know de Sambo country."

Then Dr Reynolds' crisp, friendly voice said: "Good evening, Ventress. I am glad to meet you and your good lady." Lastly the sweet, gentle voice of Ellen Dawes welcomed us. To my unspeakable joy two trumpets had lifted before us right at the start of the séance; one was slightly higher than the other, then for the first time we heard the voices of our beloved little daughter and son. They had both died at birth, and three days old respectively, owing to rhesus incompatibility. "Hello, Mummy and Daddy; I'm Zoe," came from the higher trumpet; "Hello, Mummy and Daddy; I'm Nils," came from the lower one. "We cannot stay long, the soldiers will be coming, but we will try to come back later and show ourselves." Then they both blew kisses from their trumpets. Sambo explained as they went "I've taken the children away so the soldiers will not frighten them."

My father, who died in 1939, greeted us next. "You mustn't worry about the children we will look after them until you come home." He told us: "Be happy at the cottage and don't worry about the new place." This last referred to a problem that had recently worried us. Despairing of obtaining a licence to build a house, after years of waiting we bought a cottage in May 1951; ten days later our licence was granted. Our difficulty had been to know which to retain and we chose the cottage as my father knew. I asked him: "Is Tony with you?" (our greatly loved spaniel). He replied: "Yes, and not only my dogs but also my cows and horses, too." He had been a farmer and breeder of Devon cattle. He laughed and talked with great happiness and vigour. Turning to the circle he said: "I'm afraid I'm taking a lot of your time." To which all replied, "Don't stop. We are, enjoying it." Finally I asked him: "Have you met Tim?" At once another trumpet lifted and a kindly voice said: "My sister Kay, my brother Vee." This was my brother who died at the age of three, the year before I was born. He said: "I have often wondered if your life would have been happier if I had lived – you were so lonely."

I asked Tim what work he was doing, and he told us: "One of our jobs consists of meeting people killed suddenly in train, plane or road accidents. We call it going over the mountains; and when they wake up here we are able to help them to realise where they are." Someone asked him: "If you know an accident is going to happen why can you not prevent it?" To which he replied: "Once the call has gone out, you must come. Pixie is just the same, always darting about." He added a perfect description of our volatile mother. To my infinite joy my mother materialised. She greeted us with emotion and kissed my cheek, breathing rather rapidly with excitement, then she patted my husband's cheek, and passed on to kiss the friend who had brought us before she de-materialised. Surely, we thought, there cannot be any more visitors for us tonight, but we were wrong. My husband will describe what happened next.

Here follows Mr Ventress's account: "A trumpet appeared in front of me and a voice said: "Steward," followed by words I could not make out, the voice was so husky. As the voice became weaker the trumpet was lowered almost to the floor and I talked rapidly to keep up the vibrations. Someone at the other end of the circle came to my rescue and said: "It sounded like 'was-sirt'." "I asked him (the spirit using the trumpet), "Did you say 'wash shirt?" "To my intense relief the trumpet lifted. I continued: "You must be Abudulai." His reply was immediate; "Yes, Massa, I be Abudulai, Massa Ventry," which was as near as ever he could get to my name. I asked him why he had not returned to me before

I left the Gold Coast, for he had worked for me for about twenty years. Without a moment's hesitation he snatched up another trumpet and clashed them both together, effectively simulating the crack of a gunshot, saying, "Massa, Francie s'ot me." He was from the French Territory north of the Gold Coast, and invariably spoke of the French authorities as "Francie." He could never pronounce the letter 'h'. It was ten years since he had left me, and he was greatly excited at meeting me again, even as I was to meet him. He jabbed at me with the trumpet and kept repeating "Massa, Massa," then turning to my wife, whom he had never met in this life tapped her, saying, "Missie, Missie." We could hear his feet thudding on the floor in a dance of joy as his trumpet whirled round and round near the ceiling. His voice boomed like an organ as he called out: "Hi-ya, hi-ya," a chant which the circle took up.

I should explain here who Abudulai was. Son of the Big Chief of the Gurunshi people, whose territory lies north of the Gold Coast he was heir to their Stool. He joined the Gold Coast (now Ghana) police as a young man, and after retirement worked for me as watchman, cook and steward for twenty years. In his last year with me he asked me for a short leave to visit his home country because of tribal trouble, intending to be away for only three weeks. He never returned. He was a devout Mohammedan, a most devoted and irreplaceable servant and friend. His return in the circle solved, after many years and much anxiety, the mystery of his disappearance.

There was a pause after his trumpet touched the floor, then Sambo spoke: "There is a Great White Chief from the Sambo country who wishes to speak." After another slight pause, a second trumpet rose, and a quiet voice said: "I am David Livingstone, I have come to confirm, Mr Ventress, that that was indeed your servant Abudulai Gurunshi. I worked for the Africans when on earth and am still working for them, and I know that you too did much good work for them."

Mrs Ventress continues: "On November 16th, Mrs Northage very kindly gave us another sitting in her Sanctuary, together with my mother's friend. My husband's mother, who also passed in 1943 came first and said: "I'm Mother, Mary. I'm so glad to be able to speak to you, God bless you, my boy." Vee asked if she played with the children she replied: "No, but I see them they are beautiful children. It's lovely here and I have no pain."

Then she turned and thanked Mrs Northage. Zoe and Nils followed her and both greeted us. Zoe said: "I go to school now, but it's not like your schools." Nils (quickly): "I go school soon." We then asked if they had been to the cottage, and both said they had. We asked Nils if he would like a garden, excitedly he said he would. What kind of flowers did he want? "Buttercups and daisies," he replied. Zoe asked: "Can I have one too, with roses and other pretty flowers?" Nils asked: "Will you make me a waterfall with ducks?" "He means a pond," Zoe explained. We asked what we should put on Auntie Isa's (Mrs Northage's) Christmas tree for them. Nils said: "A football, a big one to kick." "Not a big one," cautioned Zoe. I asked Nils how should we know what sort he wanted. He replied: "I come with you to shop," as one stating a fact.

Next we asked Zoe and she said: "I'd like a dolly with a blue dress. Will you make it for me, Mummy, one I can put on and take off?" Zoe told us: "Grandpa takes us round the fields to see his sheep and cows and horses." I asked if they rode on the front of him as I did they chorused: "Do you think he will let us?" I said: "Yes, you must ask him." I then asked if Daddy's Mummy was with them. Zoe said "Yes, Granny Mary." I then asked Zoe: "Is your hair dark?" She replied: "Yes, it hangs in curls onto my shoulders, and Nils has a curl in the centre of his forehead."

On February 10th, 1952, a Christmas tree séance was held, and afterwards we wrote to Mr Macdonald (as we heard our children had materialised) asking if he knew of any details of their appearance having been recorded. I quote from his warm-hearted reply: "... two children came through, the little boy gave his name as Nils. He had fair hair and .. long features and blue-grey eyes. He handled his ball and was very excited indeed and told me it was a present from his parents. He was very happy and quite at home. The little girl appeared to be about five or six years old. She was darker and had dark eyes, round face and very pretty, and was very much in love with her dolly. The dear child asked us to thank you very much for her doll. She too was very excited and full of happiness."

On January 16th, 1953, we attended Mrs Northage's Christmas tree séance. A tall tree, lovingly decorated, was covered with presents; there were extra gifts for the children, unknown to the parents who invariably pop in. Whistles, squeakers, drums, tambourines and mouth organs were heaped at the base of the tree, for spirit children are as merry as any, and love making a noise as they would if still on earth. The Sanctuary was lit by dim red lamps and scattered about were wooden, luminous plaques and torches. As each child materialised it picked up a plaque and held it up to illuminate the features.

Soon all was activity, with numerous spirit children searching for and unwrapping their parcels, talking and laughing with their parents and loudly blowing their squeakers, etc. The gentle Ellen Dawes was helping the smaller children to find and unwrap their gifts. We saw her beautiful materialised form near the top of the tree, and never had we felt so close to the angelic spheres as on this night. Naturally our attention was centred on the coming of our own children.

Nils came first. He was then about five years old we had put a little clockwork tractor on the tree for him. First we heard him saying: "Where is my present? I can't find it," with rising agitation. Then he found and unwrapped it, and coming over to us held his plaque, luminous side up, and ran his tractor up and down its flat surface. He then handed the tractor and key to my husband and said: "Wind it up, Daddy, please." When this was done we watched him follow it across the floor on hands and knees in great excitement. He then returned with the tractor and handed it to his daddy saying: "Hold it for me, please, I come back." Almost at once we heard Zoe saying: "I want my Mummy and Daddy." "We are over here, darling," I said. "I know, I can see you," she replied, and coming to stand before us she said "I thank you for my book and my bag," and then said she would like them given to the little daughter of a sitter present. I kissed her on the cheek and she moved in front of me saying: "I want to kiss my Daddy," and after kissing him she dematerialised.

Soon after Abudulai Gurunshi greeted us joyfully and snatching up a tambourine, proceeded to whisk it within a hairsbreadth of our noses, playing one of the drum rhythms of West

Africa. Later, when the lights were turned up we were astonished to find Zoe's parcel unopened on the tree, yet she had known and mentioned its contents. We can never be grateful enough that the thin veil separating us from our loved ones has been drawn aside, giving us the certainty that all is well with them.

To the friend who introduced us to Pinewoods and Mrs Northage and her inspirers we are eternally indebted. Some years ago Dr Reynolds and Mrs Northage told us that they could pick up our thoughts and would help us if we were in difficulties or sickness, and over the years this has proved true time and again.

His most recent help came when my husband cut his left eyeball. He was rushed to the infirmary and we asked Dr Reynolds for help. Doctor and specialist alike were amazed at the speed, ease and painlessness with which the eye healed. I wrote Mrs Northage on November 14th and she received my letter on November 17th. On the day I wrote, Dr Reynolds had picked up my call for help and at once treated the eye and said it would be all right. Though we have visited Pinewoods only twice, in spirit we are frequently linked, and this knowledge is a source of great comfort and reassurance to us both.

Account of Experiences.
from Olwen Scott Insall.

I had been interested in psychic phenomena for some years, having lived in a 'haunted house' for a long time. But the books on the subject were so dull and frustrating that I seemed to learn nothing.

It was not until I met Mrs Northage that the truth became apparent. It was her remarkable mediumship which finally set the seal on my faith. Then I discovered that the *Holy Bible* is the greatest Book on spiritual phenomena.

Isa Northage is the most wonderful medium the world has produced for centuries.

It is the simplicity of her séances which make them so fine – there are no tambourines, shouting and bawling, holding hands, etc., which are associated with most spiritualist séances, and which I find very repugnant.

I shall never forget the first séance we were privileged to attend. The whole atmosphere throughout, as in all her séances, was so spiritually lovely. It is her absolute devotion to God and her love of Christ which makes them so.

It was in July 1950 that we had our first experience. I was dumbfounded by the many different phenomena which occurred. For us, a spirit materialised in Arab dress – he spoke his name, Ahmed es Suleiman – and we were just speechless. Then he touched us both, my husband and myself, and said, "Sahba, sahba." We had almost forgotten the little Arabic we had learnt in Egypt before the war. And I could not remember a word to answer him, I was so bewildered. Ahmed es Suleiman was a young Bedouin who used to go with us on many of our desert trips, and we were quite unaware of his death. "Sahba" we learnt later is a very usual greeting, meaning 'friend'.

The second occasion which gave me absolute proof that there is no death was at an Armistice séance. A spirit materialised on the other side of the circle, standing in front of the medium. His thin, sensitive face and dark, straight eyebrows had a familiar look. Someone called out: "It's a sailor," and then the figure said: "It's Keith, Olwen." Again I was overwhelmed. We spoke a few words and, as he was leaving, he said: "Eternal Father, strong to save." Keith was a naval officer, a cousin and very beloved friend, who was lost in the M.1 submarine disaster.

The above are only two accounts of the very wonderful experiences I have had with Isa Northage, not only in her own séance room, but also in my own drawing room. I only wish more people in the world could have been so privileged.

(Signed) Olwen Insall.

From Mrs I. Body, 62 Birkland Avenue, Warsop, near
Mansfield, Notts. November 1958.

On June 1st my son, an only child, left home to re-join his unit in Cyprus, where he had been serving for two years. He had just finished six weeks' leave and we were all very happy with the thought that on November 12th he would be back in England for good awaiting de-mobilisation.

He arrived back in Cyprus on June 2nd, and ten days later I received a telegram to say that he had been shot and was critically ill; six days later I received another telegram to say my son was dead.

I was absolutely stunned by the shock and soon became very ill. I could not understand why God had seen fit to take my only child. I could not understand how He could be so cruel. Needless to say I lost my faith in God and the whole of mankind, because my neighbours and friends not knowing what to say to me in my grief stayed away from me. For weeks and weeks I was in black despair, not knowing what to do nor where to go, and was steadily heading for a mental collapse.

Then, one Sunday afternoon when my sorrow took me into the very depth of hell, I suddenly remembered a little church called Pinewoods, where some years ago I had received spirit healing for internal trouble and had come away cured. I remembered the gentleness and kindness I had received whilst attending there, and somehow once more I found myself entering that quiet little church. I sat with my heart breaking, wishing I had never gone, then suddenly I found myself being pointed at by the medium saying that she wanted to bring me a young soldier boy who had passed away recently through gunshot wounds in the abdomen. She said my boy wanted to tell me to stop grieving because it was only upsetting him. Tears rained down my face as I tried to hang on to every word she said. Finally the service ended and I sat with my head down, ashamed to let anyone see my ravaged face, but as the congregation began to file out many a one stopped to give me a word of sympathy which again brought the tears of dark despair.

Suddenly I found my hand clasped and my cheek kissed and someone saying: "Come on, love, your boy is all right." I looked up and into the eyes of Mrs Northage, the woman who had cured me some years ago, and there once again I saw the sympathy, love and understanding I had been starved of and which I was seeking.

I have attended that church every Sunday since then. I have found love, comfort and friendship within its walls, and tonight, Armistice Sunday, I have returned home a different woman. Why? Tonight Mrs Northage unveiled a brass tablet in memory of my son. Tonight she gave me back my faith in life, my faith in God and humanity; she gave me a new hope and a new outlook, and tonight she gave me back my son.

REMEMBRANCE

Here in this little sacred church
Tucked away among the trees,
So quiet you can hear the birds
And the rustling of the leaves.

Here within its hallowed walls
We have gathered from far and near
To pay our tribute to the Living Dead
Whose memory we treasure most dear.

Or may be it was some mother's son
Who for his country died,
She weeps, and then remembers
He still walks by her side.

Statement by Mrs Robertson, High Street, Southgate, London. December 1958.

As I sit writing this I feel an overwhelming thankfulness that I have been blessed with the power to acquire the knowledge that the spirit world is all around us and can be reached whenever we wish. I thank God that I have been given the chance to know someone as wonderful as Mrs Northage, who has devoted so much of her life to spreading this truth, and if it had not been for her and the help she has given to me and my family, I would not be sitting here at home, fit and well.

During the war I was a transport driver in the W.A.A.F. and met my husband while serving. We had many long chats on religion and there was no doubt I had arrived at the crossroads on this subject and felt I needed a longer time to enquire into the scriptures before being satisfied I was travelling on the right road. I had, much to my mother's consternation, refused to be confirmed in the Church of England because I was not sure this doctrine would answer my questions. I was, however, to find the answer sooner than I expected.

It was arranged that I should travel with my fiancé to Scotland to meet his family. We arrived in very thick fog and hours later than schedule, and George, my fiancé, was feeling very unwell with a bad throat. He mentioned this, and his mother, Mrs Robertson, asked if we would agree to sit in a circle for healing treatment. We consented, Mrs Robertson, George and I, and his brother.

I realised, although new to this sort of thing, that some other entity had taken possession of Mrs Robertson. A very peaceful atmosphere prevailed throughout the sitting the healing completed, the guide then turned to me and introduced herself as Japanese, saying that as I was new to the movement, I would require some, evidence. She then proceeded to describe my mother who, she said, was standing beside me, giving me her name, etc. then she described a gold locket I had left in London, and the drawer in the dressing table where it was. Next the guide described the house and garden where I lived as a child; all of this was quite true, even about the photographs and locket I had left behind.

I thanked her and was very impressed then she assured me I would receive much more evidence from the spirit world. For some months I had been suffering from intense headaches and fainting spells, so severe that when I had an attack I would have to lie down at once. Medical examinations had failed to find the reason. I was warned by the spirit world that I must rest as much as possible, although they realised how much this was asking, as we were in the midst of a war.

I returned to my station in the London area, and from then on became busier than ever, sometimes driving as much as four hundred miles a day. Despite strong will-power, I was compelled to report sick, and this distressed me very much, as I had not long been married during a short four days leave period. From then on I became worse, and was moved from one hospital to another. I needed rest, but was receiving drugs, etc, until finally I was given a lumbar puncture during which the needle was broken, and I became very ill indeed. I requested a friend at the hospital to ring an uncle of mine to ask if he could contact my husband, which fortunately he did, and my husband soon arrived, only to learn that I was very ill and had only a few hours to live. I sent my thoughts to my spirit friends, asking for help, and my husband sent for Mrs Robertson, who had helped him before; soon we were together sending out our prayers.

Our combined efforts reached the spirit world and Mrs Robertson had contacted Dr Reynolds, Mrs Northage's spirit doctor. At that time Mrs Northage was at the local railway station awaiting her train as she was going on holiday. She received a direct message from Dr Reynolds to return at once as I had been taken ill and we had requested help.

Mrs Northage cancelled her holiday and, with Dr Reynolds, gave me the help I so badly needed, and asked me to send my thoughts direct to Doctor when I needed his help. These two great souls did wonders for me, and at last I was able to return to my husband's parents' home in Scotland, where his mother, Mrs Robertson, such a kindly soul, cared for me during my recovery. I was very weak, hardly able to walk, and added to this I had lost three stone in weight. We now received a message from Mrs Northage saying that Dr Reynolds requested me to take a short walk in the fresh air every day and to rest as much as possible.

I was indeed very ill and had awful pain in my spine. It was as if live electric wires were sending shocks up and down it. Mrs Robertson helped me each time I tried to lie down. The pain became so intense that Mrs Robertson sent for the local doctor, as she considered that with my little knowledge I would feel more contented that something was being done. After a long examination the doctor decided to call in a specialist, whose verdict was a tubercular abscess on the spine and I was to go into hospital at once and be placed in a plaster cast for eighteen months.

After the specialist had left, the local doctor returned to say that I must go to hospital, otherwise he would not be responsible for the consequences. I thanked him for telling me the truth and for attending me, but said that, far from the probable outcome, I was going to get well and become quite fit. We talked for some time and I told him we were Spiritualists. He wished me luck, saying he was sure I would need it.

My husband returned home on special leave and we at once sat in a circle in my bedroom. In a short time the spirit guide came through Mrs Robertson. He was an Indian (North American). I can still remember his very strong voice as he said that in no circumstances must I be moved from the house. He told me I would get well as I had the faith, but would not tell me how long it would take. I thanked him and assured him I had faith.

When our sitting had closed, I told Mrs Robertson that I would need looking after physically, lying on my back and being unable to move, and asked if she would undertake this task. She, good soul, agreed, and I was then in God's hands and those of Dr Reynolds and his helpers.

As days went by the pain ceased to throw me inches from the bed every time someone walked across the room. Although in continual pain I trusted Dr Reynolds completely. I had no special medicine or instructions, taking only orange juice and milk, and I was told later that I had received my food from the spirit world. The kidney trouble from which I was also suffering had been brought on by long hours of driving. Days passed into weeks, and then months, as I lay hardly sleeping at all. Sometimes I would see Mrs Robertson standing by my side looking troubled, and I would say: "Don't worry, Anne, the Friends will not let us down," and I would pray for strength to help her carry on.

Every Wednesday evening we would gather friends for a circle to join up in thought with Dr Reynolds' and Mrs Northage's circle for healing power. One evening while sitting in circle the Japanese guide came through Mrs Robertson, giving me healing as she sang a lullaby in her own Japanese tongue.

The next morning my child was born prematurely and breeched (B. presentation). Mrs Robertson, having received my urgent call was standing beside me. It was indeed a miracle. I was overjoyed, and no one in that house knew I was bearing a child, as I had been in bed so long. We were to learn that the spirit world had not wished it to be known because it would have added to my worry, and I believe the singing of the lullaby had helped the guide to keep the information from us.

The serious condition of the spine owing to the broken needle had affected the child. The local doctor came at once and expressed his surprise at the state of events. He chatted and had tea with us, and I am sure that he would give our conversation on Spiritualism much thought after leaving us that evening. The baby was normal in every way but for the breech and I had to learn to walk again until I had enough strength to get about alone. In a very short time I was pushing a heavy pram in all weathers.

My daughter is now aged thirteen and strong, healthy and normal, thanks to the spirit world and Mrs Robertson, Mrs Northage and Friends. How happy Mrs Robertson must have been in spirit to know she helped to save two lives when she was on earth.

My husband travelled every weekend from London to help all he could, and I am really grateful to all. I hope one day to do all I can to aid the spirit world and my fellows to receive the help I was given.

It was not surprising that I longed to meet Mrs Northage, whom I had not yet met, and a great feeling of happiness came when Mrs Robertson told me that Mrs Northage was on her way to pay us a visit. When she did arrive, we sat into the small hours listening to her wonderful experiences, and she kindly promised to give us a materialisation séance.

We had this séance, and many spirit friends came to us; many others were there from spirit waiting to greet us all. My mother was the first to come through, having passed over many years ago, and she called: "Joan (my name) I am fine now, free from all pain ... well and happy." She then said: "There are a lot waiting to come through, but I will try and show myself." In a few moments she built up, and I could see her quite clearly. She then asked me to look at her robes, but not to touch just yet. She was dressed like the ancient Greeks. Then, leaning forward with her face very close to mine, she said: "You see, Joan, my arm is warm and solid; you may feel it now." She then held out her hand and asked me to look at it. I did as requested, and it was perfect. Soon she was to leave me and give way to other spirit visitors, but before leaving she told me to look after my brother and give him her love, then: "Goodbye, Joan, and God bless you."

A lady sitting next to me asked for help with her knee; at once Dr Reynolds materialised and his hands were plainly seen as he examined her knee. Doctor gave her a diagnosis and instructions, then he informed me that I would be all right. I thanked him, but he told me to thank God and not him.

Later an Egyptian materialised, standing with her feet above the floor. It was explained that she was too far advanced to touch earth conditions. If people only knew how happy they make their loved ones in spirit by acknowledging that they can return and help us; they are so close to us, yet we keep the door locked. God never intended us to be parted.

Some years later I again became ill and requested my husband to send a cable to Mrs Northage in England, (we were then in Africa), and to sit by my bed and concentrate upon her and Dr Reynolds. In a short time I improved and was able to get about again. We received an air letter from Mrs Northage to say that she was away when our cable arrived, but Dr Reynolds had informed her of my condition, and said that he had removed a polio germ from my spine and saved me from paralysis.

In 1953 I learned I was again to have an addition to the family, and at once sent my thoughts to my spirit friends and Mrs Northage. I booked a nursing home and visited a leading gynaecologist in Johannesburg. I told her I was a Spiritualist, and the circumstances of my first confinement. She kindly said she quite understood, and had an open mind on the subject. She would take my case, adding that she had seen many wonderful things. She is herself now passed into spirit. I entered the nursing home under her care, receiving every attention. Seeing me in no pain and quite calm, the nurses left me for a time to attend to others in need. Being alone, I sent out my thoughts to Dr Reynolds: "Come along, Doctor, let's get it over without fuss." So quick were events that the Sister went for Matron, and before the doctor arrived my baby was born. She weighed 8 lb. 5 oz. and was perfect. I called her Janet. Looking about me I knew the spirit friends were working with the nurses, although they were not aware of it.

One day my husband was brought home very ill indeed. I did not call a doctor, but sat and sent out my thoughts to the spirit world; then I phoned for the doctor. He was examining the patient almost before I realised it, and as he finished he informed me that it was a case for the hospital at once. He knew my views and my faith, and listened as I told him I wished to keep my husband at home, then replied: "My dear girl, who am I to say that God and your spirit friends and you cannot get your husband well?" He promised to come again during the week, but asked me to 'be sure and call' day or night if I felt we needed him. In a week my husband had recovered.

In 1956 we returned to England, and I and my family visited Pinewoods, the home of Mrs Northage. We entered her lovely church and she described the many functions and services to which she had given her life. I was too full to reply as I would have liked. Here was I, with my family, visiting the very place we had all given our thoughts and prayers to, and from which we had received such blessings.

I can only ask that God will bless Mrs Northage and her Friends, and that they may be blessed to continue this great work.

From Mrs Fisher, Birmingham. 20th December, 1958.

It was in 1948 that we had the pleasure of meeting Mrs Northage for the first time and had our first séance with her. This proved to be a most remarkable sitting as Mrs Northage knew nothing at all about us, and yet we had overwhelming evidence. The quality of the ectoplasm was superb, resembling white satin. Among the forms that manifested that night were my mother, my husband's mother and my niece, Hilda.

My sister and her husband, who were among the sitters and, incidentally, were Hilda's mother and father, had wonderful evidence. Hilda passed to the world of spirit at the age of sixteen with a paralytic condition, but she proved her survival by materialising her full form, and excitedly drew her parents' attention to the fact that she could now walk. This she proved by pulling up her ectoplasmic gown and showing them her toes. She then ran across the room several times, showing the other sitters also. Hilda playfully pulled her father's tie and embraced them both. We consider Hilda an excellent communicator as she never fails at any séance to come and talk to us all.

My mother came, and I had a long and personal conversation with her. She was only a very small person, yet my husband's mother, as I remember her, was a tall, imposing, well-built woman, and this was exactly how they appeared, the difference in them being very marked. My mother-in-law started to build up right in between my husband and myself, I would say within a foot of us, therefore, as can well be imagined we had excellent proof. The ectoplasm seemed to start on the floor and gradually rose to the height of six feet, and out of this pillar my mother-in-law emerged. During that same evening a Sister of Mercy made herself known to us and, speaking in Latin, gave her blessing, making the sign of the Cross. She singled out Mrs Hands, and stated she was one of her spirit helpers. Other guides came, one or two of whom we had heard through other mediums, which again proved evidential. This proved to be the first of many sittings with Mrs Northage whom we consider to be one of our very best friends.

Over the past ten years we have had numerous talks with Dr Reynolds, and upon such occasions we have been permitted some time to speak to our loved ones by means of trumpet phenomena. My niece, Betty, who has lived with me from the age of three, spoke to her mother for the first time on the occasion of her 21st birthday. I thought it would be an appropriate time for such a reunion, and with Mrs Northage's kind co-operation this was made possible. The sitting commenced with a visit from Ellen Dawes, who is usually the first to speak, and we assume she ascertains the conditions of the room prior to the commencement of any sitting; she is a very lovable person.

At this time Mrs Hands was still in the capable care of Dr Reynolds, and of course he took the opportunity of having a few words with her through the trumpet. After this, Dr Reynolds gave permission for the materialisations to commence; having first made sure that Mrs Northage was in a comfortable position. On our way to Nottingham from Birmingham we had purchased a single red rose for Betty to give to her mother. This fact we had to mention to Mrs Northage, as we did not know the procedure regarding de-materialisation. Mrs Northage told us to take all the thorns off the rose, for the ectoplasm is of an earthly substance and returns to the medium, and when we assembled in the room the rose was put on an illuminated plaque on the floor. The first indication that this sitting was to be much more than a materialisation was when Sister Cynthia, Mrs Edith Hands' guide, stated she would like Edith to have her crucifix. This she gently placed on her lap. The next form to build up was Betty's mother, Doris. This was the moment we had waited for. Betty stood up to greet her mother and they kissed one another. Doris expressed to the other sitters her overwhelming happiness for this opportunity to speak to 'her Betty'. Doris thanked her for the rose which was on the illuminated plaque held in her hand, and told Betty to watch while she placed her hand over the rose and de-materialised it (no trace of the rose being found at the end of the sitting), saying that she would treasure this beautiful gift in the world of spirit. Doris then handed Betty a small Cross which had been given to her in the spirit world by a Spanish lady who had befriended her from the time of her passing. She told Betty that as she had not been buried with any personal articles her Spanish friend named Marguerite had apported her own little gift. Later in the séance, Marguerite came through and spoke, saying that the Cross had been buried with her, and that she had lived in the time of King Philip of Spain. She instructed Betty to thoroughly wash the Cross before wearing it as it had been buried for so long a time. Betty wears this daily and no money on earth could purchase it. Marguerite told Betty that the more she wore the Cross the brighter it would become, which has been proved, as at the end of the sitting, when we all examined the crystal Cross, it was very dull indeed, but has now regained its brilliance.

I myself was also given a small Cross, ivory in appearance, by a very young Sister of Mercy named Therese, who also materialised and was the last to bring an apport. She appeared to be about twenty to twenty-four years of age. Smiling very sweetly at me, the only words she spoke were: "This is for you." I had no idea what she had given me until we retired to the lounge. The object at the time of being handed to me felt very warm and soft.

Needless to say I treasure this apport very much indeed. This proved a memorable evening and a very happy one.

My own dear husband, Steve, recently passed away very suddenly with coronary thrombosis on September 13th, 1958. I was able to speak to him in October to reassure him that his personal affairs were in capable hands. Dr Reynolds helped him to pierce the veil after so short a time, as the worrying about his material affairs was defeating the efforts of the friends in spirit in helping him to adjust himself to his new life. He told me, immediately he knew what had happened, when he looked down and saw his body on the floor, what a shock it had been to him. He also described the room to which he had been taken and its beauty, saying that it was much better than anything he had ever known. At the beginning of his conversation he had much difficulty, speaking as he was under emotional strain, but after a time he became much stronger, and went away with his mind at rest. At a time such as this, I can say that my belief has helped me to carry on with my daily duties, and has seen me through this sad period. I know 'there is no death' and that we shall be together again one day.

This true account is written in all sincerity and we hope that we can in some small way help others as we have been helped.

From Mr W. Molson, Cooper Road, Grimsby. 26th January 1959.

It is a privilege to be asked to co-operate by writing one chapter for this book, which recounts the wonderful experiences of those who have had the good fortune to meet and sit with Mrs Isa Northage, undoubtedly one of this country's leading physical mediums. I do not know what the author of the main chapters in this book has recorded, but, at the invitation of Dr Reynolds, one of the special spirit co-operators with Mrs Northage, I would like to record my own impressions and experiences.

I have been invited to sit with Mrs Isa Northage on several occasions, once in my own home town, and, for the remaining sittings, in her home on the outskirts of Nottingham. Never at any moment during any of those séances have I experienced the slightest degree of doubt concerning the wonderful phenomena, and it would be no exaggeration to say that those séances stand out as landmarks on the path I have followed for the past twelve to thirteen years in studying the records of psychic phenomena and, when possible, submitting the claims which are made as to the validity of such phenomena to the cold test of hard reasoning. In the short space of one chapter I shall endeavour to recount some of the incidents and tell of my own personal reactions. In order that the account may be factual and subject to any analysis to which the enquirer might wish to subject it, it is necessary for me to record details which are perhaps of a personal nature, but I have no hesitation in so doing, for my purpose is to serve the cause of truth and to help any who may read this book in an endeavour to glimpse some of the great wonders which await us when we pass from the physical body.

I first met the medium in 1948 when, in response to an invitation, she agreed to come over to my home town and sit with some of my friends, so that we might all share the wonders of her mediumship. The medium had never met me, and my only contact with her prior to her visit to Grimsby had been the one trunk call I made requesting the privilege of a sitting. While that first meeting is more than a decade away, the memories of that evening still remain bright in my memory, and it is doubtful whether anything will ever erase them from the store of treasured memories which everyone accumulates during one's earthly life.

The medium knew nothing whatever of my circumstances, personal beliefs, or religious outlook, nor did she in any way seek to elicit such information before we entered the small wooden Sanctuary standing in the garden of my friend's house. A group of us took up our positions on either side of the Sanctuary, the medium and our hosts being stationed at either end, thus completing the circle. We opened the proceedings with prayer, and almost immediately after the prayer, visitors from the other side began to make their presence known. Firstly, Sambo, the coloured guide, welcomed us all, and during the course of his short conversation with us the medium became deeply entranced. As soon as this state was complete her main guide and helper, Dr Reynolds, appeared, fully materialised. He was particularly concerned with my own health condition at that time and chatted with me just as any doctor would chat with a patient in his consulting room, taking my head in his materialised hands and examining it. The touch of those fingers was as normal and natural as the touch of any human hand, and after he had made the kindly inquiry: "Nervous, Molson?" he proceeded to adjust a splintered bone in my head which had caused trouble for many years following a serious accident. As a result of the brief manipulation which he performed I was completely free of all ill-effects which had previously troubled me as a result of that particular injury for a period of over three years. Thereafter there was a slight recurrence of the old trouble, but never in the degree I had known it previously, and when, on a subsequent occasion I discussed this matter with Dr Reynolds, he warned me that I was over-working and over-doing things generally, and that I had to ease up unless I deliberately sought a return of the old conditions. Even more serious physical trouble was indicated as being very near to me if I did not heed that warning. It would have been foolish of me, faced with such evidence, not to have taken an easier course in my life and so avoid straining the physical body beyond that point where it can stand no more.

To return to that first sitting, all the time Dr Reynolds stood by my side, Mrs Northage was in deep trance, the only indication of her presence being a very deep breathing. When the doctor had finished his mission for that evening, he bade us farewell and we saw him gradually disappear from our view. His was not the last materialisation on that evening, however, for he was quickly followed by the spirit guide of another member of the group. The features of this visitor, the clear speech, were all so firmly stamped upon our memories that it was difficult to realise later, when we discussed the events of that evening that their visits had each lasted for but a few minutes. The memorable visit that evening was that of my mother who had been in the world of spirit a little over four years. She appeared beside me fully materialised and expressed herself in the way which only a mother can express herself when talking to her only child. So the evening went on, beautiful and touching reunions, while the medium was entirely oblivious of everything that was happening.

Finally the sitting came to a close with greetings and good wishes from our friends on the other side, and we came out of the Sanctuary into the cool air of a late summer evening, conscious that we had been privileged participants and spectators in a scene which orthodoxy would, in its blindness, fail to see as being possible, and which science might attempt to explain away by one theory or another. When once one has had such great experiences, one knows within one's own heart that they cannot be explained away by any popular theory which might be evolved to suit the desires of those who would scoff.

My second sitting with Mrs Northage took place some time later, and I asked whether I might bring a friend, who subsequently became my fiancée and very dear wife, with me to Nottingham. On this occasion there were only three of us present besides the medium, and no materialisation took place. The purpose of that sitting was not for materialisation but so that I and my friend and the other sitter might have the pleasure of communion with our dear ones who had passed from this life. Mrs Northage knew nothing whatever concerning my friend who accompanied me, but within a few minutes of my opening with prayer her husband spoke to her through the trumpet in his old familiar style, his characteristic tones being unmistakable. He knew everything that was transpiring in his wife's affairs, and, turning to me, asked me, with deep feeling, to take care of his wife, for she had been a priceless jewel to him in his earthly life and the long illness which marked his final months. Dr Reynolds followed him within a minute or so, and it was clear that he could sense the relationship which was developing between myself and my friend, for he remarked that we should understand that there was no such thing as jealousy in the world of spirit, and that our eventual marriage would be richly blessed by those who loved us both. We both felt gratified and uplifted in this knowledge and subsequent events in the years that have followed have more than justified all that was promised us that afternoon.

It is difficult to single out one visit from someone in the world of spirit as being more impressive than another, and one felt deeply moved by the visit of Dr Reynolds, Walter (my friend's former husband), my mother, and the lady who addressed the third member of the circle. Yet one incident stands out in my mind as truly impressive. Here I should indicate that I had been married previously and that the wife of my first marriage had once had a child prematurely born to her. While we were sitting marvelling at the clarity of the communications which had been received, and the breadth of the knowledge which they had concerning each one of us personally, the trumpet slowly rose, in a nervous, halting fashion, and came towards me. I encouraged the unseen one endeavouring to communicate by bidding whoever it might be welcome to our gathering, while Mrs Isa Northage, who had remained fully conscious, did likewise. After a few moments of such encouragement, a child's voice spoke quite clearly to the medium, saying: "I want my daddy." This perplexed her for a moment for there were only two males present, but the trumpet turned slowly to me and said, "Daddy, Grandma Molson has brought me."

The child then went on to explain that she was the child of my first marriage and asked to be given a name. The reader will realise that, faced with such a revelation, it is not easy to answer such a request immediately, but I thought quickly and suggested that she might like the name Alice, which was the second name of my mother. This appeared to please her, and she seemed satisfied, although I have noticed on subsequent sittings that this is not the name she commonly uses, announcing herself as Fragrance, the name doubtless given to her by those in the spirit world.

Following that brief conversation with the child, my mother spoke firmly to me, saying that if only I could see the child standing there I should feel none of the bitterness in my heart which I had allowed to gain hold when my marriage was broken, not through death, but through circumstances beyond my control.

That was the first visit of the child, speaking with all the tenderness which a child of but a few years of age displays when speaking to her father or mother. I have been able to speak to her on several occasions through the mediumship of Mrs Northage during succeeding years, and have witnessed her development and growth to the stage where she is now a young person, showing many of the characteristics which one attributes to one in adolescence.

The knowledge that young children, or children who have known no earth life, continue their lives after passing and grow in age and understanding, but maintain close connections with their parents and grandparents, who have often joined them, should be a source of comfort to many.

On the last occasion I sat with Mrs Northage we used a tape-recorder during the séance and thus not only had the joy of meeting and talking with our loved ones while in the Sanctuary, but were able to play the tape back afterwards and re-live every moment we had spent within those hallowed walls.

This is but a brief and quite insufficient account to do justice to the wonderful powers of mediumship of Mrs Isa Northage, powers which she realised from early youth are most sacred and not to be abused. I would that circumstances had permitted me to write a whole book concerning the many aspects of her mediumship, which includes clairvoyance, healing and apport mediumship, besides the physical mediumship which I have described. Her clairvoyance is of an equally high standard, and whilst I have only sat once in her church while she has been demonstrating, there was such a power of assurance behind every utterance that one was left in no doubt as to the reality and sincerity of her messages from those whom we cannot see. Names of communicators, personal incidents unknown to anyone except the recipient flow out in such rapid succession that one is left in no doubt whatever. To those who have been privileged to sit with Mrs Northage – to have received healing through the operations of Dr Reynolds – life must have taken on a quite different purpose and reality than that they had entertained before meeting with such wonderful experiences.

Words are quite inadequate to describe all that one feels when thinking or speaking of Mrs Northage. She has opened the door to many a sorrowing heart, so that they have glimpsed something of the wondrous beauty and peace that awaits us all if we will but strive to be worthy and seek to progress here, while in the body. Equally grateful to her are many loved ones from the world of spirit to whom she has likewise opened the door to on this earth so that they might bring words of comfort, consolation, hope and encouragement to those they have left behind. Our unseen friends are not unmindful of the great services she renders by being the medium through which they can link with their earthly friends, and, on several occasions, after a conversation has been brought to a close, I have seen the communicator turn away and, pointing the trumpet towards Mrs Northage, thank her most sincerely for the opportunity she has provided.

One day the world will come to recognise the invaluable part such people as Mrs Northage have played in the development of understanding between both worlds' inhabitants, in the relief of sorrow and distress and in the performance of the so-called 'impossible'. For the moment such people go unsung and unhonoured, and orthodoxy would doubtless have it remain that way, but sooner or later mankind will burst its bonds and demand to know the real truth.

Until that day dawns we must hope that those who are privileged to sit with mediums such as Mrs Northage will not try to escape the responsibilities which the wonderful revelations in her séance room place upon those privileged to witness them, and participate in the intimate discussions which take place between the two worlds. Our friends from the spirit world do not come back simply in order to bring comfort and assurance to their loved ones – their mission is greater than that. They come back to tell us of the truth that life is a continual progression and that the death of the physical body is but one incident in everyone's progression. That knowledge they give to us, not that we might hide it within our own bosoms, but rather that we might proclaim it abroad. Only by the spread of such knowledge, only by a realisation of the truth, can we hope to mould men's minds to think above the material to that plane of thought where war will be outlawed, where want and fear shall be but shadows of the past, and where men shall live in the knowledge of God's great blessings to all mankind. Then will the contribution which such people as Mrs Northage have made to mankind be rightly understood and valued.

A Testimonial to the Mediumship of Mrs Isa Northage.

In my forty years of experience with Spiritualism I have sat with many physical mediums and witnessed every kind of phenomena and it is therefore very difficult to deceive me where mediumship is concerned. My name is Mrs R. Galvin of Wigan, Lancashire, and I myself have been blessed with the gift of clairvoyance and have had my own Spiritualist church for forty years. My son, who has accompanied me to many séances, has also developed psychic powers and is a keen student of all types of super-normal phenomena.

Mrs Isa Northage has been a friend of mine for thirty years, and each time I attend a séance of hers I am astonished at the wonderful mediumistic powers that she – with the help and guidance of her spirit counsellors – has acquired. To my knowledge, Mrs Northage has always mainly devoted her time to the scientific and experimental side of physical phenomena, whilst carrying out her self-imposed duties of Church Leader and Healer, always coupled, of course with the role of housewife and mother.

My first contact with Mrs Northage as a medium took place in the year 1941. The séance to which I was invited was held in a house at Poulton-le-Fylde, near Blackpool, in Lancashire.

On this occasion there were twenty people present, including my sister. This was the memorable day when Russia had declared war on Germany. There were many manifestations, and most of these could be seen clearly by luminous plaques that were held by the materialised spirits.

Then in front of me there appeared a pair of eyes, then a nose, and then the full face. There was no need for me to ask who it was, as both my sister and I immediately recognised our mother. No one in that group of people knew that my son had gone into the Forces only a few days before, but in a very clear voice my mother said: "I shall bring Dick home safe." This was a big thing to say, as at that time the war was beginning to be really bad. But her words were proved to be true in spite of all the difficulties yet to be faced by my son and his comrades.

During this séance the most wonderful perfume was sprinkled on all of us and continually voices were heard and faces were being materialised by the power of this wonderful medium.

When the séance – which lasted two hours – was over, Mrs Northage was completely exhausted and had to be carried out of the séance room in a warm blanket and have complete rest.

With the advice of her spirit co-ordinators, Mrs Northage devoted the next five years of her life to her own circle for development, to further and increase her own mediumistic powers.

It was in March 1948, at her home in Bulwell, Nottingham, that we next held a séance with Mrs Northage. I took along with me, my son and a number of my own friends, including one whom I shall call Mr W. . Unknown to any of us, a few months before this sitting, Mr W. had an appointment with Mr MacDonald, the psychic artist, and had in his possession a psychic drawing of his Egyptian guide.

During the séance a great many forms materialised and at times there were as many as four voices at once coming from the direction of the ceiling, the spirits using luminous trumpets to assist the production of their voices. Children's voices could be heard shouting and singing with happiness, others chattering away with their parents, so happy to be re-united again. Even the languages of other nationalities could be heard clearly. In the background other voices were clamouring for attention. Some of the people present on this occasion had the privilege of speaking directly to their sons, who had passed away during the war years, on the land, on the sea, and in the air. A great many tears were shed on this occasion, but most of them were happy tears of reunion.

After the séance had been in progress for a while we were asked by the chief control to watch for the next form to materialise, and standing next to Mr W. was the Egyptian guide. Now Mrs Northage at this time was thin and small in stature, but the materialised form was not only quite different from her in build but had a perfect beard and was naked to the waist, and the hair on his chest was to be seen quite clearly by all.

This perfect example of a fully materialised Egyptian spoke to Mr W. and made him understand in no uncertain way who he was and why he had come. Only hours after this séance ended did Mr W. inform us that the psychic drawing done three months previously had been seen by only two people, the psychic artist and himself, and according to Mr W. the drawing and the materialisation were identical; this is to me undeniable proof of spirit return, spirit intelligence and unquestionable mediumship.

It is not often that I ask or look for any proof of spirit return for myself, as I have had sufficient to last a lifetime. My whole life has revolved around this work and the happiness it has brought to many people. Therefore I was most surprised to be informed during this séance that a spirit visitor was coming from the cabinet to greet me. I watched with interest as the curtains opened. The materialised spirit walked down the centre of the room in her beautiful flowing robes, and in the centre of the room she stooped and must at that time have picked up a red-light torch. As she came closer we did not need to ask who it was, as she was immediately recognised by at least five people. She was well known in the town where I live. I must admit that even I was shaken as I looked at her standing before me, just as if in real life. She was a woman who prided herself on her appearance, and although some sixty years of age at the time of her passing, her hair was beautifully thick and black, and not in the least like Mrs Northage's. When in evening dress she was very proud of her arms, and when I remarked on this she switched on the torch and removed with her other hand the ectoplasm covering the upper part of her body and showed us her bare arms and her shoulders, and then took the light up to her face and her hair. It just took my breath away.

Also sitting with me was a friend of hers, and the materialised form pushed me on one side and called the lady by her name and said she wished to speak to her. They then held a conversation which more than proved her identity. My son called out to the materialised spirit and she then walked over to him for everyone to see her. She patted his cheek and just said to him: "Hello, Dick," and suddenly dematerialised in front of him. We then sang a hymn which was quite appropriate to the occasion, *Blessed be the tie that binds*.

When this hymn was finished there appeared at the top of the room the form of a nun, and she began to walk towards me. I noticed that she wore a large white collar and as she came closer I saw that also round her neck was a black cross and chain, which showed up very clearly on the white collar. I asked the people around me if they could see it, and they remarked how very plain it was. When I mentioned this cross to the nun she came very close to me and said very quietly: "It is for you, my dear." She must have picked up a luminous plaque as she first came down the room, for she put it just underneath her white collar, thus showing her face, her head-dress and the cross more clearly. All of a sudden the cross seemed to slip through her neck on to the plaque and slowly it solidified link by link. The spirit of the nun took it in her hand and blessed me, then kissing me on the forehead she placed the cross and chain in my hands and then seemed to vanish through the floor.

As a point of interest, this apport of the cross and chain *(see page 203)* carried with it a very strong smell of damp and mustiness which lingered for weeks. Its colour at first was slightly tinged with green, which later turned to jet black.

There were many incidents during the course of this séance, all of which warrant recording. Amusing episodes, such as the small, doll-like materialised face of an old woman, who in no uncertain terms told her relation: "You were always the mischief-maker in our family," and her relation agreed, amid much laughter.

A perfect example of the spaceless laws of the spirit world occurred when the head and shoulders of an elderly person appeared in front of two people who were said to be relations. This was most remarkable, for the materialisation was upside down. This was soon put right, but what proof it was of true phenomena – part of – yet apart from, the medium, Mrs Northage. This séance was of three hours duration.

My next séance with Mrs Northage took place about February 1956, and on this occasion I had with me my son and a friend. Mrs Northage sat for us alone, apart from just one of her circle members. This séance was held in the Sanctuary of the Church in Newstead Abbey Park, Nottingham, where Mrs Northage resides. This is only a very small room and is kept for séance purposes only. The floor is of concrete and there are no windows.

Once again this séance was of the highest quality, the materialisation and de-materialisation of spirit forms was a wonder to observe, the voices were more powerful than ever and even more plentiful. My spirit visitor from our previous séance in Bulwell again came to me, and we held a most happy and quite matter-of-fact conversation regarding our mutual friends.

We have since again had the pleasure and privilege of sitting with Mrs Northage, and I have only written here a little of what took place at these séances (I could have written page after page) but maybe whoever reads this testimony will stop and wonder. I advise such people to investigate for themselves for is it not written: "Greater works than this shall ye do, if it be done in My Name."

Many words have been written concerning the work of great mediums of the past. With the publication of this book we now have some facts about a truly great medium of today.

(Signed) R. Galvin.

An Appreciation

Dear Mrs Northage,

Thank you so much for such a wonderful sitting; it's so difficult to put on paper my thoughts and happiness. I know what I want to say but somehow cannot just find the words; it also makes it more difficult when I know you were not conscious of what was happening. You see, my grown-up daughter, through you, was able to come and talk to Edna and me; a daughter who had only one month of life on this earth, twenty-five years ago.

To be greeted by: "Hello, Daddy, you didn't know you had a grown-up daughter." Then she discussed personal things of our home life; it was too wonderful, the simple things such as: "You choose your own name for me." – her reference to present days, and her statement: "I am always with you in the house," meant an awful lot to us both.

Your Church and its progress, its work in relieving sick minds and bodies, its quiet worship, is a blessing indeed.

(Signed) Sid,
Mansfield, Notts.
November 20th, 1958.

Note:.– These original letters can be seen any time. – *Editor*, (1960).

Chapter Four

Healing – by Isa A. Northage

The mediumship of healing is one that is seldom thoroughly understood, often grossly abused, and generally the most difficult to develop. It requires a great deal of patience and an immense amount of faith, determination, and confidence. Success will ultimately be achieved if these requirements are fulfilled, and the following explanation is a brief guide to those whose ambition it is to become used to exercise the most divine of all the gifts of God.

To deal with this subject in its many phases and aspects would require volumes, because to describe God – the purpose of our being – and to understand something of human nature would need a deep study of the various sciences of life, so it is only possible here to give a brief but general survey of this form of mediumship.

The greatest Healer the world has perhaps ever known, was also a great Teacher, yet He taught the simple laws of life, at the same time demonstrating the power of the spirit, so that a simple survey of the subject will suffice to help any who are entrusted with the power to heal, in their development.

Power

The source of the power that heals is God. Not a supreme being who sits upon a throne somewhere in the heights of the world of ether and surveys and rules over heaven and earth as portrayed by some people, but a cosmic energy, the energy of life – that vibrates in all things created, so it can be truly and briefly described as a vibration. Everything that has life, pulsates or vibrates with its own energy; no form of life is still. There is a spiritual counterpart of every form of life on the physical plane, and its energy is spirit. It is the spirit or life-energy of man that causes the physical body to function, for it is but the temporary home of the spirit, through which he can express himself while on earth. When any part thereof becomes affected by sickness or disease, the spirit cannot make proper use of it, and as it becomes out of tune with its spiritual counterpart, it does not vibrate correctly and keep its poise. If this becomes chronic and general, the spirit, finding the body of no further use, leaves it, and the body then becomes lifeless and that which is known as death takes place. When it is not general, but just organic or a weakness of certain parts, this can be adjusted in several ways. In the case of temporary sickness, health is often restored by supplying certain minerals from the earth which build up the physical body, i.e. physician's medicine. In the case of organic diseases, etc., the affected part can be entirely removed and the body continue to be used.

Sometimes both these remedies fail, and sometimes either or both are not practicable. The body is then in a state of disorder, and the spirit of the person is called upon to bear the pain and discomforts of the frame it is using. If the person understands this and is willing, the cosmic ray or life energy (healing power) can be applied to the spiritual counterpart of the body (aura) which reinforces it to such an extent that it can make the affected part vibrate at the correct rate and so restore lost health. This is called 'Aura Healing'. If the person does not understand sufficiently to permit this to be done, the life-giving energy can be applied to the physical body direct through the hands of a healing medium. This is known as the 'laying on of hands', the most popular form of healing. When this takes place, the energy directed through the hands of the medium, passes through the affected part of the body and re-energises it. Poisonous matter, germs, etc., cannot live in such a high vibration as that of the energy or power, any more than the physical eyes can continue to stare at the blazing sunlight, and so it becomes burnt up and dispersed, leaving freedom from affliction. This power or energy is of the spirit, the source of which is the Creator – God, which is in all life, created from the fountain of life. God, then, will be found to be the essence of the spirit: in the higher vibrations of life more powerful and energetic, and in a lesser form in the lower vibrations: from the highest intelligence of man, to the lowest form of mineral and vegetable matter.

The Healing Guides

The Guide is a person living in the spheres of the world of spirit who supplies the healing power and is generally known as a healing guide, for although all their psychic faculties are very much more advanced than our own, these particular guides specialize in healing. Like medical men on earth, they may have other qualities and gifts, but healing is their outstanding speciality. They are usually discarnate spirits of Indians or Chinese, because these races are well known to be the most psychic and having lived longer are more experienced. Another reason is that they are naturally more developed in the science of human nature and have a far greater understanding and intelligence than most other races. (They originate from the oldest tribes of mankind).

As already stated, healing power is supplied through the guide, but the force of the power depends upon the 'light', or the state of progression of the guide (more will be said about the 'light' in the section headed: 'The Medium'.) This again depends upon the medium's state of progress. Guides vary in intelligence and spirituality just as do people on earth. The guide's instrument is the medium, and if the latter is not very advanced in these qualities, the more spiritually advanced guides would not work through him or her because they could not achieve any success. Therefore, the mental and spiritual progress of the medium determines the quality of the guide. Guides usually have a great regard for their mediums, who should always respect their guides, and treat them as their best friends and constant companions, for by so doing a very strong attachment and comradeship is formed. Often a guide can influence the medium to greatly increase his spiritual progress and by so doing advances his own. This is often done between people on earth, for what you sow, so you reap.

The life-energy that pulsates from the body of the guide is a much higher vibration than that which comes from a physical body, for that of the guide is of a finer substance and it is this high vibration which energises the physical part of the medium, and streams from him or her as healing power. The method the guides adopt to charge the medium with power varies according to physique and mentality. Some are able to withdraw the spirit of the medium from his body and to occupy it themselves, but comparatively few adopt this method (known as trance control), because it is a very delicate and difficult operation. The most popular method used by guides is to stand just behind or at the side of the medium and the vibrations charge or energize the aura of the medium so intensely that everything he touches gathers a power that could not possibly come from a normal make-up. The medium is perfectly conscious of this power within, and this will be described later under the heading 'The Medium'. The effect of this power often overcomes the medium as though he were doped, but he can learn to control this effect on his senses if he wishes. It is a form of mental control which varies according to how far the medium 'lets himself go'. Additionally, the developed medium not only feels the presence of the guide by the power, but the guide is also able to talk to his medium by impressing his brain with his thoughts which he expresses to the medium either by what is known as mental clairvoyance or clairaudience, according to the development of the medium. Even if a medium is clairvoyant, he or she seldom sees the guide because he is usually too close to be seen, but the characteristics of the guide will be so keenly sensed that they work together as one and the same person.

It should always be remembered that the guides are human beings like ourselves and have their likes and dislikes, also their opinions, and each differs in character and personality as we do. Many people seem to think that our guides have nothing else to do but remain always at the beck and call of the medium through whom they work. This is quite wrong, for guides have their work to do in the spirit world just as we on earth; the only difference is that while we generally work to get money for our necessities, they work because they want to, and once they start on any particular mission, they never leave it until it is accomplished, however many years it may take.

Instances have been known when a guide, being otherwise engaged has left his medium to treat a patient alone. This has only been when he patient is not seriously afflicted, and the medium has a sufficient store of power to meet the demand. (This has been my own experience on more than one occasion). This may appear rather strange to some people, but in fact it is quite simple. When a medium is healing continually through having so much power passed through him or her, a certain amount of power is absorbed by the aura. It is similar to a transformer, choke, or fixed condenser in a wireless set. Through so much electricity passing through these component parts they remain partly charged for a long time after the set has been switched off. In like manner, if the guide considers it to be satisfactory, a medium can treat slight cases occasionally, by the power contained in the aura, without the guide attending in person. However, the guide is always at hand when needed.

The Medium

Upon the medium depends for the most part the success or otherwise of healing treatment, for inspiration is governed by the channel through which it flows. The same applies to healing. The medium is the last link in the chain of power from the Godhead to the suffering patient. Much depends on the mental attitude and mood of the patient, so that failure cannot always be attributed to the medium and never to the guide. The medium when properly trained and developed will know when the patient is not receptive, in which case this should always be remedied before giving out any power, as it is obviously useless to give healing treatment if it is not going to be properly received. Guides can heal to a certain extent without a medium, but only when the patient is in the required circumstances and conditions, such as the sleep state, when they can only heal the astral body from which the physical draws the extra energy. The use of a medium is the general method and the most powerful one, because while a person is functioning through the senses of the physical mind, they are only conscious of the power from another physical body. Provided that a medium can become a channel for receiving and expelling the healing vibration, it is not necessary to be clairvoyant also, though this gift usually automatically develops in time through the continued raising of their vibrations. People who are very sensitive and emotional, warmhearted and sympathetic, make the finest healing mediums. Those who are easily irritated and quick-tempered and lack patience, are unsuitable. Assuming that the medium possesses the right temperament, he or she should first ascertain what guide is working through them for healing, as this knowledge will help at all times to maintain a strong link, always necessary to ensure co-operation. This can be done by invoking the aid of those known to possess the clairvoyant vision, and this should be sufficiently evidential when a similar vision comes to more than one. Each guide usually gives a name for recognition purposes, but there is often every reason to assume that the name is a pseudonym, though sometimes it will be the name by which they were known on earth. Everyone has a guide, (their own personal guide), who has been their constant guardian since birth, and remains so throughout their earthly life. Whatever the medium's outstanding psychic gift, is correspondingly possessed by the guide. For example, if the medium's special gift is healing, the personal guide is the healer. Should they develop other gifts additionally it is possible there may be other guides working in their various capacities, for guides specialise in certain gifts, just as mediums do.

As previously stated, the strength of the power from the guide depends upon the guide's state of progress, as the higher the spiritual sphere from which he or she comes, the finer the substance of the spiritual body; the finer the substance, the higher the vibration, for healing power is vibration. This is known as the 'light' of the guide. The medium naturally offers a certain amount of resistance to the guide's power, as it has to flow through the body in a similar way to which a condenser offers resistance to electricity. It will be understood then that the 'light' or state of progression of the medium will determine how much resistance is offered to the healing power. If the 'light' is powerful, the resistance will be very much lessened, and likewise if the 'light' is dim (progression low), the resistance will be great and the power weak. To increase their 'light' then is, or should be, the aim and desire of the medium, so as to heal well, powerfully, and successfully. This is what the Master meant when He said: "Let your light so shine before men, that they may see your good works, and glorify your Father which is in Heaven."

It will now be realised what an important part the medium plays in the exercising of a Divine Gift, and it will also be seen how wisely and justly the laws of God operate: for it will be apparent that only those fit to heal, can heal and that a Divine Gift cannot be operated by those who are incompetent.

Many profess to heal and many attempt to exercise the gift, but to what extent they succeed can only be judged by the results. They who would do the work of Christ must first learn to live the life of Christ; not in the literal sense, of course, but by taking His principles as their example, and living their lives accordingly.

A medium should not only possess all the finer human qualities but should exercise them always in every direction, so that only what is highest and most perfect in their nature shall be revealed and expressed.

Man's character is revealed in his aura. Quality of character is shown by the colours in the aura, and each colour denotes the various qualities in his character. Not only is the strength of the power an essential factor in the success of healing, but its quality also, for the higher this is, the deeper does it penetrate.

To cause your 'light' to shine before men, or to increase one's spirituality should be the first step in one's development and should be one's general practice throughout development, and in fact, always. Many attempts may be made and often we may seem to fail, but never should we lose heart or faith, but try again and again until at last we manage to conquer ourselves.

Let us study ourselves while alone with our own conscience, listen to its voice, and learn the truth about ourselves; our weaknesses, imperfections of nature and character, weakness in overcoming temptation, bad habits, etc. Let us unashamedly see ourselves as we really are, and then put forth a great effort to cleanse ourselves of our impurities of mind, instability of character, etc. Be determined to cultivate sympathy, tolerance, patience, understanding, charitable thoughts and actions only, and, in brief, attempt to live as clean and as perfect a life as Jesus Christ did. Many times we may possibly slip back, but one can always go forward again and refuse to give up.

Perhaps conditions around us may be trying and irritating, but we must remember to be tolerant, and not permit ourselves to be affected in any way by the actions, speech, or thoughts of others.

Prayer will play an immensely important part in our progress, because when one prays, the mind is lifted to a higher plane of thought where the finer qualities of our nature can express themselves. This uplifting of ourselves can be achieved only by us, aided by our spiritual helpers who know the desires of our hearts.

Now let us enter the developing circle with this as the most important factor in our development, firmly fixed in our minds, so that as we sit, our 'light' may shine forth strongly.

The body should be healthy and functioning normally, and the nerves good and not tired, otherwise the body does not make a clear channel for the high vibration that is shortly to pass through it. Plenty of fresh water should be drunk, as this clears the body of its impurities, besides being a good conductor of power, as it is of electricity. The mind should be free from worry of any kind, as worry poisons the blood stream. Sit always with people you are perfectly in tune with, for there must always be perfect harmony in the developing circle. Relax completely, physically and mentally, and be sure that your seat (which should be a wooden chair, for a soft seat 'soaks' up power) is quite comfortable. Sit in perfect quietness and occupy your thoughts by thinking of the guide, visualise him or her, so that you can learn to become 'connected' quickly. As you cannot see the guide when he comes to you, you must learn to feel his presence, and to allow this to happen, quieten the vibrations of your own body by concentrating for a few moments on your pulse and heart beats which you can easily feel if you are sitting down quietly. Take a few deep, quiet breaths, then mentally command your heart to slow down, and after a little practice you will find you are able to control the action of your heart. You will then be very relaxed and very quiet. When you actually start to do healing, you will be able to follow all these instructions and prepare yourself for the guide (in time) in perhaps a few seconds.

If you are going to be controlled, when you are quiet enough, you will feel a slight 'singing' noise in your head, and you will feel yourself rising up and up, and everything will seem to go black. Not too pleasant until you get used to it, and then you will go unconscious. After going out of trance you will probably come to, feeling rather sick and a pain in the stomach. This condition will wear off as you become used to it.

Assuming that you are doing normal healing (for very few are entranced), as soon as you are in the right condition you will feel the guide as he comes in touch with you, in the following way:

You will suddenly come over hot (his vibrations coming into contact with your aura), and all your senses will become quickened in direct contrast to the relaxed state you were in a moment ago.

The heart will probably start racing and you will literally throb, limbs and nerves together, for all your vibrations have been greatly increased by those of the guide. Because all the senses have been quickened, you will become extremely sensitive, and will probably pick up the very thoughts of your patient.

Your instincts will be so sharpened that you will feel the very character of the person you are contacting. You will learn to diagnose the health condition through the easiest channel by which the guide is able to impress you. For example, picking up the person's conditions by the vibrations around them, you may actually take on these conditions yourself; or you may 'see' a dull patch on the part of the body affected; or the guide may be able to impress your mind by telling you in thought conversation, so that you know exactly where the trouble is.

It is rather difficult to explain why some people attempt to convey the impression that they are being 'controlled' when they are not. It is a very weak thing to do, very ignorant, and definitely weakens the power, because their minds are not free. They are acting falsely and spoiling the quality of the power. Again, it holds the guide back, putting a barrier between him and the medium, thus doing nobody any good. It is also quite unnecessary to puff and blow, and wave your arms about. No guide ever causes you to do that. That is almost as bad as feigning trance, because this also interferes with the power. You are interrupting the functioning of your nervous and respiratory organs so that the guide's vibrations are broken up and flung all over the place. Anyone using these unnecessary and undesirable methods is doing the patient little good, because they actually prevent the power from flowing properly.

The effect on the medium of contact with the guide will be to increase the respiratory and heart action, and cause the limbs to throb, but the medium can always to some extent control his own body. He is useless as a medium if he cannot; we all have our own will-power. The effect of the high vibrations on the senses of the medium, will often cause him to be dopy, and this is known as 'mental control', because the mind of the guide is to a great extent using the mind as well as the body of the medium. If you have confidence in your guide, you will have the same in yourself, for confidence will break down all nervous barriers, leaving you complete master of any job you undertake. Any healer who is sure of himself will fear nothing, particularly disease or sickness, however contagious, because he or she is sure of a wonderful fellowship in the presence of the guide. This is most important, because to fear a contagious complaint is to encourage it or keep it with you. It can never affect you in the least, if your will-power is sufficiently strong to defy it. Actually, the high vibrations from the guide would make any condition harmless while he is with you, but it is possible to carry that of the sufferer about with you for some time after having drawn it away. This will however, be quite harmless if you have the confidence and faith to treat it with defiance.

The feeling of heat caused by the guide's vibrations, previously referred to, depends a great deal on the medium's temperament.

Some mediums have complained that they feel cold under the guide's influence, and not hot. While this may be possible because of the various ways in which different temperaments can be affected, the fact remains that the guide's influence raises one's vibrations and never lowers them, and raising one's vibrations naturally raises one's temperature. The real explanation may be that the medium is not sensitive enough to feel the high vibration of the guide, and thus it will not appear to affect physically and the coldness could be caused by what are known as 'psychic breezes', which are the vibrations of our etheric body affecting only our physical exterior.

To mediums who are not clairvoyant, the only evidence available that spiritual entities are present is the warmth to be felt; if they cannot feel this warmth, they are working entirely 'blind', in which case their faith alone can give them confidence. However, any medium who has sufficiently developed for healing work would either see the spirit lights, or feel the warm presence of the guide, as evidence of such guidance. There is no hard and fast rule as to how the medium passes power over or through the patient's body, as no two mediums work exactly alike, each one having his own characteristics. Should a medium ever fail to satisfy the guide, the latter can usually find ways and means of rectifying this. Of course there are one or two general rules to be observed; for instance, power is only given off when the hands are open, and the general rule is to make downward passes with fingers apart on the patient's body, but this does not apply to neck and head. The passes always vary according to need.

Some mediums at first do not seem quite sure when to stop treating a patient. This shows that they have not yet acquired complete confidence in themselves, for once they learn to work in perfect harmony with their guide, their mind and the guide's will be one, and they will know when the treatment is over. However, experience has proved this certain way of knowing when to stop. Take particular notice when healing a patient if you feel after a certain time you are losing interest in the patient. If this feeling of lost interest comes over you, it is a certain and definite sign that the guide has finished with that particular patient. You can never judge by time. To the guide there is no time, only insomuch as it affects the medium personally. Some patients need longer treatment than others for two reasons: firstly, according to their complaint, and secondly, according to the way they are receiving the power.

In conclusion, this is but a brief summary of a very wide subject. More could be written about healing than any other form of mediumship, and any points I have omitted, and any further questions I will gladly answer.

Always pray to God to give you power to strengthen someone in need, and your prayer will always be answered by a following assurance.

The Two Worlds – **24th November, 1939.**

One of the most valuable phases of mediumship is that of healing the sick, and I would like to relate some of the remarkable cures which are being effected through the mediumship of Mrs Northage, of Bulwell. Some months ago a healing centre was established at her home, and this is being conducted in the true spirit of helpfulness, no charge being made, though patients and friends are at liberty to contribute to a collection.

There are several healers working with Mrs Northage, under the supervision and instruction of Dr Reynolds, the guide of the medium. Most of the cases treated have been considered difficult; in fact some have been declared incurable by the medical faculty.

One case concerns a lady of some thirty years of age, who has been a cripple since birth. Numerous operations have been performed, but she has been unable at any time to stand without support. She is now able to stand alone for 10 minutes, whilst her friends look on in amazement. (She is now back in business, 1950).

Another patient has had removed a cancer of long standing. Another case was one of pregnancy; quite an abnormal case, which has baffled the doctors. She had been ordered to hospital for examination. Mrs Northage's guide, Dr Reynolds, was told of the case and promised to visit her personally and perform a 'spiritual operation' after which he intimated that when she went to the hospital the authorities would wonder why she had come, since everything would be found to be normal. I personally accompanied her to the hospital some days later, and after examination the medical man declared her perfectly normal, and wondered why she had been sent to the hospital.

One of the unique features of this circle is that Mrs Northage's guide, Dr Reynolds, speaks to his healers and patients by the direct voice, through the trumpet, after each sitting. He will often talk for half an hour, the sitters asking questions, to which he replies freely.

He will diagnose each case and give details as to its exact nature and treatment, though he is cautious if the patient is personally present. Further, Dr Reynolds apports pills, tablets, liquid medicine and details of prescriptions to be made up, and in every case he is careful to give instructions as to their use.

At times Dr Reynolds will request a special sitting with the healers and will give in detail a diagnosis of the case under treatment, and careful instructions for treating it.

When tablets or pills are brought, the Doctor himself places them in the hands of the healers and they claim that they are able to feel his materialised hands in solid form. Generally the objects apported are quite warm, and we are instructed to allow them to cool before consumption. As each separate lot is brought, the doctor states definitely the name of the patient for whom they are intended. Thirty to forty pills or tablets are usually brought for each patient.

When liquid is brought, it is poured into a vessel and handed to sitters in the circle to place in safety. One has only to converse with the patients at this centre to be assured of remarkable evidence concerning the work being done.

The phenomena occurring through this medium are varied and remarkable, and include materialisation, apports, trance speaking, direct voice, etc., and the way in which they are all co-ordinated is remarkable.

By D.M. Antliff.

Account by W. J. Molson of Grimsby.

When I was fifteen years of age I lost a leg through being knocked down by a drunken motorist. My head was also badly knocked about in the accident, and I lay unconscious in hospital for several days. The effects of this accident were not all shown while I was in hospital, but soon after I was discharged I experienced flushing bouts, which increased in frequency and intensity in later years.

During these attacks I would grind my teeth and a multitude of the most ridiculous thoughts would chase through my mind. All the time these fancies coursed through my mind, I tried to tell myself, "You are all right. It will be over in a minute."

These attacks only came on at long intervals during the first ten or twelve years after my accident, but in the early years of the war they became more frequent, sometimes occurring two or three times a day, and when they happened during the night they were frightening, waking me up with my teeth grinding.

In 1942, I consulted a Wimpole Street doctor who advised me to give up my A.R.P. work, and he prescribed a small daily dose of pheno-barbitone. This treatment was useless and the following year I consulted one of the world's leading brain specialists. I was X-rayed and subjected to certain electrical tests, the result of which was the discovery of a bruise on my brain, caused by the pressure of a small splinter of bone which had evidently been displaced when I met with the accident. The daily dose of pheno-barbitone was increased to two and a half grains. The attacks certainly lessened in frequency, but became more severe and left me greatly depressed for several days afterwards. I still experienced three or four attacks every six or seven weeks. My eyesight now began to fail and I had the utmost difficulty in reading print. I consulted leading eye specialists, and in 1946, visited one in Harley Street. He examined me thoroughly, and told me that nothing could be done as malgeneration had set in. This consultation made me exceedingly depressed.

During the early part of 1948, I had these attacks rather too frequently for my liking, and I feared that they were going to become as frequent as in 1942-43, when I had had to visit the specialists. I happened to mention my trouble one evening to a Spiritualist friend of mine, Mrs A. Mork, and she asked me to tell Mrs Isa Northage, of Nottingham, of my trouble, and ask her if she would ask her spirit doctor, Dr Reynolds, to come and see me one evening and make a diagnosis. I accordingly rang up Mrs Northage that same evening and told her of my head trouble, describing the ridiculous thoughts which poured through my mind while the attacks were in progress. I made no mention of the fact that I had once had a serious accident and lost a leg. Mrs Northage had never met me and did not know of this. She promised that she would ask Dr Reynolds to visit me one night when I was in bed, between the hours of midnight and 2am and diagnose. This telephone conversation took place during the second week in March, and on the 20th March, I received a letter from Mrs Northage stating that Dr Reynolds had found, on examination, a slight injury to my skull, which was causing the trouble. This was of twenty years' standing. There was also a slight internal disorder which needed attention, and this would be put right. This report was most interesting, for it confirmed the diagnosis made by the specialist after the X-ray.

I acknowledged this letter and asked whether I should continue with the nightly doses of two grains of pheno-barbitone. Mrs Northage replied on the 5th of April, stating that Dr Reynolds wished to operate when I had been built up, and that I was to try to reduce the dose of pheno-barbitone to one grain by the time of the operation. I immediately reduced the dose by half a grain, and after a fortnight on one-and-a-half grains, reduced it by another half-grain, thus taking the one grain dose as desired by Dr Reynolds. I continued on this dose until the operation on May 26th. There were seven of us who entered the Sanctuary in the garden of Mrs Mork's house on the evening of Wednesday, May 26th. The party was composed of Mrs Isa Northage, of Nottingham, (the medium), Mr and Mrs Cox of Sheffield, friends of the medium, Mrs A. Mork and her daughter, Betty, of Grimsby, a Grimsby Spiritualist, Mrs Turner, and myself. I opened the sitting with a prayer, and we sang two hymns, after which Sambo, Mrs Northage's guide came through and welcomed the party. All except myself had met him before. He said that he did not wish to take up any time at this stage of the proceedings, as Dr Reynolds wished to come through. There was silence for a few moments, and then we observed that the small red capped torch was moving about on the right-hand-side of the Sanctuary, hovering over the table on which we had placed the cotton wool swabs, two small trays, antiseptic, etc., which Dr Reynolds had ordered for the operation. The doctor appeared to be satisfied with his examination and the torch was lowered again. Within a matter of seconds a plaque arose in the air, and we were soon able to see the materialised figure of Dr Reynolds. He briefly welcomed the sitters and then came to me, standing on my right. He asked, in a friendly tone, "Nervous, Molson?" to which I replied in the negative. He then said that he proposed to examine my head and he took it in his hands. I could feel the pressure of his fingers, quite gently, on certain parts of my head, and he made a thorough examination of the outside. He appeared to be satisfied and then said, "Now I am going to lift a bone which has been pressing down for many years. If I hurt you, give a yell, but I do not think I shall. I am also going to clean the bone."

He then called for two of the ladies to bring the trays. He took one of the swabs, dipped it into the antiseptic, and rubbed the right hand side of my upper forehead. I could distinctly feel the cold, wet sensation of the antiseptic on my skin. Then, in a quiet voice, he said, "This is where I do my trick. I am going to put my hand inside your head, clean, and lift the bone." I was able to observe out of the corner of my right eye, his hand come up as he rolled back the sleeve of his robe. I sat perfectly motionless, looking straight in front of me, and the half circle of sitters in front of me saw his hand enter my head from the right hand side. I was conscious of no unusual sensation, and it would appear as though the nerves in this part of the head were temporarily shut down during this part of the operation. The doctor withdrew his hand after a short while and dropped a swab into the empty tray. He repeated this operation again, withdrawing and dropping another swab into the tray. In all, this was repeated four times, after which the doctor said, "Now I have cleaned the bone. I want you to look at the swabs afterwards. I have also lifted it so that there is now no pressure. You are very fortunate in having this done after so many years. I want you to cut down still further on the pheno-barbitone. During the next few nights, you may experience a sense of tightness in the head. We are filling in the small cavity which has been left by the lifting of the bone. Do not worry over this. I shall visit you between the hours of midnight and 2am, so if you see a flash when you are getting into bed, do not worry, it is simply me." With those words, he bade us 'Good-night', and dematerialised.

To say that each of the sitters was greatly impressed by what had transpired would be an inadequate expression. It is difficult to find words with which to express our feelings after witnessing that wonderful spectacle: we were filled with awe and wonder, rejoicing together in the privilege which we had enjoyed. But the sitting was by no means over, for more was to follow. Within a minute or two of the completion of the operation, Dr Savage, the spirit healer helping Mrs A. Mork, presented himself to the company, standing on my right. His features could not be seen clearly in the faint luminous light by the sitters facing me, and he invited Mrs Mork to step forward so that she might obtain a closer view, which she did. He smiled in welcome to the company, and then dematerialised. He was followed almost immediately by the Chinese guide of Mr Cox, who although he did not materialise, spoke rapidly through the trumpet. He was followed by Gloria, Mrs Mork's daughter, who spoke lovingly to her mother and sister, referred to her brother who was away at school, and sent her love to her aunt and father. For me, however, there was still a great joy in store. My mother materialised, standing on my right, smiling at me and the company, and telling me, in the voice which I had come to know so well while she had been in the flesh, "You will be all right now." She had known of my head trouble, and I fear that it had worried her greatly. There was that note of quiet reassurance in her voice which was deeply impressive to me, had I been in need of conviction after what I had already experienced.

Sambo, Mrs Northage's control, then told us that there was someone coming who had never spoken through the trumpet before and he asked us to be patient with him, adding that the communicator wished to speak to me. Within a few seconds the trumpet began to rise, and then a strong voice addressed me. He told me that he was not used to holding these things. I promised him that we would help him, and immediately it was borne in upon me that it was my father who was speaking. He responded at once to the old name of 'Pop' and showed himself thoroughly familiar with all the circumstances which had affected my life since his passing in 1942. He urged me to make a fresh start, to put the past behind me. He told of how he had awaited the coming to spirit life of my mother, who had passed on just over two years after him, and how happy they were together, and I told him that I remembered them every night in my prayers. He said that they did not need my prayers, but rather my kind thoughts.

Before leaving the Sanctuary we lifted the used swabs which had been placed on the tray by Dr Reynolds. There was the unmistakable evidence. Each of the swabs bore the sign of blood, but two of them, presumably the first two which the doctor had used, were soaked with thick, black, dirty blood, which had been cleaned from the bone before it was lifted.

These wonderful events took place on May 26th, 1948, but I have allowed six months to elapse before completing this record. I am happy to say that at no time during this period has there been any return of the ill conditions which distressed me for so many years.

For several months now I have not taken any pheno-barbitone, and I now enjoy regular, normal, and peaceful sleep. It is not easy to express in words the relief and happiness which I feel from this experience, which was the most moving and impressive of any in my life, but my desire is to show my gratitude and appreciation of the great blessing of healing bestowed upon me, through the power of the spirit, by devoting my life to the service of others.

Such evenings as the one I have described come but rarely in our lives, and I realise that I am greatly blessed in having had such an experience. The great comfort and knowledge that I was not really alone in the world, that there were those on the Other Side watching over me, helping and inspiring me, was made manifest to me that evening, and will for ever remain a source of continual inspiration and confidence.

W. J. Molson

The Two Worlds (by the *Editor*) – 24th June, 1949.

This is a story without parallel. It is the story of a highly skilled man, who passed from this life over one hundred years ago, and who has been in the habit for several years now, of returning to earth again, assuming a physical form and continuing the kind of work he used to do when on earth. This work is not ordinary labour, but consists of performing skilled operations upon the bodies of patients who have been abandoned as hopeless by the medical profession. He is able to do this astonishing work through the physical mediumship of Mrs Isa Northage.

On the 11th of March we published an account of how Dr Reynolds lifted a bone from the patient, without using any instruments or anaesthetic. It was the convincing testimony of the patient concerned who, after many years of agony has since had no further trouble with this complaint.

On May 21st, I was privileged to witness, in Mrs Northage's operating theatre, two further amazing operations by Dr Reynolds and the following is a plain statement of facts concerning the proceedings.

On arrival at her home I was introduced to Mr Newman, a tall, and well-built gentleman from Northumberland, who was assisting Mrs Northage for a few weeks in gratitude for his own sensational recovery. He had been discharged from the Services with an acute duodenal ulcer, his weight had been reduced from thirteen stone to nine and a half stone, his stomach could not retain the smallest portion of food, and he was rapidly wasting away, when a friend took him to see Mrs Northage.

Mr Newman was operated upon in September, 1948, and today he has regained his former weight, is happy, healthy and has been able to find employment once more. After hearing this further testimony of the genuineness of Dr Reynolds' work (there are dozens of such cases), a small party of eight, including Mrs Northage, assembled around the operating table in the wooden building, used for this purpose, in her garden.

Mr Stocks, her secretary, opened in prayer after the electric light had been switched off and the door secured. Mrs Northage was now entranced in the cabinet and after a verse of a hymn had been sung, Ellen Dawes, a young spirit girl, picked up the trumpet and said that she had been sent to examine and test conditions.

After the trumpet had been lowered, Dr Reynolds' materialised form appeared and was first discernible as a black silhouette against the red glow from the lamp on a trolley on which were laid forceps, two red electric torches, one white electric torch and two luminous plaques.

Picking up one of these torches Dr Reynolds switched it on and turned towards the operating table on which lay a patient suffering from an acute duodenal ulcer. He greeted everyone present, and as he did so his face and ectoplasm draperies were visible to us. He was of average height and shorter than Mrs Northage. I was standing immediately opposite to him on the other side of the patient and was able to follow, very closely, the whole proceedings. As two of the party were not wearing masks Dr Reynolds insisted that we should have these fitted before he commenced the operation. He handed mine to me personally and told me to put it on and watch closely. We had met before at a previous seance, and so we held a brief conversation before he commenced.

Dr Reynolds than prepared the patient, placing a collection of cotton wool swabs on his abdomen and reassured him that he would feel no pain whatsoever. No anaesthetic was used. The doctor then said he would 'freeze' the portion of the body to be operated upon and then pass his hand, which would become dematerialised, into the side of the body and remove the ulcer. His hands moved to the side of the body and as he did so he asked the patient if he felt any pain. The patient replied in the negative. Then I heard a gurgling sound like the passage of wind inside the body. At this stage Dr Reynolds paused and said that the ulcer was in a very bad condition and would not come away in a whole piece and that he was afraid of haemorrhage. This was apparently overcome and the portions of ulcer brought through what Dr Reynolds described as a temporary opening in the abdomen, and placed on the swabs on the surface of the body. He next cleared an opening amongst the swabs and asked me to look down into it. It was difficult however, in the red light, to see anything very definite through this opening. He then proceeded to remove some of the swabs with the forceps and placed them on a tray which was held by one of his assistants.

At this stage Dr Reynolds told us that he was going to call in another doctor, Dr West, from the spirit world, to check up on the condition of the patient. After de-materialising he was soon followed by another spirit. Now whereas Dr Reynolds has a comparatively large angular face, Dr West's features were quite different, being smaller and more round. This difference was clearly noticeable when he appeared, because after examining the patient and approving what had taken place, he lifted one of the plaques and held it in front of himself, so that we could see his features and apparel. He was a smaller man than Dr Reynolds.

After Dr West had gone, the patient's 'deceased' daughter, Miss Smith, materialised and came to speak to her father. Mr Smith raised his head, as his daughter greeted him. "Hello Daddy, you are going to be all right now," she said, and after speaking a few words more she was forced to return to the spirit world as she was unable to sustain the materialised form for long. Before she returned she kissed her father and spoke to her mother who was also present. Jim, Mr Smith's son, likewise in spirit, also greeted his father and mother in the direct voice, with the aid of the trumpet. He told his father not to do any more dragging with the garden roller.

Then Dr Reynolds returned once more to perform a second operation. This patient had recently had an accident in which the bone in his nose had splintered and had prevented him from breathing through his nose. This time the spirit doctor picked up a white electric torch and for a few seconds we saw him in the full glare of white light. He next picked up a red torch and proceeded to examine the patient saying that he would dematerialise his hand, pass it through the back of his head, clean the bone and remove the splinters with a piece of lint.

Dr Reynolds' hand was then seen to approach the back of the patient's head and apparently pass into it. When it was withdrawn his hand stretched out to place something in a second dish held by Mrs Stenson, one of his assistants. Dr Reynolds stated that he had collected three small pieces of bone.

Before leaving, Dr Reynolds discussed another case which he had in hand, and asked Mr Stocks to make arrangements for the next operation. After he had gone, Sambo, Mrs Northage's guide, asked me to look at the medium still in trance. The electric light was switched on and Sambo continued to talk to me, through Mrs Northage, as I was looking at her, sitting in the same position as at the commencement of the seance, her green dress, silk stockings, court shoes and her shock of curly hair still undisturbed. Before the seance ended there were further manifestations, including three other doctors, who said that they had been watching the operations with great interest. Mrs Stenson closed with prayer.

As soon as the seance ended Mrs Difford, Dr Reynolds' assistant, and I collected the two containers holding the used swabs, took them into a room in Mrs Northage's house and with the aid of forceps salvaged the tissues and two pieces of bone, and immersed them in a bottle containing surgical spirit, throwing the bloodstained swabs into the fire.

Before leaving I interviewed both patients, the first stating that he felt quite well and had now no pain whatsoever, whereas he was in great pain before the operation. The second patient testified to the fact that he could now breathe freely through his nose whereas this had been impossible since his accident.

A few days later I was fortunate in securing the sympathetic co-operation of one of the highest authorities in the medical profession (unfortunately I have not permission to disclose his name), who promised to make an analysis of the ulcer under the microscope in his laboratory.

His subsequent report was as follows:– "It is an acute duodenal ulcer, contains Brunner's glands and shows from its condition that it was about to penetrate the intestine and would have proved fatal at a very early date." He was surprised at the freshness of the tissue which was very soft, and also at the fact that there was no trace of modern surgical methods having been used in the operation. Naturally he was greatly puzzled by all the circumstances of the case.

The Two Worlds – 24th June, 1949.   By Richard L. Serin,

Hon. General Secretary of Universal Brotherhood Federation.

I was very interested to read the article in *The Two Worlds* about Mrs Isa Northage, of Nottingham, and the wonderful cure by Dr Reynolds. I have known Mrs Isa Northage for some years and when I was living in Nottingham during 1941 and 1942, I had the pleasure and the privilege of attending her circles and her healing services. Mrs Isa Northage is one of the most spiritual mediums I have known in these last twenty-five years, and also one of the most developed instruments I have seen or heard. You only have to enter her home to feel the presence of spirit.

The following case of healing, although of small importance, is of interest. One day during 1941 my hairdresser pointed out to me that I was losing my hair rapidly in one place. He declared it to be 'an alopecia patch' and advised me to consult a chemist of Nottingham who had made a speciality of this kind of complaint. The latter gave me a bottle to rub into the hair, but told me that he had not the proper ingredients as some of the oils came from France and that I should consult a doctor, as my trouble was probably due to my general condition. The doctor informed me that I was going bald and there was little he could do. As he himself was as bald as a billiard ball, he treated the matter very lightly and dismissed me! The patch was now the size of a half-crown, completely denuded of hair.

The following week my wife and I attended a sitting at Mrs Isa Northage's Sanctuary at Bulwell. The medium was controlled by Dr Reynolds who, when the healing was finished, asked if anyone else needed help. My wife and I were sitting right at the back of the room and my wife whispered to me, "Ask him about your hair!" I was whispering back that it was too trivial when Dr Reynolds spoke and said, "Have you any trouble, Serin?" I then told him what I was worried about and Dr Reynolds said, "All right, I shall see what I can do. Tonight you may wake up and see a blue flash. You will then know I have been with you." Effectively at about midnight that night I woke up suddenly and observed what was like a parting blue light.

A week later there were short stubs of hair showing on my alopecia patch. A week later again the patch had shrunk to the size of a shilling piece and a fortnight after that my hair was completely restored and has been ever since.

It is nothing unusual, when sitting in Mrs Isa Northage's house to hear the gramophone playing by itself on the floor above and to hear the record turn over, and that when no one is in the house excepting the people with us, on the ground floor.

I would also like to say that the only materialisation seance I have had with Mrs Northage impressed me so much that I am certain she must be one of the very best physical mediums of modern times. To see entities build up from the floor and later disappear through the floor would convince the most sceptical observer.

But above all, it is the spirituality of Mrs Isa Northage which is her outstanding quality.

A Report from D. Dimbleby. 17th July, 1941.

For ten years I suffered with internal stomach pains and lived chiefly on milk and soft diet. I had medical treatment for Ulcerated Stomach, Duodenal Ulcer, and not getting any better I was told that the lining of my stomach was gone. Some time previous I had received an invitation to visit Mrs Northage; who was a medium used for healing, etc. As I was getting worse instead of better I decided to accept the invitation, and I visited her home at Bulwell in May, 1940. I was operated upon by a Dr Reynolds, who I learned afterwards, had performed operations beyond the skill of earthly doctors. After my operation the doctor said he had removed a cancer from the pit of my stomach. I believe that he did. But I do know that I can now eat and enjoy many things that I have not eaten for ten years.

I have had the pleasure of seeing, talking, shaking hands with this doctor, just as I would with any one of my own friends.

Signed: David Dimbleby,
Yew Tree Close, Ashover.

From George Spence

I had suffered with stomach trouble on and off for several years, but it was not till August 1946 that I had an X-ray at Derbyshire Royal Infirmary which confirmed that I had a large ulcer on the rear wall of my stomach.

I was under treatment of my panel doctor from that time till January 1949, which was the time I started treatment from Dr Reynolds, the spirit doctor who worked through Mrs Northage. Prior to contact with Mrs Northage I had treatment from a Harley Street specialist in 1947, but the pain and suffering still continued, in fact it got worse and worse and I was contemplating suicide. I was at home more than at work, and my wife was having to take in boarders to make enough money to live on and I could not see myself being a burden to her.

It was at this time that I kept receiving messages from the spirit world though mediums who attended Charnwood St. Spiritualist Church, which I had been a member of since 1928, telling me not to lose faith in them as my prayers would be answered, and through this I would witness some most wonderful happenings and have wonderful spiritual experience.

The outcome of this was that a visitor to my home told me of a friend of hers who was a patient of Mrs Northage and was improving after doctors had given up hope. I wrote to Mrs Northage asking if anything could be done for me as I had had stomach trouble for several years. The following week I had a reply stating that Dr Reynolds had visited me and his diagnosis was Gastric Ulcer which he would treat if I called on Mrs Northage. I was just about all in when I arrived at 'Pinewoods' as it was a two-hour journey from my home. On meeting and shaking hands with Mrs Northage I had a strange sensation within me of comfort and a certainty that here if anywhere I would find that which I had been searching for, for so long, yes, even before my illness. There was that power which seemed to flow to me from her which made me realize the spirit world had led me to this place. I had a talk that same day with Dr Reynolds through the trumpet and what a wonderful experience it was! He told me he could cure me, and I praised God for the confidence I felt in Dr Reynolds and Mrs Northage.

I felt I knew from that moment I would be cured; I had no doubt about it. I was uplifted in mind and body. Dr Reynolds said he would give Mrs Northage some powder for me to take night and morning and I had to return the following Wednesday for a report. I was under the impression that Dr Reynolds would operate on the ulcer (I have since assisted at three operations of this kind, at which Dr Reynolds materialised and performed the operation after which we were allowed to inspect that which had been removed: a most wonderful experience this has been to me), but after attending about three weeks during which I had been very much improved, experiencing very little pain, Dr Reynolds told me in my case he did not think an operation necessary, as he believed he could remove it without. He stated that he would loosen the ulcer and when ready I would probably vomit and bring up the ulcer, so I had to watch out for this and when I saw the blood which would come with it I had to take a dose of powder and lay quiet for a while. After a month of the powder he put me on another medicine which he gave me the prescription of. This I had made up at the chemists, and took half an hour before meals.

By this time I was feeling much better, by the end of about 12 months I was a new man, only very infrequently was there any discomfort, till one Saturday I ate some plums. They were lovely and sweet, and I could not see them doing me any harm as Doctor had not restricted me on my food in any way. That night I had a recurrence of the old agony and sent my thoughts to Dr Reynolds to come and help me. I decided to write to Mrs Northage for some more powder.

By Sunday morning the pain had abated so I put off writing as I was due to go over to 'Pinewoods' on Wednesday. The day came and while on the bus the pain began to increase, till by the time I arrived I was on the point of collapse. Imagine my surprise when before I could tell Mrs Northage how ill I had been and was, she told me that Dr Reynolds had been to her and told her how I had sent for him at the weekend and that I would need some powder on Wednesday when I arrived, a dose of which I took immediately and within two minutes the pain had gone.

His message to me was to leave the plums alone, as I had more than enough acid in my body without adding to it. I had said nothing to Mrs Northage about the plums, proving Doctor's nearness when called.

As the years went by I carried on with the medicine, this was to control the acid so Dr Reynolds informed me. I now felt on top of the world, able to do a good day's work and no trouble. All this time I had been a regular sitter in seance and had wonderful experiences. They proved to be the meeting of my two brothers from spirit, talking to them through the trumpet, and receiving advice on various matters which only we were conversant with.

Now we come to July 1955, it was the last Saturday in the month and I had what I thought was a touch of food poisoning;

terrible pains in the stomach and a feeling of sickness. I was so ill that my wife was compelled to send for my doctor but before he arrived I had a vomiting bout and I noticed the blood which came with it. Not a lot, but it made me rather worried as I had forgotten Dr Reynolds' instructions, as I was under the impression that the ulcer had been removed and had passed through the bowels. This Dr Reynolds had told me was a possibility, but he would do all in his power to avoid it. Within a few minutes my panel doctor arrived, but by this time I was feeling such a lot better. After several questions on what I had been eating, etc., he said he would send some medicine round immediately he got back to his surgery and then came the thought to me – you have some of Dr Reynolds' powder, take a good dose as you were told and lie down. This I did, and from then till now, I have never suffered any discomfort and have not taken any medicine.

I have tried in this statement to keep to facts and avoid my feelings towards Dr Reynolds and Mrs Northage, and her other helpers, but I cannot finish without giving expression to my innermost thoughts of Mrs Northage. I feel from her that sympathetic understanding personality, which is the hallmark of the healer. Of her I also know from my own observations, that devotion to what she calls her duty to mankind, her unselfishness, even to the extent of neglect of her own physical well being. May God be with her and bestow on her His blessing for her services to mankind.

Signed: George Spence.

From Mr R. Smith

At the age of twenty-two I began to suffer from headaches and depressions which were severe in nature. I was so ill that life was only an existence from day to day. Even my doctor could not help me, nor could the psychiatrist whom I visited. My cousin, Billy Gillette, came from Sheffield to Nottingham where I lived, to see a football match and saw my plight. He being a Spiritualist told me of Mrs Northage, an old friend of his who was a wonderful Spiritual Healer, and she would help me.

Now I would like to say, having met Mrs Northage, I've never in all my life known anyone so understanding and unselfish. I came to her as a stranger and told her of my condition, and she explained to me that she would send her spirit guide, Dr Reynolds, to me while I was asleep, between the hours of 12 and 2. On my next visit a week later I was told that Dr Reynolds would like to speak to me.

At a later date I was allowed to sit at a trumpet seance at 'Pinewoods' where I met Dr Reynolds, who told me he had diagnosed my trouble. My nerves were in a very bad state and also he had found inside my nose pieces of broken bone. He promised to help me in the future and I was to send my thoughts to him whenever I needed him. He would arrange an operation on my nose, which took place on 21st May, 1949, in Mrs Northage's operating theatre. Casting my mind back into the past I can remember as a small child playing on a slide made out of the snow, when I fell on my face and broke my two front teeth. Although I didn't know, I must have damaged my nose, I remember it was difficult to breathe down my nose, this must have caused a blockage, thus the headaches. My father who suffered from duodenal ulcer in the meantime had spoken with Dr Reynolds and he had arranged to operate and remove the ulcer at the same time. At the operation there were eight people including Mrs Northage, Mr Stocks, Mr Newman, Mrs Stenson, my mother and father, Mr Thompson and myself. Mr Stocks opened in prayer and Mrs Northage asked for the light to be switched off and then was taken in trance. A hymn was sung and the trumpet which was placed on the floor at the side of the operating table on which my father lay, was raised, and the voice of Ellen Dawes spoke, and said she had been sent to test and examine conditions.

After the trumpet had been lowered Dr Reynolds materialised; we saw him in the red glow of a lamp which had been lit. He greeted everyone present, and as he did so, his face was visible to us and also his robes.

After witnessing the wonderful operation of removing the ulcer from my father's abdomen, Dr Reynolds had me sit with my back to him, then after plugging my nose with cotton wool he explained that he would dematerialise his hand and pass it through the back of my head and remove the splinters of broken bones in my nose with a piece of lint. Dr Reynolds' hand was then seen to approach the back of my head and pass into it. I should like to say that I felt nothing at all, while this was going on. When his hand was withdrawn, he stretched out his hand and placed something in a dish along with the ulcer which was taken from my father. All those people present could clearly see the ulcer and the three small pieces of bone.

To conclude my story, all it remains for me to say is that my spirit brother, Jimmy Smith, spoke through the trumpet to my father and mother and myself. My spirit sister, Hilda Smith, was allowed to materialise, and all present saw her standing in her beautiful robes. She bent over my father and kissed him and told him she would help him: turning she spoke to my mother and myself, and then we saw her dematerialise.

Well, readers, this concludes this wonderful story of my operation under Dr Reynolds, and I would like to add that I owe everything to Mrs Northage, my marriage – which couldn't have been possible – and my son, which completes my happiness.

Signed: R. Smith,
Nottingham.

Chapter Five

Experiments

Séance held at the 'Eleanor' Sanctuary: 21st August, 1946.

Medium: Mrs I. A. Northage, Bulwell, Nottingham.

When all had assembled and were seated in a circle, Mrs Northage entered the room and immediately sat in the cabinet. In a very short time, after opening with a brief prayer, the lights were lowered and Mrs Northage was heard breathing deeply.

Soon the voice of Sambo gave us greetings and said that the power was good, and he hoped we would have a happy and enjoyable séance as there were many loved ones waiting to speak.

The trumpet was then seen to rise from the floor and circle the room. The voice of Ellen, Mrs Northage's introductory helper, was heard confirming the remarks made by Sambo, giving us greeting and hoping that we should have an enjoyable evening. She also informed us that she was handing over to Eleanor for the evening.

Again the trumpet rose and Eleanor spoke, giving her name and stating that this was her Sanctuary and that she was pleased to see so many friends present. Soon the trumpet sank and then Eleanor began to materialise. Whilst this was being done, the voice of Sambo was heard saying: "The plaques are not so good for light to-night, Bro. Nixon, so the Eleanor she will try to show herself with the red light." Eleanor was then seen to present herself, and flashed on a red torch to enable more detail to be seen. For a considerable time she turned the torch upon her body, pointing out its aid various parts such as arms, body, head, features etc., and each person present was able to see quite clearly. She also stooped and shone the light on the paper whilst the recorder was taking down these notes, her face being illuminated at the same time.

Many of the messages and talks between sitters and their loved ones were of too intimate a nature to be recorded here and so a brief account is given of the friends who visited us, and of some of the talks or instructions, etc.

First to come, after Eleanor, was Mr Gill's mother, speaking through the trumpet, and showing herself and talking directly to them. Quite a conversation was held, and 'Grandma' said how glad she was that Mr Gill's son, Teddy, had returned home safely, and that 'Granny had been looking after him'. She mentioned how much joy it gave her, and how happy she was to speak with them, and that: "The boy is growing and is not afraid of me." Mr Gill's son was present at the séance. 'Granny' kissed them all and bade them farewell.

Dr Reynolds then spoke from the trumpet to Mr Read, and said he was glad to see him looking so well, and how much he would have liked to see John. Still, he understood he was on holiday, and he would like to see him later. Regarding John's treatment he said: "I am pleased that John is looking up. We arrested the kidney trouble in time. See that he drinks plenty of water so that the kidneys can be flushed. Watch the winter, and tell him to go very carefully for a time." There was a little more to do, but he would attend to this, and send a report to Nixon. Mr Read then asked Dr Reynolds if he could do anything for Mrs Read, so the Doctor addressed her directly and enquired about the pain in the leg. He said there was fluid round the ankle, but he would remove it. He would attend her in her sleep state, and asked her not to be frightened, but to ask for him on occasion so that he could make the contact more easily.

Dr Reynolds then spoke direct to Mrs Gill, asking her to drink plenty of orange juice which would assist him in removing the fluid from the chest, etc., so that the phlegm and mucus could be easily dispersed. After this, Dr Reynolds said: "Well, I suppose you want to get on with your séance, so I will just say 'goodnight'," and with that, the trumpet sank to the floor.

Next came 'Dad' who wanted to speak to 'Billy', and he kept repeating "Speak to me." After the vibration was established and made easier, he went on: "Business is all right, and if you want assistance just send word to Grandfather." Much conversation was held and a reference was also made to 'Granny' in spirit.

Ivy now appeared, and those who had met her previously could not mistake the voice or actions. She was shortly joined by Jill Savage and the pair conversed at length. They spoke of an oil painting they had each done, and also that Jill had eaten a chocolate off her birthday cake. One of the sitters wished to have a photograph of them, so they promised to let one be taken at any time Dr Reynolds gave them permission. Ivy made reference to her earth life and gave also the address of her parents, etc. She referred humorously to her grandfather whom she often saw over there; he thought he was still killing Germans and crawling under barbed wire. In Ivy's own words: "He is always deeing that. He luks daft craaling aboot like thaat."

Two trumpets were seen to rise and we were told that Georgia had come to convey greetings to Mrs Tribe and Pearl. Sid, Mrs Tribe's brother, was the other visitor. Georgia, being a woman, was permitted to speak first, but as she appeared to intend speaking for some time, Sid became rather impatient and kept on telling her to finish so that he might have something to say. At last Georgia bade her friends adieu and Sid addressed his sister. He answered many questions and said, among other things, "I'm not with Mother, but with Dad. I don't too much want to come back. I am quite happy where I am." Replying to a question, he said: "Help my brother's wife, Sis. Tell – that he must remember that he married his wife for good," – and that when he came back to this country he was not to judge his wife by the same standards as the girls at home, and thereby be led away. He should remember this, etc.

'Granny' next came to Miss Evans and talked with her.

Dorothy spoke through the trumpet to Mr Read, and spoke of family matters. She then 'disappeared', but was soon seen to be materialising. She again talked with the family, saying she was so happy to see them there. Kissing them all, she promised her help; especially she asked Mrs Read to look after her brother.

Jack Murch came to Mrs Murch, and although she did not recognise the name he told her that he was Uncle Jack Murch, and had been away many years. He had since passed over and was of her husband's people.

Barouck again spoke through the trumpet to Mr Rushton and gave salaams. Eleanor interpreted and said that he intended helping Mr Rushton to experiment with photography.

Chang, a Chinese guide to Mr Gill, spoke in his well-known high pitched voice, and caused some merriment in his excitement.

Eleanor, in a long talk with Derek said she would watch over him during his career. He had passed his examination, – (no official news had been received of this, and Derek was not too sanguine as to the result, but this will be an indication of 'pre-knowledge' from the spirit world). He would be going into danger, but she would always be near to help him, and when he needed it he was just to say her name and she would be there. She extracted a promise from him which he should remember.

Duncoo, healing guide to Mr Gill, showed himself to the sitter.

Another materialised form showed herself to Mr Murch, and gave the name of Beaty. She was asked if there was any message for Philip, and answer was made accordingly.

Black Cloud then said that the power was good and he would show himself; his materialised form was visible to all.

Dr Reynolds then spoke through the trumpet asking whether the sitters were tired and was emphatically assured by all that they were nor. Mrs Murch then asked Dr Reynolds if he could help her in health, and he promised his assistance.

Johnny Keith, the next 'visitor' went across to Mr Gill and family, and said he also was a sailor and had been in Australia. He addressed Mr Gill's son by the name of Edward and said among other things that he had brought with him Horace Slade who had passed out on the 'Byron' and had previously served on the 'Repulse'.

Kathleen and Victor (two names, given when the two trumpets rose together) expressed disappointment at not finding those they wanted, but Kathleen asked us to convey a message to her mother.

She said: "Tell Mother that it is I, Kathleen, and that Victor came with me to-night. Give her my love and tell her I am happy, and that Victor is now beginning to make progress. Love to Mother," and one trumpet sank. From the other was heard: "This is Victor, and will you please tell my aunt that I have been released from the 'plane. Ask her to tell my mother and give my love to her and Mother."

Again the trumpet rose and went across to Mr Gill. A voice said: "Florrie; Aunty Flo, Aunty Mabel has been to-night. Tell Flo I do visit her."

A voice spoke to Mrs Murch in what appeared to be a foreign tongue not understood by those present. Suddenly another trumpet rose alongside the other and Eleanor was heard saying: "This is Eleanor again, and I have come to interpret the message. She says she is Sister Catherine and was a French Sister of Mercy from a convent in the south of France. She died helping the French patriots in 1942-43. She had assisted in the Underground Movement." Several present offered guesses as to the language spoken, but Eleanor turned to one of the sitters and said: "It was Latin, Daddy."

Another voice was now heard saying: "I came, not of your country. I came from White Russia. I am Polish. I was looking for my brother. I am Maria Agonchitika. I escaped from Poland 1939-40. I am with my brother now, and we come to help you." One who gave the name of Brother Petre said: "May the Grace of God be with you to all eternity." He said that he passed out in Charwood (or Sherwood) Forest, 50 years ago, but that he was now 'well alive' and came to help again.

Nancy, (apparently a child guide) came to Mr Gill and asked him to get her some chrysanthemums. Mr Gill appeared to know to what she referred.

The next voice came just after Sambo had told us that the power was going, and otherwise the gentleman who had spoken previously would have tried to show himself. The strength of this voice did not indicate any loss of power, but it was noticeable that the trumpet was unable to tap the sitter as had been done by previous speakers. However, the voice said: "This is Lilian, for Frank, ... Aunty Lilian. Perhaps you will understand me better if I say Aunty Tootles. I tried and tried very hard to come before.

How's Kathleen?" Much else was said, but of interest only to the recipient, and with the words, "give my love to Mother," the trumpet sank to the floor.

Although the power was evidently receding, another tried to speak and managed to get the trumpet to rise, addressing one of Mr Read's party thus: "I am Grandmother and I have waited nearly too long, – Grandmother on your Mother's side. I am anxious to talk to you, and have much to talk about. I will talk to you again, and Mother."

The voice of Sambo was then heard saying that it was time to finish and he hoped we had enjoyed the séance. He said he would leave the medium's body and we could put on the lights when we were ready. Good-nights were said, and the lights restored as Mrs Northage returned to normal. Thus ended a wonderful and interesting evening, for we had seen, spoken with, kissed, touched, and joined in a party with those of our loved ones whom the world thought lost and gone, and we who had been thus privileged would ever remember. Truly death had lost its sting, and the grave had no victory!

(Present at the above séance were: F. W. Rushton, E. Evans, F. M. Nixon, W. H. Gill, and ? The original signatures of the sitters, together with those belonging to the other records contained in this chapter are in the author's possession).

Experimental Sitting: 16th September 1946
                                                    Bulwell, Notts

15watt Red Light and 25watt White.

Ellen Dawes and Dr Reynolds materialised in red light, speaking about *Links and the excellent power for a great experiment. It was good to know so many were helping the Links. Grey Wolf, North American Indian, materialised, giving a message from his 'White Chief' in the Californian link, a Mr Johnson, who had previously sat with us while serving in the U.S. Army, now resident in California. Glasgow and Newcastle links were sitting. Jeanette and Ruth Hutton spoke in Direct Voice to Mrs Cooper. A 'Sister Hyacinth' and 'Brother Richard' spoke to Mrs Stevenson. Doctor Reynolds requested the lights be ready for next sitting, changing the Watts. Various voices spoke through trumpet.

The Links: The name given to 'Circles' sitting each week at the same hour, to create a reserve of power or energy, for the spirit doctors to draw upon for the healing of the sick Each week these Circles received a report from us which we obtained from spirit. Sitting closed in Prayer.

Experimental Sitting: 23rd September 1946

25watt White Light.

Sitting commenced at 7.30 pm. Reports re: patients.
Reports from Links.
Experiment with Ectoplasm.

Dr Reynolds requested White Light to show Ectoplasm clearly.

First to materialise was a Lady, very aged.

Ectoplasm now shown in movement, showing how the different forms built up, with first, a young girl aged about ten years, standing clear in the white light. A young man next started to build up from the floor showing head first until fully materialised, another just seemed to walk out of the air. Doctor then allowed each one present to feel the different types of Ectoplasm, Solid, Illuminated, and as a mist. Requesting the Sitters to remain quiet, Doctor said he would try all links. In a few minutes materialisation of two Indians (N. America) Slim Buck and Grey Wolf, followed by the materialisation of Guides of all links. An Italian Doctor then addressed us as he materialised. He too was helping experiments.

Sitting closed in Prayer.

Experimental Sitting: 30th October 1946

Sitting opened in Prayer.

Sitting commenced at 7.30 p.m. to enable reports and diagnosis of patients before experimenting. This Sitting was marred at the start owing to a lack of harmony in one of the links through a misunderstanding. Doctor informed us a gap such as this was holding up progress with white light but he would allow a few voices.

Ellen, Sambo, Slim Buck, Eleanor Nixon, Grey Wolf, Sacadina, Jeanette, Gloria March, John and Cyril (Airman and Sailor) Mr Radford and Conan Doyle. Conan Doyle and his brother Barry Doyle (had been of Catholic Faith before passing) were helping experiments but tonight had been disappointing owing to this break in complete harmony. Ellen told us to close.

Sitting closed.

Experimental Sitting: 13th November 1946

Sitting commenced 7.30 pm. Harmony restored helping to provide a much more successful sitting (Not trance).

Doctor opened sitting in direct voice commenting upon good conditions, and was followed by Rhumar of Bombay who had been many years in spirit. In broken English he told us he had been 'set apart' by 'Shiva's seal'. He returned to help our work and Doctor Reynolds' experiment, and while he talked, a very beautiful young lady materialised. As she stood before us a blue light enveloped her whole form. We passed our hands (with permission) through her etheric robes and body and yet did not disturb her form. As she spoke, her voice was very musical. Doctor Reynolds materialised (in white light) showing his head without a hood. His hair and beard were grey, eyes brown, height about 5ft. 8ins. Doctor stood for 10 minutes showing us his hands whilst talking. Ellen spoke (Trumpet) for a while commenting on good sitting and then requested us to close.

Sitting closed.

Experimental Sitting: 20th November 1946

Sitting opened in Prayer.

Ellen Dawes opened the sitting by addressing us (trumpet) saying there were many present who were helping the experiment and had returned from spirit to speak with us. Doctor Reynolds said h:e was leaving us for a little while to visit the other links; in the meantime he had a friend with him who wished to speak to us. We were then addressed in a drawling voice by Hudson Tuttle, an American who when on earth lived at Berlin Heights, Ohio, U.S.A. He stated that at the age of sixteen: "I became a physical medium; also I did both Automatic and Inspirational Sittings. I wrote a number of books, scientific and philosophical, also songs and stories. I have returned to help you in your great work. I was born in a log cabin and had to educate myself. Nevertheless I did my work as a servant of God, and wish to carry on in helping you." Dr Reynolds returned to address us and to experiment with Ectoplasm in various lights. 30watt white, 30watt red and 30watt blue. A Chinese girl materialised under a 40watt white light for 5 minutes. Sambo addressed us and suggested we draw to a close.

Sitting closed in Prayer.

Experimental Sitting: 27th November 1946

Sitting opened in Prayer.

Ellen Dawes addressed us in direct voice stating all links were sending out their thoughts; conditions were good.

Sambo spoke in direct voice, giving advice and comfort.

We were addressed now by David Anderson, of Glasgow, in direct voice. When asked for some evidence he replied: "I was born in Armagh, Ireland, and had been a Methodist, Unitarian, Swedenborgian, etc., but could never find what I wanted until I was introduced to Spiritualism by a friend in 1876. From then on I became very interested. I became very successful in diagnosis and healing and later was a Trance Medium for Speaking." We then requested him to show himself. He did so at once. His hair was curled, his forehead bare. Brown eyes, small beard and moustache.

Doctor came again and told us to prepare to try out Ectoplasm next week in 40watt White Light.

Sitting closed in Prayer.

Experimental Sitting: 4th December 1946

Sitting opened in Prayer.

White Light ready as requested by Dr Reynolds.

Doctor requested us to relax for a while whilst he visited links, if conditions were good he would try to lift their trumpets.

Doctor returned and after addressing sitting he allowed spirit friends to materialise in the white light.

First to come was 'Aghan' (Indian) Brown face, black hair, piercing dark eyes, standing about 6ft. 0ins. tall.

Now a small boy materialised. He stated he was South African and he had come to show earth people that we do not alter our personality when we make the change called death. We progress and become highly evolved, but we always return as we were when passing over, for recognition. Ellen Dawes materialised in her etheric body (like a mist).

Sambo requested the sitting close.

Experimental Sitting: 11th December 1946

Sitting opened in Prayer.

Doctor Reynolds in direct voice discussed Psychic Research and various religions, finally accepting that Faith and Love were the true religion.

First materialisation was a Bedouin from Moroccan Desert (25watt White Light). He spoke in his own language; however Doctor Reynolds materialised and translated for us: "A greeting to my English friends, for you are all children of the Divine Spirit and GOD giveth you all divine gifts by the spirit. To one the word of wisdom, to another the word of knowledge, and by that same spirit the gifts of Faith; to another Healing and working of miracles, and discerning of spirits, divine gifts of tongues, and to another interpreting of tongues. We cannot tell why to one should come the gifts of song, to another music; gifts that are sometimes inherited and sometimes so unexpected as to appear alarming. Many obstacles must be overcome to forward their development." Coming towards myself (Isa) he addressed me personally: "Where did you inherit your wonderful gift of healing, who gave it to you? – GOD. And who gave you the gift of miracles that we can humbly return to-night to help you? – GOD, the Divine Spirit; and so this gift of yours is greater than music. Gold can be laid at your feet, but keep your gift pure, my child, keep it pure." Touching his head in salute he dematerialised.

Sitting closed in Prayer.

Experimental Sitting: 25th December 1946
Christmas Day.

Sitting opened in Prayer.

This evening's sitting was rather poor owing to prevailing general conditions. Doctor spoke in Direct voice for 15 minutes.

The subject was research between the two worlds, the experimenting with the means of communication and the method by which the spirit world was working for the benefit of earth people, and our efforts to give greater proof of the return of spirits. A few friends materialised. Doctor then gave us a warning: "Although you have had a very mild Christmas I must warn you all to take great care of yourselves. A great cyclone is moving, bringing in its wake, floods, famine and disease, also death. So keep warm, take care and watch the coming month. I am afraid our experiments will suffer, we may have to finish them before the allotted time, but we must do our best and GOD will surely reward us. I will not keep you longer, this is Christmas and I know you are all anxious to be at your party, so Good Night." Doctor and Ellen both wished us a Happy Christmas. Sambo then asked us to close.

Sitting closed.

Experimental Sitting: 5th February 1947

Ellen opened (Trumpet) welcoming two Welsh friends to Sanctuary, and telling them they had a big surprise coming. As Ellen was speaking, their daughter who had passed at the age of seventeen years materialised (in white light). She looked very beautiful; she then conversed with her parents.

An aged lady was next to materialise and with the Welsh friends sang (*Fryniau Caersalem*) *Jesu, Lover of my Soul* in Welsh. The lady's name was Mrs Hughes; she was an old pioneer of Spiritualism before her passing. Next a Sister of Mercy stood with an illuminated Cross saying a prayer. As she prayed a Chinaman stood beside her, his name Li-Wung. After the prayer he spoke for ten minutes. He was well educated before his passing and said he knew the inner mysteries of the old Chinese temples (where the truth we were seeking was practised 6000 years ago).

Lone Star (Indian) gave a blessing.

Doctor Reynolds now asked for our thoughts as he was about to visit the links. In a few moments each Guide of the different links announced his presence including the South African link, American link; Glasgow, Ashington and Devon, London, Northampton, Portsmouth and Newcastle links.

Sambo now called upon us to close.

Closed in Prayer.

Experimental Sitting: 12th February 1947

Doctor Reynolds was first to speak (Trumpet).

All sitters were feeling cold owing to coal shortage and it was snowing hard.

Doctor had chosen tonight to show us the different mouldings of hands and faces and how the faces could appear at the passing. One Welsh miner, killed in an accident at Treforest, S. Wales, showed his face to a Mr Gronow who was with him at the time of the accident.

Then the face appeared of a Tibetan Monk who was buried in a glacier many centuries ago, it was a perfect mould, all in 25watt white light. I was not in a trance, as part of the experiment to experience materialisation while fully awake. I felt I had shrunk to the size of a child, and was numb all over. A child then materialised, face and body very badly scarred. She had been burned to death at seven years of age through her night-dress catching fire. Gradually the scars disappeared and she stood absolutely beautiful as she is now in spirit.

Ellen then came and told us to retire into the house and get warm.

Sitting closed.

Experimental Sitting: 19th February 1947

Sitting opened in Prayer.

This was indeed a poor night and bitterly cold. We had neither electric heat or coal.

Dr Reynolds and Ellen both spoke for a short while. We also had a few words from Guides from the Links. We received plans which Doctor hoped to carry out later if we kept up our health. We were instructed to keep humble, and take all our experiments in a natural way and not to look for material gain; to keep this work holy, for many would seek the Sanctuary to see if miracles could be performed. The greatest Miracle had yet to come.

Doctor then bade us all 'Good Night'.

Sitting closed.

Preliminary Talk Given by Dr Reynolds During a Séance held in the Sanctuary: Wednesday, 10th September, 1947.

Present:

Leader, Mrs Northage; Mrs Stenson, Mrs Cooper, Mr and Mrs Cox, Mrs Morck, Ken and Audrey, Mr Stocks.

Dr Reynolds greeted all sitters, thanked Mr Cox for his gift, and then proceeded to give a preliminary talk on the work he wished to be carried out prior to the forthcoming experiments, and some of the things he hoped to accomplish during the months from October to the end of April.

For the purpose of these experiments, it was absolutely essential that anything which was likely to hold germs should be removed:

– i.e. old flashlights, books, etc.

The curtains of the cabinet were to remain closed at all times, apart from the evenings set aside for the work.

The Links who were to be asked to join in would be given by the Doctor later.

Some important points were: –

(a) When the sitters have been chosen, on no account must new ones be introduced.

(b) Sitters would be expected, unless prevented by illness, or something of the utmost importance, to attend regularly.

(c) In the event of a sitter being absent, his or her chair must be set in its usual place and left unoccupied.

(d) Dr Reynolds particularly stressed the necessity for all sitters to be in their places, so that the séance could commence every Wednesday at 7.30 sharp. This is very important.

The Doctor said he wanted sitters to be as passive as possible whilst at the séance and throughout the months of the experiments. He asked that everyone should try, as far as humanly possible, to refrain from falling into fits of temper and strive to live and work in closer touch with things of the spirit. It wasn't his wish that we should abandon innocent pleasures, but riotous living would certainly be a hindrance to this special work.

With each sitter, from October until April, there would be present, at all times, a Guardian from the world of spirit to watch over us whilst at work and even during sleep.

Anyone who was likely to be a disturbing influence was not to be allowed in the Sanctuary and, on any occasion, when visitors were shown in, the curtains of the cabinet were still to remain closed.

Dr Reynolds said he was sending out thoughts to higher spheres for help in these experiments, and we were to witness some truly marvellous things. Spirit people from higher spheres would visit us during these months, and the Sanctuary would be filled with light as bright as day on occasions. In fact, the world would not be ready for such phenomena for a great span of time.

The Doctor explained that it was because of the unusual nature of the phenomena he had asked for a certain number of articles to be removed from the Sanctuary. He said he fully realised that everything which was introduced was with the idea of making it a place of beauty and, he was, indeed, proud of it, but for the purpose of this special work, he asked for their removal temporarily.

Experiments in photographic work were to be carried out, and it was arranged that, when Ken was home from time to time, special evenings would be given up to this end.

Whilst we were passing through this period, unusual things might happen to any sitter, even during daylight, but as we had been forewarned, there should be no cause for alarm since no harm would befall anyone.

Report of the First Experiment carried out in the Sanctuary: Wednesday, 8th October, 1947.

Present:

Leader: Mrs Northage; Mrs Stenson, Mrs Cooper, Mrs Difford, Mr and Mrs Cox, Mr Patterson, Mr Home, Mr Stocks.

A few moments after Mrs Stenson had opened in prayer, Ellen greeted all sitters. Sambo then spoke through Mrs Northage, told us the power was very good, and that Dr Reynolds was waiting.

Dr Reynolds then spoke through the trumpet, greeted everyone and said he would visit the Links, sending the Guides along to speak to us as he did so. The first Guide to speak was the London one and the rest came in the following order:– Ashington, Northampton (Mr Ives), Exeter, Grimsby, Northampton (Mrs Barratt), Govanhill, Glasgow, Airdrie, Newcastle (the Guide said there were only a few sitters, but all were in earnest), Pontypridd, California and South Africa.

Dr Reynolds then returned and said all were in harmony and the power was very good, which made conditions satisfactory for him in which to work. The Doctor warned us that on these occasions anything might happen, but there was no need for alarm.

The first manifestation was a foot, perfectly formed, and this was raised several inches from the ground. A fully materialised form was the next, and the first thing the red torch revealed was a beautifully shaped right arm and shoulder (both uncovered), then a face of exquisite beauty. Attention was particularly drawn to a pair of lovely eyes which appeared light in colour. The robe had a sheen, like fine silk, which covered the head, and fell in small folds over the left shoulder.

The form disappeared and Dr Reynolds came to explain that an Egyptian lady from a high sphere had visited us. She had been in spirit for many years.

The next form was a Bedouin lady in a long white robe. Forehead, hair and body were completely covered. A notable feature was a thin veil which came from under the band across the forehead, thus screening her face from view, but the end of what appeared to be a pointed nose could just be seen.

Next a young Egyptian materialised. She wore a long white robe, with arms and head covered, but round the wrist was a band from which went a cord to the body. Dr Reynolds explained that this girl had been a slave when in earth life and the band on the wrist and connecting cord to the body were symbolical of the chains by which she was bound. On the death of her mistress, she was thrown into her tomb where she passed on herself into spirit.

We commented that these spirit friends all seemed to be very tall, but Dr Reynolds explained that they came from very high spheres. In manifesting they never touched a material condition, but remained suspended several inches from the floor. The Doctor said we should probably be wondering how it was they appeared in the Sanctuary if they did not touch a material condition, but this was accomplished by dematerialising part of the partitions to allow them to enter.

Explanations were given after the departure of the forms because, Dr Reynolds said, these souls were so sensitive that had he spoken whilst they were present, they would have returned immediately.

An Italian Sister of Mercy then showed herself. She banged the plaque on the floor several times and we were a little puzzled as to why she should do this. On looking closely she seemed to be legless. Her parents had given her over to the Convent and, on reaching a certain age, she was subjected, for want of a better term as the Doctor put it, to a certain discipline. Because she refused, she was victimised and given all kinds of menial tasks to perform. As she grew older, her body, of course, grew weaker through this treatment, and she was finally dropped through a trap door into the river which flowed by the Convent. Her legs were tied back to her arms, which explained why we could not see them when she first materialised. Although she suffered so much whilst on earth, she had progressed greatly in spirit and returned to-night without bitterness towards the people who were responsible for the tortures she had endured whilst in the body.

Dr Reynolds then said the power was very beautiful and all the loving thoughts from the Links were joining together in the form of a bright roadway down which the spirit friends were descending to make themselves seen to earthly eyes.

On one occasion, whilst Dr Reynolds was making preparations for the next manifestation, a relative (John Patterson) spoke to Mr Patterson and said that from the spirit side the vibrations were wonderful to behold, and the best way of describing what he saw was that the Sanctuary represented the standard of a Maypole and the vibrations emanating from the Links were streams of blue light circling round it as if they were being fanned by a gentle breeze.

Dr Reynolds then showed us three forms of ectoplasm – ethereal, solid and illuminated.

He then proceeded to show us how it was drawn from Mrs Northage. A red torch was switched on and from the region of the solar plexus a thin cord of ectoplasm could be seen coming through her dress, broadening, until it reached the entrance of one of the trumpets lying near her chair. The trumpet was moving slightly all the time. We then had the experience of seeing ectoplasm being drawn through the mouth. This time it was in a thick silken rope and extended down to the floor. Dr Reynolds asked if we had noticed how the ectoplasm was moving gently all the time and said the movements were those of the heart of the medium. It was this living ectoplasm that enabled our spirit friends to move and speak. He went on to say how we should realise from this the importance of having perfect conditions in which to work, since we should see that anyone attempting to cut or hold the ectoplasm in any way would have the effect of seriously injuring our wonderful instrument. In fact, haemorrhage could be brought on, which would take her to the fringes of the spirit world, if not, indeed, to the other side completely and, on this account, we should understand why the doors of the Sanctuary must be closed to other than the right sitters.

Dr Reynolds then said he would ask Sambo to leave the body, so that we could just see the 'shell' as he termed it. Sambo did so, materialised behind one curtain of the cabinet, said: "I am here now," and pushed it out with his hand. Dr Reynolds then asked Mrs Stenson to come forward and place her hand over Mrs

Northage's mouth and then close to her nose to convince us, for a brief span of time, there was no breathing. Sambo then returned to the body. This was done in a red light for all sitters to witness.

Dr Reynolds then said he would try the direct voice whilst Dr Thompson and Dr Savage were speaking to us on the trumpets. The Doctor said, "Good evening," and this was heard more clearly than the two voices on the trumpets.

During one of the experiments Dr Reynolds said he would dematerialise Mrs Northage completely and materialise her again several miles away from the Sanctuary.

The experiment was then closed in prayer by Mrs Cox.

Signed: James Patterson, John Home, Audrey Difford, W. Cox, F. Cox, L. Cooper, H. Stenson, G. Stocks, I. A. Northage.

Report of the Second Experiment carried out in the Sanctuary: Wednesday, 15th October, 1947.

Present:

Leader: Mrs Northage; Mrs Stenson, Mrs Cooper, Mrs Difford, Mr and Mrs Cox, Mr Stocks.

Mr Stocks opened in prayer and shortly afterwards Sambo greeted us through Mrs Northage. Ellen then tested the power and told us it was quite good.

Whilst Dr Reynolds was visiting some of the Links, Ellen informed us it had taken them a little longer to get Mrs Northage 'over', because she had been doing so much, and her body was tired.

Dr Reynolds then came on the trumpet and said all the Links had settled down with the exception of the Californian one. Members were there, but were not yet sitting. As it was only 4 o'clock in America, it was not quite so easy for them, but he hoped they would be concentrating in a few minutes. He then left us and Ellen said she would help some of our Guides to materialise.

Whilst she stood fully visible herself, one of Mrs Cox's guides, Sister Katherine, also showed herself. She was a very beautiful spirit in a long robe, with a short cape covering the upper part of the arm, but leaving the forearms bare. Mrs Difford's guide, a young Egyptian, with a lovely face, then materialised. Mr Stocks' Tibetan guide followed on the trumpet. He spoke in his own language, but Ellen translated and said he was very pleased to be with us and hoped to speak again soon.

Dr Reynolds returned and said he wanted to try out various voices to-night, and that we might find our voice boxes a little sore in the morning, because power would be drawn from them.

Two Bedouins from the Moroccan desert picked up the trumpets – a sister and brother. The brother greeted us, but as he spoke in his own language, nothing can be recorded. His sister spoke very good English and said her brother and his whole caravan were lost in the desert in a sandstorm. This girl said she had passed into the spirit world between 1909/10. After their return, Ellen told us they were both of very high caste, and an English governess had been employed to teach the girl English.

A Russian lady then spoke and gave her name as Nina Nowkowski. She and her man had fought side by side in the last war. She went on to say that the women in Russia were not afraid to fight with their men and die by their sides. They had lived in a village near the borders of Siberia in earth life. She asked us not to believe everything we were told about their country. "We are civilised people," she said, "and are allowed to worship our God as you do." She was sorry that some of our political leaders seemed to be against her country, and when listening to an address by one of the church dignitaries recently, was surprised to observe that even he had some hatred in his heart for her people. She explained that when we get to the spirit side, we would find that all men and women are brothers and sisters – class distinction and colour bars are unknown. Nina and her man died of starvation. She promised to speak to us again and on this occasion would bring him also.

Dr Reynolds then told us he had been speaking on the trumpet to Mr Hall at the London Link. He also mentioned that he had tried to move the trumpet at some of the other Links but, when anyone thought they saw it move, a discussion had immediately followed and this, of course, broke up the vibration.

A Frenchman spoke next and told us he had been brought down whilst on a reconnaissance on the borders of France and Belgium, resulting in his being burned to death. He had lived in the neighbourhood of Paris.

One of the band who had received bread from the Sanctuary *(see page 209)* was the next to communicate and said he had been shot whilst attempting to escape. He wanted to thank Mrs Northage for all that had been done, and said before long one or two of them would be visiting her. General de Cazale sent his thanks and a message that he would apport something from the ruins of Notre Dame in gratitude for all that had been done.

The Doctor said that the Californian Link starting late had prevented him from doing all he had planned to-night, but he hoped an early start would be possible next week.

Mr Cox's mother then spoke and brought with her Mrs Everett, who had only passed on the previous Monday; in fact she was to be cremated the following Friday. Mrs Everett just gave her name and said she would return again after she had rested.

The experiment was then closed in prayer by Mrs Difford.

Signed: I. A. Northage, H. Stenson, L. Cooper, F. Cox, W. Cox, A. Difford, G. Stocks.

Report of the Third Experiment carried out in the Sanctuary: Wednesday, 22nd October, 1947.

Present:

Leader: Mrs Northage; Mrs Stenson, Mrs Cooper, Mrs Difford, Mr and Mrs Cox, Mrs Blake, Mrs Smith, Mr Stocks.

The experiment was opened in prayer by Mrs Cox. During this prayer, and before Mrs Northage was able to go into trance, a pair of hands materialised. Mrs Northage was the first to comment about their moving over her face. They went over to Mrs Stenson, then to Mr Cox, and finally to each sitter, touching them somewhere on the face.

Ellen spoke on the trumpet, and Mrs Northage asked her what was happening. She replied that it was experimenting night and it would be better for Mrs Northage to go into trance. We then sang a hymn and Sambo took possession of the body. He said that the power was building up and quite a number of forms were already in the cabinet.

Dr Reynolds came after this and told us all the Links were on time to-night. They were all joining up and he left us to visit one or two.

The first form to materialise was an Egyptian lady. The right arm and shoulder were uncovered, but the covering over the head came down over the right shoulder. Her robe was fastened tightly across her chest and under the arms. Ellen requested Mrs Difford to switch on the side lights, so that we could see her more distinctly. She remained in full view of the lights to the slow count of five.

Dr Reynolds then spoke and said he had visited some of the Links, who had heard his tappings on their trumpets; he had been able to speak to some and we would be hearing from them about it.

Following this a young Egyptian girl showed herself, and we observed that she wore a thick band of material across her chest. Ellen told us she was very young and her attire was representative of what she had worn in earth life. She came from one of the higher spheres.

Sambo at this stage mentioned to Dr Reynolds that a great deal was being drawn from Mrs Northage now that the power was so high, and asked for a moment before the next manifestation. He told us the cabinet was full of forms and he was having a very busy time giving instructions and holding them back.

One of the plaques went up to the ceiling and remained there for several minutes. This was to show us that the forms come through the ceiling in the first place. After a short pause, a hand appeared in front of the plaque followed by a head. The plaque was banged a number of times on the ceiling, then it moved slowly to the centre of the Sanctuary. Next it came back to the left-hand side and finally descended. In doing so a foot was placed on Mr Cox's shoulder and the form then stood in front of Mr Cox and was recognised as his mother. She then went over to Mrs Cox.

After dematerialising, she spoke on the trumpet and said it was mother.

The Doctor, told us that although it might seem that much more time was being taken to show the forms to-night, a lot of work was going on that we could not see.

Dr Reynolds said he would now materialise a lady from a very high sphere, and we were to observe as much as possible. She wore a beautiful flowing robe which covered the whole of her body; her hair was also covered and there was a band across the forehead. Her face was of unusual shape, and a nose pointing slightly upwards with long nostrils were particularly outstanding. She also wore a pair of beautiful ear-rings, the colour of which may have been pale blue or mauve, but gold could be distinctly seen near the edges. We were again informed that she came from a very high sphere, was of Indian nationality and in earth life had been a Priestess in the temple of a Rajah from the Himalayas. Dr Reynolds asked us if we had noticed the mark on her forehead, which denoted her faith. She was a Brahmin of very high caste.

After this a North American Indian showed himself in front of one of the plaques and particularly drew attention to one feather which was seen by all present.

Sister Katherine also materialised and brought over an illuminated cross to Mrs Cox.

Dr Reynolds said he was extremely pleased with the night's work, as it had enabled him to lay a solid foundation for the things which were to come. He then said the experimenting was over, but he would allow one or two friends of the sitters to speak.

Amongst those communicating were Dr Savage, Dr Thompson, and a Viennese doctor. On this occasion, three trumpets were up together. All had been watching with great interest the experiment from the spirit side, and said they had witnessed some marvellous things. A Dr Jensen, who gave his nationality as Norwegian also spoke, repeating in similar words the thoughts expressed by the previous doctors. He said he would be pleased to do all he could from the spirit side to contribute to the continued success of the wonderful work he had witnessed to-night.

At one period during the séance, Sambo said flowers were being brought from the spirit world and we were asked to close our eyes.

Moisture could be felt dropping into the Sanctuary and all present had the experience of inhaling a beautiful aroma.

The experiment was closed in prayer by Mrs Difford.

Signed: I.A. Northage, V. Smith, E.A. Blake, W. Cox, H. Stenson, L. Cooper, F. Cox, G. Stocks, A. Difford.

Report on the Fourth Experiment carried out in the Sanctuary: Wednesday, 29th Ooctober, 1947.

Present :

Leader, Mrs Northage; Mrs Stenson, Mrs Cooper, Mr and Mrs Cox, Mr Stocks.

Mrs Cox opened in prayer. Ellen told us a few minutes later that Dr Reynolds was visiting the Links and the Guides were sent in the following order. – Slim Buck said all was well and brought greetings from Northampton (Mr Ives). Dawn spoke next and said she had passed Slim Buck on the way and that the Doctor's tappings on the trumpet in that Link had been heard. All was well and she asked us to give her love to her mother, father and other members of the family. The Guides from London, Newcastle, and Blackpool Links then made themselves known.

John Mains came on the trumpet from Ashington with a message from his mother. She was anxious to know who Dr Reynolds had chosen as the Leader of their circle. A promise was made to ask the Doctor during the evening, and to pass the information on the next day. The Guides from South Africa, Glasgow No. 1, Glasgow No. 2, and Airdrie spoke afterwards. It was the first visit of the Guide from Airdrie, and he said he would know more about us later.

A gentleman then spoke, who said he had come from New York City. He wanted to speak to Mrs Northage, as she was wanted very much in America. On being asked where he came from, he said Lilydale Spiritual Camp and he had been sent to try and persuade Mrs Northage to go there. He came from the Fox

Sisters. Before his death he had lived in Boston and was an old Spiritualist. He went on to say that many mediums were sitting and were awaiting his return to hear what Mrs Northage's reactions were. Sambo explained how busy his medium was, but he was very persistent and said he would do everything he could to bring off this visit.

A little boy followed and said his instrument was sitting in the London Link. This was one of the Guides of Mr Clair. Helen Nixon greeted us and said her mother and father were sitting. Her mother was not too well, but both were sending out thoughts to us.

The Guide from South Wales was followed by Dr Savage, who brought love and greetings from Grimsby. He said the Link had been reduced and there were now only five sitters. Next came Mrs Barratt's Guide with greetings. A gentleman who had lived in Boston, Massachusetts, then told us it was quite true that Mrs Northage was being watched very closely and was wanted in America. He had been the Editor of *Light*, had passed on in 1870 and was an old Spiritualist. He said he would speak again some time.

Ronny Butler (known as Ron) said he was not a Guide but had been sent from the Link at Fleetwood. He had passed on whilst serving with the Royal Air Force in the last war. His mother was sitting for Dr Reynolds and had sent him to greet us. Sister Katherine materialised and brought over the illuminated cross to Mrs Cox. Ellen said this would be the symbol Mrs Cox would always see before being taken in trance by her. A Bedouin followed and thumped his chest heartily several times. His profile (a very fine one) could be seen distinctly by all. The Chinese guide of Mr Cox came next but he was so excited and waved the plaque about so vigorously that no one could see his face, but all heard his voice.

Dr Reynolds then said: "All the Links have joined up and everything is going very well." He was asked about the Leader for the Ashington Link and said: "I have been looking round this circle and have decided to ask Mr Dick to carry on for the remainder of the experiments. It has been possible for me on visiting the Links to-night, to tap on some of the trumpets and lift others. You probably think you have only been taking messages here, but much more than you realise has been done. The foundation laying for the moving of some of the trumpets has been accomplished. Taps have been heard on some, but it was not possible to give a message. A few words have been spoken to members of the London Link. Mr Hall has been told he must take the chair and occupy it always on these occasions. I have gained very easy access to-night to all Links; they are all eager, and are giving out their love and thoughts. Once we get the trumpets going, we will be able to hold them until they are strong enough for the Guides to speak."

He then spoke on Mrs Northage going away: "In the future I have a great work to do and, although it may seem selfish on my part, going away does break up things just as I want everything closely guarded here. Although strange sitters were friends, it means breaking or holding up the experiments. It is necessary that the experiments should be held in one place only, the place that is to hold all the power from week to week. The Sanctuary makes it possible for me to lift the curtains between the two worlds, and much easier to bring souls from the higher spheres. I must have a talk with 'Doctor' Isa, and hope that she will not arrange to do anything until the experiments are over. There is a great deal to do, not only in experiments, but also in healing. There are many cripples outside waiting to enter and we cannot keep our doors locked much longer or the spirit forces will break them open. Sacrifices on your part will be great, but your names shall live for ever. They will not appear in print, but will be passed on from mouth to mouth. During the past two months, much has been made of 'Doctor' Isa, and her name is in print in England. She will be much in demand now they know, and you are not to be surprised if in two or three weeks you receive papers. You must just smile and carry on in your own way.

"I will now allow a young lady, who cannot speak English, and who comes from the Temples, to show herself. I want you to watch closely, taking particular note that her feet do not touch the floor and observe what a wonderful profile she has. You will see the body of one who has been watched over and preserved in earth life. She is a Priestess who has been shut away from her own people and only looked upon by her Priests. She is desirous of bringing to the Sanctuary some of the wonderful treasures which were buried with her in her tomb in Egypt. She wants to start as soon as possible to gather all these together and you must arrange for a special night. There are things that have been buried many thousands of years, and archaeologists do not know of their existence. There will be some very valuable treasures.

"One evening I will arrange for a trumpet to be hung in the Sanctuary. I will then go into the temple in the desert and you shall hear the sounds and gongs used there and, although these are earth sounds, they will be brought by spirit. One evening, at the right time, you shall hear the Bedouins praying to Allah. I will also bring to you the sounds amongst which the Buchanans sit for these experiments. You shall hear the birds and the beating of the tom toms in the distance from the compound of the Black People; thus you shall know that one of our Links, although not in England, is drawn very close in friendship across the sea with all other Links sending out loving thoughts to the Sanctuary.

"When Mr Beavis hears anything on the trumpet he gets very excited and hopes there will be a message. The harmony in the Links is very pleasing and enables me to slip in and out so easily. I picked the trumpet up from the floor at Airdrie, rocked the one at Glasgow and have spoken in London from five to eight minutes. This is why I have been so long in returning. In Rhodesia, of course, it is their bedtime, about ten o'clock, and they have to sit to the beating of tom toms.

"I have been able to draw so much power from the Sanctuary to-night to each Link that it seems we only have to press a button as it were, and the music begins. Very shortly, I hope to be able to speak on all the trumpets. There are two friends with the Buchanans who have motored 100 miles to sit, and do this every week.

"I have promised Sambo that Mrs Northage shall one day go to South Africa and during this visit he will be able to speak to some of his own Chiefs. There are still one or two who would understand him. The young ones would not know his language, but Sambo will guide Mrs Northage to one old Chief who, when he hears him speaking, will think it is one of his old Chiefs returned. He will also be able to bring others who have passed into the spirit world to speak.

"I have not drawn from the higher spheres to-night, but have joined together the Links in one band. It is as though we have one huge Link and all are in harmony.

"The reason why I allowed Mrs Sutcliffe's guide to come along was because she also is sitting for me, although she has no instructions. Probably 'Doctor' Isa will receive word asking what they can do further. Then will be the time to send along instructions. I know they are very eager and will be of great help."

Nancie Crowcroft then came on the trumpet and said: "I wanted to speak to Mrs Northage and had hoped that she would be normal."

Mrs Stenson closed in prayer.

Signed: I.A. Northage, H. Stenson, W. Cox, F. Cox, L. Cooper, G. Stocks.

Report on the Fifth Experiment carried out in the Sanctuary: Wednesday, 5th November, 1947.

Present

Leader: Mrs Northage; Mrs Stenson, Mrs Cooper, Mrs Difford, Mr and Mrs Cox, Mrs Terry, Mr Stocks.

Mr Stocks opened in prayer and shortly after two trumpets went up. Sambo greeted us all through Mrs Northage, then Ellen spoke. We asked who was on the second trumpet and were told it was Dr Reynolds; he was testing the power. "Smoke from the many bonfires is interfering a little, but the power is quite good," he said. "I am now going round the Links."

A very tall lady then showed herself; she had a cape of unusual shape over her shoulders, but the arms were uncovered.

A small figure in a turban appeared. A similar figure followed; this time the head-gear extended down the sides of the face, but stood away a little as though reinforced. The profile was shown and a name given, but the voice was so gentle that we didn't quite get what was spoken. When asked if she was an Indian, she bowed all round the circle.

Ellen then explained on one trumpet, whilst the child listened on another, that she was an Indian and her name was Chandra-

Lila. She was of the Brahmin faith. In earth life she was married at an early age, but was unfortunate in that her husband died. It was believed this young wife was possessed by an evil spirit because of this. She was tortured, made a child Priestess, and had to spend the rest of her life travelling across India with many other child widows.

At one stage of her journey she was exposed to the cold of the Himalayas; at another she witnessed how the superstitions of the people were played on by the priests. There was an island nearby on which stood the figure of a huge idol, and from time to time the eye of this god would light up. When this happened, the people became very disturbed and afraid and offered their money, food and anything they had, believing that this would appease the anger of this god. This child discovered that the eye was lighted by the hands of the priests, who went over at night in a boat to do it. It was whilst this was taking place that she escaped, and finally fell exhausted near a hut, in which there was a white woman, who was writing a book on India. This lady gave her food and helped her in every way, but she was in such a poor state that survival was of short duration. Before her death, however, this lady told her of the Christian faith, and she passed to the higher life feeling very happy. It is still her desire, because of this great kindness, to help English people. Ellen said she would visit us again, and next time will bring along the lady who did so much for her.

Dawn then spoke in the direct voice. "I am fully materialised and standing out of the cabinet," she said: "I am watching over the Northampton Link, so I must go back," but Sambo was quite a few minutes in persuading her to do so.

Sister Ruth materialised, came over to Mrs Terry and said: "Give my blessings to Zoe," made the sign of the cross, and slowly dematerialised.

Ivy and Jill then came into the circle for a few minutes and talked about a photograph on which she and Jill appeared. Mr Cox was asked to request Mrs Northage to write to Auntie Millie for this photograph.

A North American Indian then showed himself. Dr Reynolds gave his name as Red Leaf, said he was highly evolved, and was not attached to anyone yet. Brother Benedictine spoke to Mr Stocks and said it was many hours since he last did so. "I have treasures I want to bring from Tibet," he said.

Mrs Terry's mother followed and said: "I have brought father." (Dr Midgeley) He spoke for several minutes on the trumpet, but this was not recorded because of the personal nature of the message.

A very tall lady then walked into the circle. She would be quite 6 feet in height, wore a long white robe covering the feet, and stood showing profile as though in a pose.

Dr Reynolds followed: "Another evening I intend to show you the beards of some old and young men and, if you like, I will allow you to pull one. I think I would like to do this to show you the difference between personalities as they come back. To-night there have been many foreign influences and the last one was a Greek. You have often seen a model of a Greek. This lady stood as she used to do when being modelled. The others were Indians. Now I have had to do this to-night, because of the thickness of the air and also the bangs. The experiment I had arranged for to-day I have had to switch over, and next week you will see the beards.

"The first Indian was a boy, and his name was Kashmar. These entities as they come back attach themselves at some time to someone. This is their first experience, but they will come back. You will notice the difference of the robes worn. I wish you could have seen the colours. We have the wrong kind of light, but before long we shall be able to see the pastel shades of the robes. I am very satisfied; all the Links are very eager, are sending out sympathy, and all seem happy. This is a splendid uniting of Links; keep it up and then we shall win through to success.

"We have been a little slow to-night, but this was on account of the air. I hope you managed to see clearly the friends we have brought. Perhaps you would like to know that the Indian girl has been over many hundreds of years, and the Greek lady passed on over 1,000 years ago. If we can get them to hold in the red light, we might manage one evening to show them in a white light, then you will notice every detail of the robes. The Greek lady had a splendid figure.

"Ivy told you she had managed to rock the trumpet and I knocked on it. I think it will be very marvellous when we have their reports. Some of them have seen me, and some have heard the sounds on the trumpets." Dr Reynolds then addressed Mrs Terry and said: "Your father is progressing and has forgotten many of the earth things, but he likes to come along when you need him. Your cataract will soon all be gone."

The experiment was closed in prayer by Mrs Difford.

Signed: I. A. Northage, A. Difford, H. Stenson, W. Cox, F. Cox, L. Cooper, G. Stocks.

Report of the Meeting held in the Sanctuary: Wednesday, 12th November, 1947.

Present:

Leader: Mrs Northage; Mrs Stenson, Mrs Cooper, Mrs Difford, Mr and Mrs Cox, Mr Stocks.

Mrs Cox opened in prayer. On entering the Sanctuary, Mrs Northage remarked on the strong smell of death, but at this period we had no idea of what was to follow.

Dr Reynolds came through and said the experiment would have to be cancelled this evening, because the Armistice conditions had brought many earth-bound souls around and it was his wish that they should be released.

John and Cyril helped in this work and took turns with the trumpet, speaking to these souls and encouraging them to speak to us. Everyone in the circle did their best to help by telling them they were amongst friends, and that they would feel very much better if they would try to speak.

Three boys were out of the cabinet at one time, and Sambo got quite excited, telling them to come out steadily and be gentle. They returned, of course, bringing back the condition with which they passed on, and as these boys had been lost in a submarine, they brought into the Sanctuary quite a lot of sea water. Mrs Cox, Mrs Difford and Mrs Stenson received several small waves of water and, after the séance, the carpet and curtains of the cabinet were saturated. Water had even been thrown as far as the curtain near the door. When these boys first came through, they remained on the floor tapping out messages to each other. They were finally encouraged to pick up the trumpets and speak to us, and all said they felt better for it.

Sgt. Fallenwell, who was with the Gunners, spoke and said he went down with the Gloucesters outside Crete in 1941. Wilfred Walsh from Lancashire also spoke, telling us he died in the Far East. Harold Lee told us he had his leg shot away, received injuries to the head and body and was finally taken prisoner with many other boys. He had nothing on his body by which he could be identified. He passed on through loss of blood and had been in spirit for five years. Morris Head from Gateshead spoke, but he returned quietly, because he knew of the after life. He had already spoken to his mother and father, but not in the direct voice, as to-night. He said he would return to the Sanctuary and give their address, so that we could pass a message to them on his behalf.

A doctor spoke during the evening and said he, together with his nurses, had been caught when the Germans over-ran France. He, his nurses and patients had been shot by them. Mrs Difford commented that she thought doctors and nurses were spared and how inhuman this was, but the doctor replied that the men who did so were not to blame; they were merely carrying out their orders. One of the nurses materialised.

Sambo allowed us to see the materialised form of one of the sailors. The ectoplasm was very dark, his face was ashen grey, and a growth of beard could be seen all round the chin. Sambo also allowed us to see the materialised form of a girl who had been burned to death in one of the raids on London. The ectoplasm for the greater part was black, but white spots could be seen here and there. Her face was hardly recognisable. She spoke on the trumpet and said she had been a plotter. Several boys who had served in the R.A.F. spoke to us, but as Sambo requested us not to use the light, their names were not recorded. They said they would return again sometime and it is hoped then to be able to report more fully.

Mrs Difford closed in prayer.

Signed: I. A. Northage, L. Cooper, H. Stenson, F. Cox, W. Cox, A. Difford, G. Stocks.

Report of the Sixth Experiment carried out in the Sanctuary: Wednesday 19th November, 1947.

Present:

Leader: Mrs Northage; Mrs Stenson, Mrs Cooper, Mrs Difford, Mr and Mrs Cox, Mr Stocks.

Mrs Cox opened in prayer. Sambo was the first to greet us, then Ellen spoke and Dr Reynolds followed. He gave a very interesting talk on what he hoped to do, the part we should play, and how he was looking forward to the new Surgery.

People would come from far and near; some would arrive on crutches, but would return home leaving them behind. It was his wish that all should be welcomed, no matter of what religion or nationality, and he wanted us to greet them with a smile; to make them feel perfectly at home and try to help them to feel something of the peace of the spirit which prevailed in the Sanctuary. There would also be a band of helpers from the other side, and many wonderful things would be done.

Referring to our meeting of last week, the Doctor said it was necessary to draw quite a lot of power from each sitter, and he hoped we did not feel this too much. Whatever had been taken would, of course, be repaid tenfold, and he said we would be happy to know that it had been possible to help many souls.

Because so much had been drawn last week, he proposed to-night to have only voices to give all a chance to rebuild. It had been a big strain on Mrs Northage, but he was watching closely and all would be made up.

Before visiting some of the Links, Doctor said he would tune us in to one so that we could hear what was going on. The Northampton Link was heard and someone was saying: "Move your chair then – did you hear that – Percy has gone over to-night. Can you hear him snoring?" A gentleman in the Ashington Link was heard praying, at the end of which he said: "Please see to each one of us here, help our homes, help our bairns, bless this circle to-night, Amen."

Several guides followed and spoke to their instruments. The sister of General de Cazale spoke and said she was very pleased to return. She was interested in our work and would come another time with her brother, who was, at the moment, very busy with other things. We should be having a visit sometime from some of the survivors who had been helped and, on this occasion, she would return and speak to them in her own language.

Mrs Difford closed in prayer.

Signed: I. A. Northage, L. Cooper, H. Stenson, F. Cox, W. Cox, A. Difford, G. Stocks.

Report of the Séance held in the Sanctuary, Wednesday: 26th November, 1947.

Present:

Leader: Mrs Northage; Mrs Stenson, Mrs Cooper, Mrs Difford, Mr and Mrs Cox, Mr Stocks.

Mr Stocks opened in prayer. A few minutes later one of the trumpets moved slowly, stayed for a few seconds in the air, then descended steadily to the floor. There seemed to be rather an unusual atmosphere and Mrs Northage commented on how strange it was and wondered what it could mean.

Dr Reynolds spoke and said he regretted he had to bring sorrow into the Sanctuary to-night. He had three relations of Mrs Northage, who had only just passed on, in fact they were not yet buried. He had been called to help them and the power this evening would be given to them instead of experimenting. Although this would hold up his work to some extent, he said these things were to be expected and when the call for help of this kind came, it could not be refused.

Whilst Dr Reynolds was doing this work, the guides spoke to us, and the sitting was closed by Mrs Stenson in a prayer for the friends the Doctor had brought along.

Signed: F. Cox, H. Stenson, L Cooper, W. Cox, G. Stocks, A. Difford, I. A. Northage.

Report of the Seventh Experiment carried out in the Sanctuary: Wednesday, 3rd December, 1947.

Present:

Leader: Mrs Northage; Mrs Stenson, Mrs Cooper, Mrs Difford, Mr and Mrs Cox, Mr Stocks.

Mrs Stenson opened in prayer. It was several minutes before Ellen spoke. She explained that the Links were drawing together a little more slowly to-night than usual, hence the delay.

Dr Reynolds spoke and said as there was an operation to follow, he would not allow any materialisations but would use the power for the strengthening of the Links. He would help the Guides to draw closer, so that this would prove most useful later on.

During the time Doctor was away he said he would allow some of the friends who were guiding us to speak. The Guide of each sitter spoke in turn, and on this occasion Mrs Northage was able to enjoy the evening as much as all present, since the Guides did not take her in trance. Mrs Difford closed in prayer.

Signed: I. A. Northage, H. Stenson, L. Cooper, A. Difford, W. Cox, G. Stocks, F. Cox.

Report of the Eighth Experiment carried out in the Sanctuary: Wednesday, 10th December, 1947.

Present:

Leader: Mrs Northage; Mrs Stenson, Mrs Cooper, Mrs Difford, Mr Cox, Mr Stocks.

Mr Stocks opened in prayer. Ellen told us the Links were rather slower to-night in getting started.

Dr Reynolds said he would spend the evening visiting the Links, and whilst he was away some of the friends who were present would be allowed to speak.

There were no materialisations, and Mrs Northage was able to enjoy this experiment along with us.

The Doctor reported that he was quite satisfied with all the Links.

Mrs Difford closed in prayer.

Signed: W. Cox, A. Difford, H. Stenson, G. Stocks, I. A. Northage.

Report of the Ninth Experiment carried out in the Sanctuary: Wednesday, 17th Decenber, 1947

Present:

Leader: Mrs Northage; Mrs Stenson, Mrs Cooper, Mrs Difford, Mr and Mrs Cox, Mr Stocks.

Mrs Cox opened in prayer. Two or three minutes later one of the trumpets went up. Sambo greeted everyone, then Ellen said the Links were a little slower to-night joining up – Dr Reynolds followed. He spoke to Mr Cox about the sailor he had brought along two weeks previously for an operation, and told him what had been happening at the hospital and the reactions of the person concerned.

Last week in the Airdrie Link some of the sitters had seen blue smoke and had hoped the trumpet would rise, the Doctor said before very long he hopes to make this possible.

The first materialisation was Mrs Cox's grandmother. She went round the circle and then had a short chat to Mr and Mrs Cox. Dawn, who had slipped away from the Northampton Link, materialised and patted each one on the face.

Dr Reynolds told us that he works in the laboratories of the spirit world, but not for the same purpose as he did when on the earth plane. He was able, through the knowledge he had gained, to help some of the souls who had committed suicide and relieve them of their torments. He went on to say that to-night we would observe it took much longer for the forms to materialise, because he was drawing from a higher sphere, and in the case of Guides from these spheres, although they received our calls, they were not able to be at our side so quickly as those on the lower spheres, because they had to descend through the lower ones to reach us.

An Arab with a short beard showed himself, and later Sambo told us he was a Bedouin who had come to the Sanctuary to beat the gong, but we had again forgotten to bring it down. His name was Ahmed Allah Pasha.

The next form to materialise was quite tall and wore a round white headdress. Mr Stocks said he thought his face was partly covered, but this was not so. He patted his face with the plaque to prove this and, after he had dematerialised, we were told that Ellen had asked him to do this, in order to leave no doubt. He had been a Persian Prince when in earth life 800 years ago, and as he came from a high sphere and knew no English, he could not speak to us. A small boy next showed himself, and he too wore this round type of turban. We noticed he held one hand over the plaque in a very stiff attitude and did not move it during his visit. He had been in one of the temples and was to become a priest in the days to come. The sacrifice he had made for his gods was to stand with his hand in one position until it had withered.

A lady next came into the circle with a long flowing robe, which covered her feet. She lifted this robe to show us she had on a pair of sandals. Her eyes could be seen, but the rest of her face was completely veiled. She came from the harem and was never allowed to be looked upon by any but her husband. She was not allowed out of the building, which was surrounded by high walls.

A North American Indian followed. He had black hair and a white band round the forehead. Sambo told us his hair was long and went down his back, and that the band denoted the tribe to which he belonged when on earth. He had a fine physique and thumped his chest to show how powerful he was. The robes of these souls seemed to be of fine illuminated silk.

Sister Katherine came over to Mrs Cox and Lone Star gave the full name of Mrs Difford's husband. This was even unknown to the rest of the sitters. Red Wing spoke to Mrs Cooper and White Blossom to Mrs Stenson. The Indian Doorkeeper of Mrs Cox gave his name as Running Water. Mr Cox's mother spoke next, and finally Mrs Northage's brother asked us to pass on greetings to her for Christmas.

Ellen then told us the experiment was over and said she did not think we realised how much had been done from the spirit side this evening.

Mrs Stenson closed in prayer.

Signed: F. Cox, W. Cox, A. Difford, H. Stenson, G. Stocks, I. A. Northage.

Report of the Tenth Experiment carried out in the Sanctuary: Wednesday, 7th January, 1948.

Present:

Leader: Mrs Northage; Mrs Stenson, Mrs Cooper, Mrs Difford, Mr and Mrs Cox, Mr Stocks, Mr Smallbone.

Mrs Cox opened in prayer. Sambo greeted all sitters, and told us the power was very good. Ellen said Dr Reynolds was waiting and would be with us shortly. Several minutes later the Doctor came. He said the Links were joining up and he would leave us to visit them, sending the guides on to the Sanctuary as he did so. The guides from the Links followed in quick succession, greeted us, and indicated from where they had come. Dawn materialised and had a few words with us, then returned to the Northampton Link.

Dr Reynolds came back and said: "The power is very good tonight. I shall be able to draw from the higher spheres. Arnold Clair is in the London Link and I have had a few words with them. No doubt you will be hearing of this."

The luminous cross was seen floating and a Sister of Mercy materialised. She placed the cross in the top of her robe. She was quite tall, her robe was of the finest texture, and she came round the circle for all to see. The Doctor said, after she had dematerialised, that she had been in a convent on the Swiss-Italian border and had passed into spirit from a wasting disease, now known as T.B. She had always worn a large cross on the front of her dress and this was the reason she had placed it there when coming into the circle. She had been in the world of spirit for 500 years. A small girl came next. She wore the round type of turban and her dress fell in small folds from the shoulders. She salaamed to everyone and remained in the Sanctuary for several minutes. She came over to touch the board on which notes were taken.

Dr Reynolds then spoke and said he would show us a block of ectoplasrn, so that we could see how the spirit clothed itself to materialise. The block moved slightly from the floor, a hand protruded; the ectoplasm slowly expanded both upwards and downwards; a face could be seen building in the upper portion – in a few seconds a fully materialised form stood before us. A foot was placed on one of the plaques and the toes moved about, to show what command of the 'earth body' they had for a short space of time.

The Doctor said we would notice how slowly and gently those souls from the higher spheres materialised, as compared with those on lower ones. There was no rush in coming or going, and each one brought a marked atmosphere of peace and calm. The power and harmony from all the Links, the Doctor remarked, was very good and he was very pleased with what he had been able to accomplish. Doctor said how rapidly the cyclones round the world were moving, and that seven years from now would see many changes. One or two loved ones were then allowed through, and Ellen in saying that time had gone remarked that little did we realise how much had been done from the other side.

Mr Stocks closed in prayer.

Signed: I. A. Northage, F. Cox, W. Cox, A. Difford, L. Cooper, H. Stenson, Bernard K. Smallbone, G. Stocks.

Report on the Eleventh Experiment carried out in the Sanctuary: Wednesday, 14th January, 1948.

Present:

Leader: Mrs Northage; Mrs Stenson, Mrs Cooper, Mrs Difford, Mr and Mrs Cox, Mr Stocks, Mr Smallbone.

Mrs Stenson opened in prayer and before the prayer was over and Mrs Northage in trance, Ellen materialised and spoke to her. This was followed by a hand being shown against one of the plaques, which, we were told, was a mummified one from a tomb. A very strong smell of perfume came into the Sanctuary and no sooner had this been noticed than Mrs Northage had a quantity sprinkled on her; the same thing happened to each sitter. This was being brought from vases in a tomb.

Dr Reynolds spoke and said he would materialise in one of the links, and endeavour to lift the trumpets in others. The smell of perfume would go with him to each of the Links and no doubt some reports would be forthcoming concerning this. On returning, Doctor said they had definitely noticed this in the Glasgow Link.

Ellen said she would try materialising in the red and blue lights. This she did; the form was clearly seen by everyone – robe, feet and arms, but the face could not be clearly defined. A white light was used once, and the whole form was easily discernible, but could only be held for a few seconds.

Whilst Doctor was away, an African Doctor and his friend came into the circle and told us he had been able to help his people a good deal. He promised to bring, in three weeks' time, an African piano, and would return on occasions to play it. Two trumpets were up together whilst this Doctor and his friend remained.

Ellen said she would materialise in the etheric body and allow Mr Cox to put his hand through it. In the light of a red torch his hand could be seen pushing its way through this body. After the experiment Mr Cox said it seemed as though he was pushing his hand through a thin curtain. Dr Reynolds remarked that he had dematerialised his hand as it entered the etheric body. He went on to say that Mr Cox would understand much better after this, the procedure adopted by himself for performing operations, namely – how he dematerialised his hands to get inside the human body. One or two of the Guides came through with greetings, and the experiment was closed in prayer by Mrs Difford.

Signed: I. A. Northage, H. Stenson, L. Cooper, F. Cox, W. Cox, G. Stocks, B. K. Smallbone, A. Difford.

Report on the Twelfth Experiment carried out in the Sanctuary: Wednesday, 21st January, 1948.

Present:

Leader: Mrs Northage; Mrs Stenson, Mrs Cooper, Mrs Difford, Mr and Mrs Cox, Mr Stocks, Mr Smallbone.

Mr Stocks opened in prayer.

When the Doctor came through, he said many of the Links were short of sitters, owing to illness and, in some cases, it would be necessary to cut the vibrations.

Ellen materialised and the red and blue lights were tried out.

After this Doctor said he would allow some of our loved ones to speak, and the experiment was closed later in prayer by Mrs Cox.

Signed: A. Difford, W. Cox, F. Cox, L. Cooper, H. Stenson, G. Stocks, B. K. Smallbone, I. A. Northage.

Report on the Thirteenth Experiment carried out in the Sanctuary: Wednesday, 28th January, 1948.

Present:

Leader: Mrs Northage; Mrs Stenson, Mrs Cooper, Mrs Difford, Mrs and Mrs Cox, Mr Stocks, Mr Smallbone.

Mrs Difford opened in prayer. It was several minutes before Sambo greeted everyone, after which one of the trumpets went up and Ellen came through. They both told us the power was good. Ellen said she was picking up the vibrations from the Links and Dr Reynolds would be with us in a few moments.

When Doctor arrived, he said the Links were joining up very well to-night, and it seemed as though they were making up for last week.

The first materialisation was a lady in a long robe. Her head was covered, but on close examination, a piece of material hung from each side of the face, approximately from the level of the ears, and this swept down over the right arm the left one was – bare. She stood in the circle for several minutes. A little girl was the next visitor, and later Sambo told us she had been the victim of one of the blitzes.

A tall dark figure then built up; a very small face was shown, the left half of which was covered by a cowl. He remained with us for several minutes, but did not speak. The Doctor said he was a Monk and would be bringing some of the apports.

Ellen showed herself again in the red and blue lights. She was able to hold much longer in the red one and everyone saw her quite distinctly. She materialised again and stood in such a manner that it was possible to see Mrs Northage's shoes – one on either side of the right foot.

The Doctor had a little talk and said the apports were almost ready and that within the next two weeks we should probably be receiving them. They would be brought in a red light, so that we could see them coming. Some, he said, would be very valuable and were not to be seen by everyone who visits Mrs Northage. Whatever was brought Doctor wanted us to realise that it was sacred to the spirit bringing it and he wished us to value it just as much as the more precious things. Some of the treasures to be brought by the Monk had never been looked on by the eyes of the world; it was his wish for them to be treated with reverence and kept away from covetous eyes. It would be as well for the Sanctuary to be securely locked, because of any attempt at burglary. If anything like this did happen the articles stolen would be returned by the spirit people to the Sanctuary, but it would be wise to take reasonable precautions.

The electric globe with the cross enclosed sparkled with light from time to time, and Sambo told us we would notice this now constantly when the power was high and prior to materialisations.

He asked that the bulb in the centre of the Sanctuary should be replaced by one with a smaller voltage, because this also would be lighted up by the spirit people when the power was at its height.

At one time, two trumpets were up. A North American Indian spoke and said he would bring some apports, but we did not learn who our second visitor was. Also, another spirit said he had lived on an island and there were many treasures buried in the sea, some of which we understood he would be bringing.

Mai Fen Chang came into the circle during the evening.

Mr Smallbone closed in prayer.

Signed: A. Difford, W. Cox, F. Cox, L. Cooper, H. Stenson, G. Stocks, B. K. Smallbone, I. A. Northage.

Report of the Séance held in the Sanctuary: Wednesday, 4th February, 1948.

Present:

Leader: Mrs Northage; Mrs Stenson, Mrs Cooper, Mrs Difford, Mr and Mrs Cox, Mr Stocks, Mr Smallbone.

Mr Cox opened in prayer. Several minutes later Ellen came through on the trumpet and said Dr Reynolds had been called away to a serious case and would be with us a little later.

Robin Pringle, a baby two months old, was very ill in The Cottage Hospital, Bromley, Kent, suffering from pneumonia, and meningitis had set in. Dr Reynolds had gone to answer the prayers of the father, who had been sending out his thoughts to him. The doctors at the hospital had done everything possible for this child and said they could do no more. The father then asked for Dr Reynolds and said he had faith that something could be done from the spirit side.

Ellen said Dr Reynolds wanted to take two blood transfusions and would like Mrs Stenson and Mrs Difford to give them, if agreeable. Both said they would be only too glad to do this to assist, and Ellen requested that their left arms should be bare to the elbow when the Doctor arrived. Dr Reynolds said that the child was in a very poor way, and he hoped these blood transfusions would materially assist in saving its life. Doctor then materialised, went over to Mrs Stenson and then to Mrs Difford to take the blood. Both were requested to keep their handkerchiefs over the places selected by the Doctor until after the séance. Doctor said he would take the power from all the Links to-night for the purpose of helping this child.

One or two loved ones were allowed to speak and materialise whilst the Doctor was at the Hospital. One spirit, who, in earth life, had lived on the Indian-Burmese border materialised. He was wearing a headdress with two pieces of material hanging at the side, and his black moustache could be clearly seen by all sitters. He had been killed in the last war.

Towards the end of the séance, Ellen asked everyone to concentrate on the Doctor until word was received to relax. A few minutes after the silence a continuous noise, like the snapping of fingers was heard, which seemed to move from the side of the Sanctuary to the centre. Ellen came through and said we could relax, and the heart of the child was beating again.

Dr Reynolds spoke later telling us the child's breathing was just perceptible and asked that we should remember it in our prayers. He said if it could survive the difficult hours from 12 midnight until 2am there was every chance of saving it.

Mr Stocks closed in prayer.

Signed: I. A. Northage, F. Cox, W. Cox, A. Difford, L. Cooper, H. Stenson, B. K. Smallbone, G. Stocks.

Report of the Séance held in the Sanctuary: Wednesday, 11th February, 1948.

Present:

Leader: Mrs Northage; Mrs Stenson, Mrs Cooper, Mrs Difford, Mr and Mrs Cox, Mr Stocks, Mr Smallbone.

Mrs Difford opened in prayer. Ellen came through and said the power from the Links was not quite so good to-night, and she was not sure what Doctor intended doing.

When Dr Reynolds came, he said there were gaps in the Links – four empty chairs in Ashington No. 1, and no sitters at Grimsby or Exeter.

It had been intended to bring some of the apports which were ready but, owing to this break, it would be impossible.

For the rest of the evening, Guides and other spirit people were allowed to communicate. Mrs Northage was not taken in trance and was able to enjoy the séance with us.

Signed: I. A. Northage, L. Cooper, W. Cox, F. Cox, B. K. Smallbone, G. Stocks, A. Difford, Mrs Cox.

Report of the Séance held in the Sanctuary: Wednesday, 18th February, 1948.

Present:

Leader: Mrs Northage; Mrs Stenson, Mrs Cooper, Mr and Mrs Cox, Mrs Difford, Mrs Hodgkinson, Mrs Stocks, Mr Smallbone, Mr Stocks.

Mrs Cox opened in prayer, and it was longer than usual before the trumpet went up. When Ellen came through she told us Dr Reynolds had been called, and he would tell us what had happened when he came.

A little later Dr Reynolds told us Mrs Nancy Sinclair had been taken to the nursing home, and it looked as if things were nor going too well. Thoughts had been sent out to the Doctor earlier in the day and he had just returned from the bedside. He went on to say that the umbilical cord was entwined around the baby's neck several times, and he did not know at the moment whether it would be possible to save it. However, Doctor said: "I will go back and fight for the life of the mother." Whilst he was away, he asked us to send our thoughts out to him from time to time. Meanwhile, Guides and loved ones would speak with us.

When Dr Reynolds returned, he told us the mother would be all right, and asked us again to send our thoughts to him on retiring for the night.

An Airman spoke on the trumpet and gave his name as Eric Lees; he asked if we would write his mother whose address was c/o Hallam and Company, Castle Street, Hinckley, Leics. He had come down in the sea with his plane and consequently had never been traced by the Air Ministry. Mrs Difford promised to do this for him. Mrs Stenson closed in prayer.

Signed: I. A. Northage, H. Stenson, A. Difford, L. Cooper, F. Cox, W. Cox, D. W. Hodgkinson, B. K. Smallbone, E. M. Stocks, G. Stocks.

Report of the Séance held in the Sanctuary: Wednesday, 25th February, 1948.

Present:

Leader: Mrs Northage; Mrs Stenson, Mrs Cooper, Mrs Difford, Mrs Stocks, Mr Stocks, Mr Smallbone.

Mr Stocks opened in prayer. After the singing of the first hymn, Ellen spoke and said she did not know just what Dr Reynolds intended doing to-night, because there were breaks again in the Links.

When Dr Reynolds came, he said there were many gaps in the Links and he considered it advisable to cut the vibrations. He thought this a good opportunity for our Guides to draw closer and said it would be up to us to get what we could from our own power. We were told to concentrate on whoever we wanted to come to prove that thoughts were living things. Sambo spoke to all of us on the trumpet, and a Guide spoke to each sitter in turn.

The Airman, who appeared in the Circle the previous week and asked us to write his mother confirming his death, spoke again. Mrs Difford posted a letter, but this was returned marked 'unknown'. He said he was sorry about it but on getting through he was so excited he gave the name of his friend Eric Lees and not the full address. He then asked for the letter to be sent again, and this time the address was given as follows – Mrs Manion, c/o Cameron, c/o Hallam and Company, Limited, 33 Castle Street, Hinckley, Leics. Mrs Difford promised to write again for him.

Mr Smallbone closed in prayer.

Signed: I. A. Northage, H. Stenson, A. Difford, L Cooper, B. K. Smallbone, E M. Stocks, G. Stocks.

Report of the Séance held in the Sanctuary: Wednesday, 3rd March, 1948.

Present:

Leader: Mrs Northage; Mrs Stenson, Mrs Cooper, Mrs Difford, Mrs Stocks, Mr Stocks.

Mr Stocks opened in prayer. Ellen came on the trumpet immediately after the opening prayer and said she was not sure what Dr Reynolds had in mind to-night, but as he was waiting we would soon know his intentions.

Doctor said there were still gaps in the Links through illness and he would take this opportunity of having a talk with us. There would be much work to do in the future and some wonderful things would happen. Many people would present themselves at the doors of the Sanctuary, including visitors from abroad. More helpers would be needed, but they would be brought along at the right time. At the opportune moment the world would be shown something of the wonders of spirit, and instructions would be given. Time and place would be decided by the Doctor and, whenever invitations were issued, the decision of acceptance or refusal was to be made by him. Although we might not always understand the decisions made, the Doctor asked that patience and tolerance be shown, because he had a longer vision in these matters.

It was decided to make an attempt at photographing materialisations the following week.

Signed: I. A. Northage, H. Stenson, A. Difford, L. Cooper, E. M. Stocks, G. Stocks.

Report of the Séance held in the Sanctuary: Wednesday, 10th March, 1948.

Present:

Leader: Mrs Northage; Mrs Stenson, Mrs Cooper, Mrs Difford, Mr and Mrs Cox, Mrs Stocks, Mr Stocks, Mr Smallbone.

Mrs Cox opened in prayer. A container was put down for Dr Reynolds to bring some lotion for a patient's nerves. A few minutes after Dr Reynolds spoke the liquid could be heard running into the container. Sister Katherine materialised and handed it to Mrs Cox.

An attempt was made to photograph two materialisations by Mr Stocks. The Doctor said he would not tell us who the visitor was, because if the plates were successful, they would show clearly.

One or two spirit people then spoke to the sitters and the séance was closed in prayer by Mr Stocks.

Signed: I. A. Northage, H. Stenson, A. Difford, L. Cooper, F. Cox, W. Cox, B. K. Smallbone, E. M. Stocks, G. Stocks.

Report on the Fourteenth Experiment carried out in the Sanctuary: Wednesday, 17th March 1948.

Present:

Leader: Mrs Northage; Mrs Stenson, Mrs Cooper, Mrs Difford, Mr and Mrs Cox, Mrs Stocks, Mr Stocks, Mr Smallbone.

Mr Cox opened in prayer. Ellen, Sambo and Dr Reynolds came through, and we were told that several Guides would come through to bring their gifts.

Mai Fen Chang materialised and brought into the circle a beautiful perfume. She spoke a few words and said she was very pleased to visit us. As she tested the power, her arm could be seen, and the draping from her spirit robe looked like very fine net.

Dr Reynolds told us to take our apports in the left hand, because this gave the heart-beat and would help the Guides.

Sister Katherine was the first to materialise. She came over to Mrs Cox and placed a cross in her hand. Brother Benedictine followed and gave the cross he had worn in earth-life to Mr Stocks. Sister Teresa then manifested and gave Mrs Stocks a cross. Mr Smallbone's sister materialised and told him that whilst it was impossible for her to bring anything, because she had passed through the veil without actually knowing earth-life, she would, nevertheless, at the opportune moment, bring him a flower from her garden in the world of spirit.

By this time much of the power had gone and Sambo said the gifts to the rest of the sitters would have to be brought the following week, as much power had been drawn from Mrs Northage during the evening and she was now in need of a rest.

Mrs Stenson closed in prayer.

Signed: I. A. Northage, H. Stenson, A. Difford, G. Stocks, B. K. Smallbone, L. Cooper.

Report on the Fifteenth Experiment carried out in the Sanctuary: Wednesday, 24th March, 1948.

Present:

Leader: Mrs Northage; Mrs Stenson, Mrs Cooper, Mrs Difford, Mr and Mrs Cox, Mrs Stocks, Mr Stocks, Mr Smallbone.

Mr Cox opened in prayer. Ellen greeted all sitters, then Sambo came through. Ellen remarked on the flowers and said how beautiful the Sanctuary was to-night. Dr Reynolds was waiting and Ellen promised to speak again later.

Dr Reynolds spoke and said the apports for the rest of the sitters were to be brought through, but he just wanted to thank us for the way we had attended throughout the experiments and for giving up our time to him. He said that the experimental work carried out in the past had enabled him to prepare the way to show to the world the wonders of spirit; he was now ready to materialise in bright lights and speak in a public hall for twenty minutes. His thanks were not only extended to the sitters in the Sanctuary, but to each sitter in the Links. It was their unselfishness and patience in giving up their time to him each week which had made this great test to the outside world possible. This would be one of the greatest tests to prove survival.

As there were apports to come, the Doctor said he would have a talk with us some other time, and would leave us to assist in getting them through. Sister Monica came on the trumpet and told Mrs Cooper she would bring her the cross and girdle she wore during earth life. It was not valuable in the monetary sense, but she had treasured it and desired Mrs Cooper to have it. She then materialised and brought them through.

The North American Indian Guide of Mr Smallbone spoke next, but we were unable to understand, because he spoke in his own language. Sambo translated and said he was very upset to find that his loin cloth when picked up had fallen to pieces; this was because he had been so long in spirit. It had been his intention to bring this, but as this was now impossible, he would bring another gift which he had managed to get. He picked up one of the plaques and passed it down for Mr Smallbone to receive. It was a small box of porcupine quills, and Ellen said each one had been placed in by hand and was perfect. The Guide was very excited in bringing this through.

Blue Wing then came to Mrs Stenson and said he would bring her a spoon. He materialised and the spoon was dropped on the floor. A few minutes later Sambo said the lights could be switched on so that the spoon could be picked up, as he did not want it to become mixed up with the ectoplasm.

When the lights were switched off again he said there was a big Chinese bowl which he wanted, if possible, to get materialised to-night and out of the way. He asked Mr Cox to switch on the red torch and concentrate the light on the centre of the ceiling. He did this and the ectoplasm could be seen going up towards the spot. This effort to materialise the bowl was not successful, and Sambo said they would have to try again. The next attempt was also unsuccessful, but this time the bowl in dematerialised form was shown round the circle on a plaque. Sambo said it would now have to be left until a later date. There were other things to bring, including rings from many countries, more Indian and Chinese articles, and the last to be brought would be the Egyptian treasures. Red Wing brought a spoon to Mrs Cooper.

Mrs Difford closed in prayer.

Signed: I. A. Northage, H. Stenson, L. Cooper, A. Difford, G. Stocks, B. K. Smallbone.

Experiments in Autumn 1948

Report of the First Experiment carried out in the Sanctuary: Wednesday, 20th October, 1948, at 7.30pm.

Present:

Leader: Mrs I. A. Northage; Mrs Stenson, Mrs Cooper, Mrs Stocks, Mr Stocks, Mr and Mrs Pashley, Miss Tyers.

The experiment was opened in prayer by Mr Stocks. Sambo, Ellen and Dr Reynolds greeted us and said how pleased they were to see us once again.

The Doctor said he would not be doing any experimenting this evening, because the greater part of the time would be taken up by visiting the Links, having a look at the sitters and bringing back any reports for transmission to them.

The Doctor thanked Mrs Stenson for all the hard work she had put in during the day in order that the Sanctuary could be ready for the evening. He then proceeded to the Links and one or two spirit friends were permitted to speak meanwhile.

On returning, the Doctor said he was quite satisfied with the Links on the whole. There were one or two little things in some of them which would be put right for next week.

He left us again for the Links and said he would send along the Guides from each. As he moved from Link to Link, the Guides came into the Circle and announced themselves.

The Doctor returned again, and said they were all doing splendidly. He asked for the lights at the back of the Sanctuary to be ready for next week, also red and white torches.

Sambo and the Doctor promised that, prior to commencing next week, our Guides would be allowed to introduce themselves, so that we would know who was with us for the remainder of the experiments.

The Doctor said he desired us to be ready to start on the stroke of 7.30pm as there was much to do and the time passed so quickly.

Mrs Stenson closed in prayer.

Signed: I. A. Northage, H. Stenson, L. Cooper, E. Tyers, G. Stocks, E. M. Stocks.

Report of the Experiment carried out in the Sanctuary: Wednesday, 26th October, 1948.

Present:

Leader: Mrs Northage; Mrs Stenson, Mrs Cooper, Miss Tyers, Mrs Stocks, Mr and Mrs Howman, Mr and Mrs Pashley.

Mrs Stocks opened in prayer. Dr Reynolds welcomed sitters and asked that in future no oils be used in the Sanctuary as these were blocking vibrations. He then left to visit the Links, and Ellen explained that by use of telepathy she would be able to give a running commentary.

Glasgow No. 2 Link – very good. Ruthergien – very good (Mrs Robertson in the chair). Airdrie – Miss Simpson – big light seen, five new sitters present. Ashington No. 1, thirteen in the Link; all old friends present. Ashington No. 2 – Doctor picked the trumpet up; eleven present. Mrs Galvin – five sitters, trumpet half-way up. Doctor spoke. Grimsby – trumpet rocked, but Doctor unable to do more. Northampton – Slim Buck and Dawn very busy. Mr and Mrs Barratt sitting in their Sanctuary. Pontypridd – Chinaman in charge. St. John's Wood – trumpet up; splendid power. Doctor said he would speak at the next sitting. Exeter – several new faces. Trumpet tapped. Eleanor and Blackfoot Indian there. N. Rhodesia – seven sitters. California – good Link.

Several guides were then permitted to speak.

The Doctor then allowed a spirit to build, so that the perfection of the eyes could be seen, and to show – contrary to general belief – that friends return with their eyes closed. The Doctor went on after this materialisation to say that there is no deformity or blindness in the world of spirit – all returned with a perfect body.

Dawn materialised very clearly in a red light and allowed us to feel her spirit robe.

A monk from Tibet (interpreted by Ellen) said he would bring to the Sanctuary a gift from his Monastery. An Indian with turban, draped on one side, and with perfectly moulded features, came into the circle. He had been in the spirit world for 3,000 years.

Sambo warned us to close our eyes as children were coming to bring perfume from their flowers. The essence is squeezed out of them and this was sprinkled around the circle.

George Cox returned and explained that, owing to a doctor's mistake, his life on the earth plane had ended. An injection of gas had been given whilst he was asleep and on waking he had found himself on the other side of life. Mrs Stenson closed in prayer.

Signed: I. A. Northage, H. Stenson, E. M. Stocks, D. M. Howman, L. Cooper, E. Tyers, A. Difford, J. M. Pashley, T. H. Pashley.

Report of the Second Experiment carried out in the Sanctuary: Wednesday, 3rd November, 1948.

Present:

Leader: Mrs I. A. Northage; Mrs Stenson, Mrs Cooper, Mrs Stocks, Mr Stocks, Mr and Mrs Pashley, Miss Tyers, Mr and Mrs Harman.

Mr Stocks opened in prayer. Sambo greeted all sitters through Mrs Northage; Ellen spoke on the trumpet, followed by Dr Reynolds.

The Doctor, said Mrs Northage's body, was very tired tonight and as those of all sitters were not quite up to par he would have to depend on us concentrating our thoughts on him, so that he could draw from them. He then left us to have a look at the Links, during which time one or two spirit friends spoke.

Ellen announced the Doctor's return and said that he was now busy conditioning the Sanctuary ready for the experiment. This would take a little longer in view of the fact that he could not draw too much from the body of the Medium.

The Doctor told us all the Links were doing very well and said he only wished we could see the vibrations from them being drawn into the Sanctuary. One night he hoped that conditions might be favourable for him to give us just a fleeting glimpse of how they look from the spirit side.

Tonight he would be drawing from the higher spheres and the materialisations would not speak. We were asked to observe closely.

There was a strong smell of perfume and the first materialisation was a lady, in spirit robes, with left arm uncovered. She stood in the circle for several minutes moving round for everyone to see her. The top part of her robe seemed to be very much brighter than the rest and stood out very clearly. Doctor said this soul had been in the world of spirit for many hundreds of years and was highly evolved. Doctor went on to say that when souls have been in spirit for so long they cannot remember anything connected with earth-life and this lady was now known in the spirit world as 'The Presence'. This, he said, contrasted very differently with those of our loved ones who had been passed over for five, ten, twenty or thirty years, and returned to give their names and talk about incidents connected with things they had done and to help with problems confronting those to whom they were communicating.

Dr Reynolds continued by saying that speech in the spirit world is unnecessary; thoughts are just sent out and received. He gave an example – when he wishes Ellen to descend for a séance, he sends out thoughts to her and these are answered by thoughts. There is never any doubt about the result, because Ellen is always present. We could, he said, do the same sort of thing on the earth-plane if only we gave the time and thought to it.

A small boy then came into the Circle; he bowed to everyone, but did not speak.

A materialisation then followed of what appeared to be a spirit person, but the whole of the face was covered by a veil. The Doctor said this also was a very highly evolved soul from the fifth sphere. In this particular sphere souls are getting nearer to God and the faces of those dwelling thereon become shrouded in a kind of mist; they are unable to use their voices when they reach this stage of development. Sometimes it takes thousands of years to progress from one sphere to the next. It depended entirely on the person, as to whether he or she really wished to make headway.

It was noticed that the garments of the more highly evolved were of very much finer texture than those from a lower sphere, and they took much longer to show themselves.

We then heard someone thumping himself heartily on the chest. When the plaque was raised we discovered it was a Gurkha. He leaned over the plaque to show the draping from his headdress and remained in the circle for several minutes.

Doreen Wilford, of Melton Mowbray, then spoke on the trumpet and said she had recently passed over. Her husband had been in the Air Force in the last world war.

Mrs Harman closed in prayer.

Signed: I. A. Northage, H. Stenson, L. Cooper, E. Tyers, E. M. Stocks, G. Stocks, D. M. Howman, G. W. Howman.

Report on the Séance held in the Sanctuary: Wednesday, 1st December, 1948

Present:

Leader: Mrs Northage; Mrs Stenson, Mrs Cooper, Mrs Difford, Mrs Phillips, Mrs Pashley, Miss Tyers, Mr —, Mr Stocks.

In the middle of the first hymn the trumpet rose to the centre of the Sanctuary, then went over to Mrs Northage, who was not yet in trance. Ellen greeted her, then spoke to the rest of us. She said the Doctor was waiting and she would have a word with us later.

Sambo spoke next, then the Doctor followed. He told us there were many gaps in the Links owing to the bad weather and to illness. He then left the circle to have a look round the Links.

Sambo said there was a soul trying to manifest and asked us to sing a hymn to help. A few minutes later the brother of Mr — materialised. He gave his Christian name and flashed on the white torch to show the garb in which he had come. He passed over at sea and returned now in sou-wester and oil-skin cape. He patted the oil-skin several times with the torch to show the strength of the materialisation. After speaking several words to his brother he returned.

Dr Reynolds came into the circle again and said it would be impossible to carry out any experimenting, as the attendance in the Links was not very good, as previously stated. However, those who were sitting were keeping the vibrations going and that was as much as could be expected under the circumstances. He remarked again that they were ever ready on the spirit side, but many times, owing to material conditions, work from the other side had to be held up.

For the rest of the evening guides and loved ones present were allowed to communicate, and the sitting was finally closed in prayer by Mr Stocks.

Report of the Experiment carried out in the Sanctuary: Wednesday, 8th December, 1948.

Present:

Leader: Mrs Northage; Mrs Stenson, Mrs Cooper, Mrs Stocks, Mrs Howman, Miss Tyers, Mr and Mrs Pashley, Mr Stocks, Mrs Difford.

Mrs Difford opened in prayer. Ellen spoke through the trumpet and later Sambo through Mrs Northage. The Doctor left us to look round the Links where, he said, there were still one or two gaps.

The first materialisation was a finely shaped hand and the arm was covered with a loose sleeve, the texture of which was so fine it almost looked like gossamer.

Ellen materialised in the red light, but as we could not see her very well the blue one was tried. She remained to the count of ten. The full form was clearly seen by all present. Ellen was followed by a Sister of Mercy, who stood fully materialised to the count of five – also in the blue light.

The red torch was then switched on and a foot was seen. This was several inches from the ground and we were told that a soul from the higher spheres was present. The foot was seen first to show that the form was not touching the floor of the Sanctuary. This soul stood for several minutes showing her robe. It was a very beautiful one covering the head and coming over the left shoulder in numerous folds. This lady had a lovely face and brought a great quiet and calm into the Sanctuary.

During the sitting scent was sprinkled over us; this was from flowers brought by children from the world of spirit.*

---

*For some reason this report was not finished in the same way as previous reports. (A.H.)

Chapter Six

Dr Reynolds Operates

Dr Reynolds is the spirit doctor who conducts the healings and operations through 'Dr' Isa Northage, and was on the earth plane over 160 years ago. He is an Irishman, (although the Irish brogue is not too pronounced), forthright and definite in his requirements and instructions, and a model of punctuality at all times at the sittings and consultations.

He has been attached to and watched over 'Dr' Isa since she was three years old, although his direct voice was not heard until 1918.

It was during the First World War that Dr Isa, whilst serving with the R.A.F. was in serious danger, when the voice of Dr Reynolds spoke to her and directed her out of danger to safety. Since then he has been heard by many people, and his voice has also been recorded on frequent occasions. He always seems to give comfort and courage to those who have heard and spoken to him, and his wise counsel and guidance are of immense help.

Dr Isa and the ministers of the Pinewoods Healing Church hold regular meetings with him, and discussions on many and various topics take place. The health problems of others are also always brought to him for his, advice and guidance on the treatment to be used.

To those who have talked with him it is just like having a chat with the family doctor.

A Message From Doctor Reynolds.

"My desire when I returned to the earth plane was to heal the sick and to carry on the work I did when there. However, as you know, my work has progressed more and more, so that now not only do I return to heal the sick, but to develop our work which has increased so much that we now continue with our experimenting between the two worlds. I have gained access into the highest spheres that I may bring within this Sanctuary those who will give of their powers to help the people of the earth to understand and to gain knowledge of that which lies beyond the veil.

"Now I know that you are to describe to the public much of the work that I and my beloved helper here have tried to do, and that you may wish to ask me questions to help you with this book of the future. Believe me, it is going to be the great book, and you will find that you are all only the pioneers of the work to come two or three hundred years hence. Through this chronicle many young friends of the future will be helped to develop those great gifts that God has given unto the earth children.

"I would say to those who read this account you are writing that I hope the work I have returned to do upon the earth will be greatly blessed by God in the knowledge they gain from the book.

"God bless you and God speed the writing on its journeys, wherever it may go."

October 20th, 1956.

'Pinewoods', Sunday evening service, December 4th, 1955.

Operation for removal of malignant growth from intestines by Isa A. Northage under trance control of Dr Reynolds. Patient treated, (Mrs) E. Dowsey, 3 Lime Street, Kirkby-in-Ashfield, Nottinghamshire.

"The evening service began as usual at 6.30pm and, following the address, Isa A. Northage, under the complete control of Dr Reynolds, gave a sign to the officiating ministers to draw about her, requesting that a Mrs Dowsey a member of the congregation, be brought and seated upon a stool in front of the altar and above the Star. The lady being quite unaware of what was to happen came as requested.

A receptacle containing swabs, antiseptic, surgical spirit, forceps and towels was brought forward ready for the Doctor's use. The curtains were drawn between congregation and chancel, but the lights down the centre of the church were left on. The lamp (oil and wick) was lit, giving sufficient light for everything to be seen.

Mrs Northage, still under the complete control of Dr Reynolds, then knelt at the patient's side and placed her right hand on the outside of the lady's dress and over where the trouble lay.

Doctor then asked for the antiseptic, which was poured upon his hand, and taking a swab, his hand dematerialised and entered the patient's body.

A glass container, half full of surgical spirit had been prepared and as Doctor called for this it was passed to him; he then withdrew his hand from the body and placed a growth in the container.

The tumour removed

Doctor then requested that the service be drawn to a close and permission was given to any who so desired to see the growth in the receptacle.

After a drink of water the lady returned to her former seat.

(The proceedings were witnessed by the congregation, together with several officials whose signatures were recorded.)

Statement from Mrs A. Dowsey, the patient treated,
>3, Lime Street,
>Kirkby-in-Ashfield,
>Nottinghamshire.

During the first week of December 1955 I was full of pain and during that week I kept praying to Dr Reynolds, the spirit doctor, to help me, and on December 4th, 1955, I did not feel like going to Pinewoods Church but there was something inside me urging me to go. During the service I heard the voice of Dr Reynolds calling me to come forward, and I was very pleased as I was feeling very ill. Dr Reynolds told me that it was a small growth that was making me ill. He asked me if I wanted him or the hospital to remove it, and I said, "I want you, Dr Reynolds." During the operation there was Dr Reynolds and six of the church ministers. When the operation was over I felt easier and happier, and now I would like to thank Dr Reynolds, Mrs Northage, the leader of Pinewoods Church, and all of the ministers who were present at the time.

(Signed) (Mrs) E. Dowsey.

Account of Experiences
by Group Captain G.S.M. Insall, V.C., MC.

My first experience of psychic phenomena occurred in about 1916-1917 when a prisoner of war in a German fortress. I took part in a short-lived séance of table-turning.

As a contrast to my first séance mentioned above, I will tell you what I saw, heard and felt on a red-letter day of my life in Isa Northage's little séance room, adjoining her Spiritual Healing Church.

I was asked to attend and help with a couple of bloodless operations. I met the two patients in her sitting room. They were business men who had just driven from a Midland city about fifty miles away. They were both suffering from hernias, and one had complications. I had joined the other helpers, leaving the patients chatting with Isa.

We prepared the room, donned white overalls and masks, as was the rule with Dr Reynolds. This was not new to me as I had been a student in the most up-to-date French hospital before the First World War changed my career to flying. I had attended many an operation in those days, and some I would never put pen to paper to describe. But this bloodless one is a very different story. I will now proceed.

The two patients came in. The first, the one with complications, was partially stripped and placed on the operating table. The other was given a chair nearby.

There was a trolley, and I checked over the instruments tweezers, swabs, kidney basins and bowls; no cutting instruments at all except scissors to cut lint. There was also a small white pencil light. I checked the emergency door and saw that it was locked and bolted on the inside, and draught excluded by a mat placed on the threshold. I was just closing the inner door leading into the church when somebody noticed that the medium had not arrived. I opened it again, and she came in. The light was turned low and somebody opened in prayer. I could see the medium sitting in her usual chair, a curtain hanging on either side.

Immediately the prayer was over a trumpet rose and Dr Reynolds' familiar voice greeted us all. He then reassured the patients and gave them instructions, saying he wished to leave the medium in trance the shortest possible time, so there would be a break after the first operation while the second was being prepared. I was assigned a kidney basin to collect swabs in and stepped forward to the operating table. The trumpet went down, and almost immediately the Doctor appeared in materialised form on the opposite side of the operating table. He is of small stature. The medium was in deep trance.

He first took the tweezers and swab with a disinfecting cleanser and swabbed the area. The hernia was umbilical. I collected the swab in the kidney basin.

Then I saw him place his hands on the patient's flesh, and they just went in deep, nearly out of sight. He stretched out for the tweezers and swabs and I collected eight soiled ones altogether.

He then questioned the patient: "Do you feel anything ?" The answer was in the negative. He told him he would be all right in a few days, but he must take it easy for about a week. The second patient, whose hernia was straightforward, was the driver of the car and they would both drive back that evening.

Dr Reynolds then said: "I want to rest the medium; get the next patient ready. I am off, but will be back as soon as you are ready."

His last action was to pick up the pencil lamp and turn a bright patch of light on to the flesh where he had operated. All that could be seen was a slight flushing of the skin, no break, no scar. He then left us, and full lights were gradually turned on. The medium came out of trance and we prepared the second patient.

The procedure was then repeated, and I think I only collected one swab, as there was no infection. I noted that those of the first operation were mostly stained, but in neither case was any blood forthcoming. The infected swabs were of course incinerated.

As soon as Dr Reynolds had said goodbye and departed, I opened up the door to the Church and we joined Isa in cup of tea. The two patients felt no ill effects, and they drove back in the manner in which they came.

I could give many more instances of other phenomena, but I will limit them to two which concerned me in particular.

An airman cousin of Isa's was killed in a bomber crash in World War II. His spirit used to like to come and play an old gramophone she kept for him. One day she said it was broken, so I repaired it for him to play at the next séance.

Also to amuse him I took with me a solid brass model of a Polish aeroplane, weighing about two pounds, given to me by a Polish contingent under my command during the war. I had marked it heavily with luminous paint and placed it in front of me on the floor When John 'came through' he was delighted and flew the model most realistically round the séance room, looping, spinning and rolling, and then ended up with a perfect landing at my feet.

At another séance I was asked to sit near a recent widower who had not attended a materialisation séance before, and he hoped his wife might come through. She came, and after a short conversation, during which I noticed that another materialised spirit was giving flowers to relatives sitting on the opposite side of the circle, I heard her say: "Just wait a minute, I will be back again in a minute." She disappeared and returning a few minutes later handed two freshly-picked pansies to her husband.

When the lights went up at the end of the séance, he showed them to me as he put them in his pocket-book to press them. I told him I knew where they had come from. I looked and found two broken stems in the clump where his two pansies had been picked from. On that occasion also I had locked and bolted the doors before the séance, and was sitting with my back to the door leading to the Church.

Of course it is very simple really. If anything can be materialised it can just as easily be dematerialized – given the knowledge and the power, but we do not yet know how it is done.

Signed: G. S. M. Insall, G/Capt. (Retd.) R.A.F.

Testimony of Mr John Hands

I, John Hands, am writing this account of the operation on my wife by Dr Reynolds. I and Mr Steve Fisher were asked to help, as Mrs Northage had been ill and the Doctor did not wish her to be too long in trance. We had to wear white coats and theatre masks, and I stood at the operating table with a nurse and Mr Fisher.

Within a few minutes of Mrs Northage going into trance (she was sitting in a cabinet at the end of the Sanctuary), Dr Reynolds appeared on the opposite side of the table. After greeting us all and talking for a few moments he asked my wife if she wished to remain normal or go to sleep, but in either case she would feel nothing. My wife replied that she would like to remain normal, and see what happened. The Doctor then proceeded to swab the parts to be operated on with disinfectant. He then set more swabs about the places and passed his hand across the affected areas. The patient's breasts were opened, and the abdomen treated likewise. Dr Reynolds then took a bright green pencil torch from the trolley and shone the light into the cavities, showing three cancers lying deeply inside.

Doctor then explained that the cancer in the intestines had burst, and with swabs he removed the pieces, carefully placing each in a receptacle. He cleaned the site with swabs, each of which as it came from the wound was covered in blood and pus. There was a strange sound as each cancer was drawn from the breasts, and after this all wounds were carefully cleaned. The doctor not only removed the cancers but also the hair-like roots which, he said, would prevent the growths from re-forming. They were over most of her chest and abdomen, and while working in the region of her left armpit a hemorrhage started which caused the Doctor some concern, and he said he would have to fetch something from the spirit world to stop it. He disappeared through the floor, but in a few moments reappeared with a liquid with which he soaked a swab and pressed it under my wife's armpit, asking her to close her arm tightly against it.

On being satisfied that the wounds were clean, he gradually closed them up sideways, until only what appeared to be scratches were left. Then he placed his hand sideways of each wound and drew it across from end to end, and as his hand passed over the edges of the wounds they were sealed completely, not even a scratch remaining. Finding the haemorrhage had stopped, he sealed up that wound likewise.

During the time that I was passing swabs to the Doctor he worked so fast that he occasionally grabbed my fingers instead of the swab. When the operation was over he said he would go, while a Dr West came to examine his work and, stepping back about two feet from the table he sank through the floor, and within two minutes Dr West appeared in his place, the latter being of different height and build to Dr Reynolds. He said very little as he went over the patient's body with a torch, taking particular notice of the place where the bleeding had occurred. Then he told my wife she had very little to worry about providing she carried out Dr

Reynolds' instructions, which he would later give to her. He then remarked that the Doctor had made a very good job of a very difficult case, and wishing us all 'good-night' he left. When Dr Reynolds reappeared he gave instructions that all the swabs must be carefully collected and the surgery thoroughly scrubbed down with disinfectant, as the cancers were of a particularly contagious type. Also, when he had examined them in the electric light they must be burned, and not taken away, as when they were kept in a spirit solution the patient never really got well. He then told my wife that the freezing he had done would last until next day, but then she would be in a fair amount of pain; he would, however, be there to help her. This took place as he said, my wife being very ill for a few days, but within a week she was up and has progressed very well since.

The operation took one hour and twenty minutes. When it was over we went outside, and Mr Fisher remarked that though he had witnessed everything that took place he just could not believe his eyes. – That is just how I feel about it.

The Patient referred to in the Statement by Mr John Hands describes her experience.

The 'Inner Chamber' at Pinewoods is sacred to me as a happy meeting place between friends of this world and that of spirit.

I am Mrs Edith Hands, of Rubery, Birmingham, and since 1948 I have witnessed wonderful and, to me, evidential phenomena. At my first sitting my mother materialised and spoke of intimate family matters, and my niece, Hilda, who had been unable to walk some time before her death, also materialised and danced before us, a slim, graceful figure in a filmy party dress, her bare shoulders gleaming in the light from the luminous plaques.

I have met and spoken to, for the first time in my married life, my mother-in-law, who stayed quite a while talking of her family and friends, and at another sitting, a young nun materialised and gave me a crucifix which had been buried with her body. She told me that she had been with me in hospital and had tried to help me through a very difficult time, and she hoped the crucifix would give me the strength that it had given her during her lifetime. Her name, she said, was Cynthia, and she is now a very dear friend of mine.

In 1949 I entered hospital for a major operation, and only the skill and attention of Dr Reynolds saved my life. After three months rest I was to return for another operation, but Dr Reynolds decided to do the operation himself, thereby giving me the most wonderful experience of my life.

Mrs Northage, or 'Doctor' Isa as Dr Reynolds always calls her, had just got over a very serious illness herself, so the operation must take less than the two hours normally taken. He requested that my husband and our friend Mr Steve Fisher should assist the nurses present. They had to wear surgeons' white coats, and all had masks over their mouths. I had a loose gown placed on me and then lay on an operating couch. We quietly sang while Mrs Northage went into trance, the hymn *Nearer My God to Thee*. After a short prayer the red light was switched on and Dr Reynolds stood before me; after greeting us he explained to the nurses what he was about to do. He would, he said, remove three cancers, but owing to the state of Mrs Northage's health he must work fast. He gave instructions to my husband and Mr Fisher, and asked me if I wished to sleep or otherwise, but I said I did not want to miss anything.

He then bathed the parts to be operated upon with cotton wool swabs and proceeded to operate, removing each cancer. While working by my armpit a sudden haemorrhage started; it was not too bad, but the Doctor did not like it (I learned later that the Doctor does not like to spill blood). He said he would fetch something from the spirit world that would stop it. Almost at once he disappeared and returned with a liquid which he poured onto a piece of cotton wool and placed on the part. He then pressed my arm against my side with the swab between it and my body, telling me to keep it there; this at once stopped the bleeding. As he passed his hand over the site of the operations it was as if each place had been opened with a surgeon's instrument, revealing my inside, and he called those present to see the cancers he was about to remove. I felt no pain or discomfort during the operation or any reaction afterwards. The amazing part also was there was no sign of a wound or mark.

Imagine the wonder of it as I lay gazing into the Doctor's eyes as he operated. He talked to me quite naturally as he worked; his was no ghostly figure, but a normal human being, dressed in a surgeon's coat and white hood. I had to think deeply to realise he was not of this world, but was indeed an angel. The operation took about one hour and twenty minutes. As he talked to me he assured me that all would be well. Now I can thank God for this illness. It was the means of bringing me face to face with the true meaning of the manifestations of spirit.

I am thankful to God that He led me to receive this healing from the willing hands of Isa A. Northage and Doctor Reynolds without which I would never have been writing these words.

Operation: Dented Skull and Blood Clot

The procedure adopted for this operation was somewhat different. The patient, a young girl aged nineteen years, had been brought from Birmingham. She had suffered for years, had frequent epileptic fits, and was quite unable to keep a regular job as typist.

It had been difficult to get a diagnosis regarding the cause of the trouble and the remedy, until they were able to visit the Sanctuary. She was taken there accompanied by her parents to consult Dr Reynolds, spirit doctor of Mrs Northage. We had a small red light, sufficient to see each person, and then opened, as usual with prayer, to await the Doctor's appearance. Five of us were present; Mrs Northage, myself, Mr and Mrs F., and daughter. The girl sat on an ordinary chair in the centre of the room. I stood at her side and Mrs Northage in an armchair, prepared for trance. Soon the Doctor materialised and talked first with the parents, then the girl, who, although she had never seen the Doctor was soon on the friendliest terms with him. We had prepared some cotton wool swabs, disinfectant and a kidney dish, as we were previously informed this was all that was necessary. The Doctor stood at the back of the girl and requested me to stand close by. Taking my hands he placed them at each side of her head. Cleansing his own hands with disinfectant he took a swab, and calling my attention to the left side of the girl's head showed where the dent was, saying it had been caused by a fall from a swing many years ago, when the girl was three years of age; (this was the first time the parents were aware of the cause).

Now the Doctor placed the hand holding the swab on the side of the girl's head. The hand entered the head, and he said: "I have now removed the dent; we will wait a while to allow the natural fluid to fill the cavity." At the same time the Doctor withdrew his hand and passed me the swab he had used, on which was a small clot of blood.

Speaking to the girl from behind her chair, the Doctor asked her what she would like. She said she would like to see him; at once he stood in front of her, joking about his beard. They laughed together and were perfectly at ease. The Doctor said he wanted to bring someone very near indeed to her, then, turning to us, bade goodnight and was gone.

To our astonishment the two persons who returned from spirit were the mother and father of the girl we had treated, and we learned that the ones who had brought her were foster parents. Although the parents had been in spirit since almost the birth of the child, they had followed every step of her life and were as interested in everything she did as they would have been had they remained on earth.

Their gratitude to the foster parents was wonderful to hear. The girl was able to resume her employment on the following Monday and has had no further trouble since her operation five years ago.

It may be interesting to note that for this operation Doctor Reynolds had fully materialised, but to get at the trouble inside the skull had dematerialised his hand only.

Since this first meeting the young lady has seen and talked often with her parents and become a great friend of the Doctor and our Sanctuary.

Operation for Strangulated Hernia

One evening we were called together in answer to an urgent request from Birmingham to help in the above case. The man was in a serious condition and was brought by car, some 60 miles to the Sanctuary. The journey was a great strain on his condition, but on arrival he seemed to have stood it fairly well.

We entered the Sanctuary at once and he was prepared for the operation, and as the prayer closed, Doctor Reynolds materialised .... and proceeded at once to expose the site of the trouble, namely, the lower left side of the abdomen He then took a pencil torch (green) and, shining it into the body, showed me what had happened, explaining, as he untwisted the hernia with his fingers, the seriousness of delay in such a case.

As the operation was of short duration and conditions were favourable, we were permitted to meet several materialised souls who had been in spirit for some time. We met and spoke to the following – Sir Arthur Conan Doyle, who gave a short talk on our work, Silver Birch, guide to Hannen Swaffer's Circle, who gave a blessing, Nurse Bruce, friend of Nurse Cavell (shot by Germans, First World War), and who is now helping struggling souls in spirit, and does not, incidentally, wish to return to earth conditions.

This will perhaps help people to understand that the work they loved whilst on earth can still be carried on in the next life without interruption, should they so desire, but of their own free will only.

Operation for Removal of Malignant Growth (Carcinoma).

For all operations of a surgical nature the Spirit Doctor always fully materialises and indeed often remains so for an hour.

One evening we were assembled for the above operation, everything having been prepared; trolley, torches, swabs, disinfectant and towels, etc.; and each assistant fitted with the usual surgical mask and instructed in the part assigned for the operation. Above the trolley is an electric light and switch, for the Doctor's use only; it is a 25watt red light. The patient strips, reclines upon the operation table, and is covered with a sheet.

After sitting in silence for a few moments, the opening prayer is offered, followed by the Lord's Prayer, and during this Mrs Northage goes into deep trance. Almost at once, Dr Reynolds materialises, dressed as a surgeon about to operate, but without rubber gloves.

A clear view of him can be seen as he switches on the trolley light and examines the contents, and declares his satisfaction or otherwise. Before commencing he approaches the patient for a brief chat and enquires whether or not she (in this case) would care to see the operation performed. In almost all cases the answer is in the affirmative, if not, the patient is at once asleep; whichever way it is, there is no pain or discomfort. The sheet covering is removed to expose the site of the operation, and as the Doctor passes his hand over the place the flesh will dematerialise (the equivalent of a surgeon making an incision) and the whole of that part of the internal organs will be exposed, and can be seen in the light of the torch which the Doctor shines into the cavity.

The Doctor will then place swabs around the opening, and one can see these becoming stained as the operation proceeds. Sometimes at this stage the Doctor will call a colleague from spirit and he too will materialise, and together they will discuss the case. On this occasion there were in the Sanctuary nine persons: Mrs. Northage (in trance), three assistants, the patient and two relatives, also the two doctors in materialised form in surgeons' attire.

The Doctor then proceeded to operate, and as each growth was removed it was placed in the waiting receptacle.

At this particular operation four growths were removed. When he had taken two from the breast, he turned to say he would bring one who was interested in this type of disease. At once a lady dressed in a nursing uniform materialised, announcing herself as Madame Curie, and taking another green pencil torch examined the patient. With a pair of forceps she slowly lifted a growth from the abdomen, and holding it above the patient remarked: "Horrible, horrible." Again adopting the same method, she removed the next growth. Madame Curie then spoke briefly to the Doctor, bade us goodnight, and was gone.

Turning back to the patient, Doctor Reynolds examined the results of the work done. Apparently satisfied, he enquired if she would care to meet some of her loved ones who had passed into spirit; the offer was gratefully accepted, and four members of her family spoke to her.

Before this, immediately after the Doctor's examination, he passed his hand over the body of the patient and removed all swabs. The wound instantly healed, and except for a slight redness, where the operation had been performed, the body was quite normal; no scar, not a mark where the growths had been. In answer to the Doctor's questions the patient replied she had experienced no pain or discomfort; it had indeed been a wonderful experience.

Thanking all who had helped, the Doctor bade us all goodnight and dematerialised. We now took the relatives into the house and they were shown the growths in the receptacle in the light of a 100watt white light, before the contents were burned. An earlier request to take away some parts of the cancers was refused, the Doctor stating they were far too contagious.

Dressing and joining the company for a cup of tea, the visitors prepared for their homeward journey of about eighty miles by car.

About four years after this operation we were informed that the lady had returned to her previous employment within a few days of her visit to our Sanctuary and was still keeping well.

Removal of Malignant Growth from Pancreas

Pinewoods Healing Church,
Sunday, December 18th, 1955, 6.30 p.m.

During Sunday evening service, following the address, Dr Reynolds took control of Mrs Northage and gave the sign for the Ministers to draw about him; then he requested a Mrs Johnson, of Sheffield, who was in the congregation, to be brought to him. The lady consented and was placed upon a chair in front of the altar and over the Star. A supply of antiseptic, swabs, lint, etc., was made ready for the Doctor's use. Dr Reynolds then knelt at the patient's side, and speaking a few words to her requested that antiseptic be poured over his hand. Taking a swab of cotton wool, his hand dematerialised as it entered the lady's body. In a few seconds the Doctor withdrew his hand holding the growth, which he put into a vessel containing surgical spirit, stating that any member of the congregation who so wished could come and inspect what he had removed. At the same time he took about half a pint of fluid from the site of the tumour. The patient, after a drink of water, returned to her former seat.

The photograph below was taken by an analytical chemist some hours after the operation. The surgery took place during the service in the full lighting of the Church.

A.M.

Malignant growth from the pancreas

Chapter Seven

Apports

We had been told by our spirit friends that they would like to bring a gift to each sitter as a token of friendship. So one night we sat for this purpose, and, as is usual on these occasions for this type of phenomena, Mrs Northage was taken into deep trance. There are various ways by which an apport can be received, and ours came in the following manner: –

Dr Reynolds asked me to cup my hands and, with the trumpet sailing upwards to the ceiling, we at once heard the sound of an object spinning round inside the trumpet; slowly descending towards me, the narrow end touched my hands and a ring dropped out. It was gold with a diamond in the centre. The next apport was a number of North American beads and these were loose, and sounded as if they were being thrown against the Sanctuary wall, as indeed they were; it was as though a handful of gravel had been thrown about.

The materialised hands of *my* spirit doctor appeared in front of me and seemed to be holding something between them. My doctor then said: "Mac, I have brought you a little gift. It is of no commercial value, but I would like you to keep it as a link and keepsake," and slowly withdrawing one hand, there was exposed an engraved silver case. I reached forward and took it from him, and as our hands met, I could feel the warm touch of his, just as one does human hands in the flesh. I have always since carried this case about with me. It had been placed in the grave at the Doctor's funeral eighty years ago. When he gave it to me, it was bright and shining. After this I was greeted by a feminine voice and saw my wife's helper, a French nun, standing in front of me. She said a blessing in Latin; then placed in my hands an ivory cross, requesting me to give it to my wife with her love.

Left: The silver case and the ring.

The apports we received this evening had been brought from various places; the silver case from Sydney, N.S.W., rings from S. Africa, the beads from N. America and Mexico, other apports from China and Tibet, and the ivory cross from France. As to the silver case which had been given me, the Doctor told me some more about it. He said it had been given to him by a fellow student, who, after finishing his studies, had entered a monastery, serving the community in his medical capacity.

Some months later, we were at a séance, this time in total darkness, during which my wife took from her pocket, the cross she had previously received, and held it in her hand: she said it always gave her comfort. Almost at once, Sister Marie, who gave the cross, appeared before her, and blessing her, said: "I came at once, as you were holding my symbol." (the cross).

Right: The ivory cross

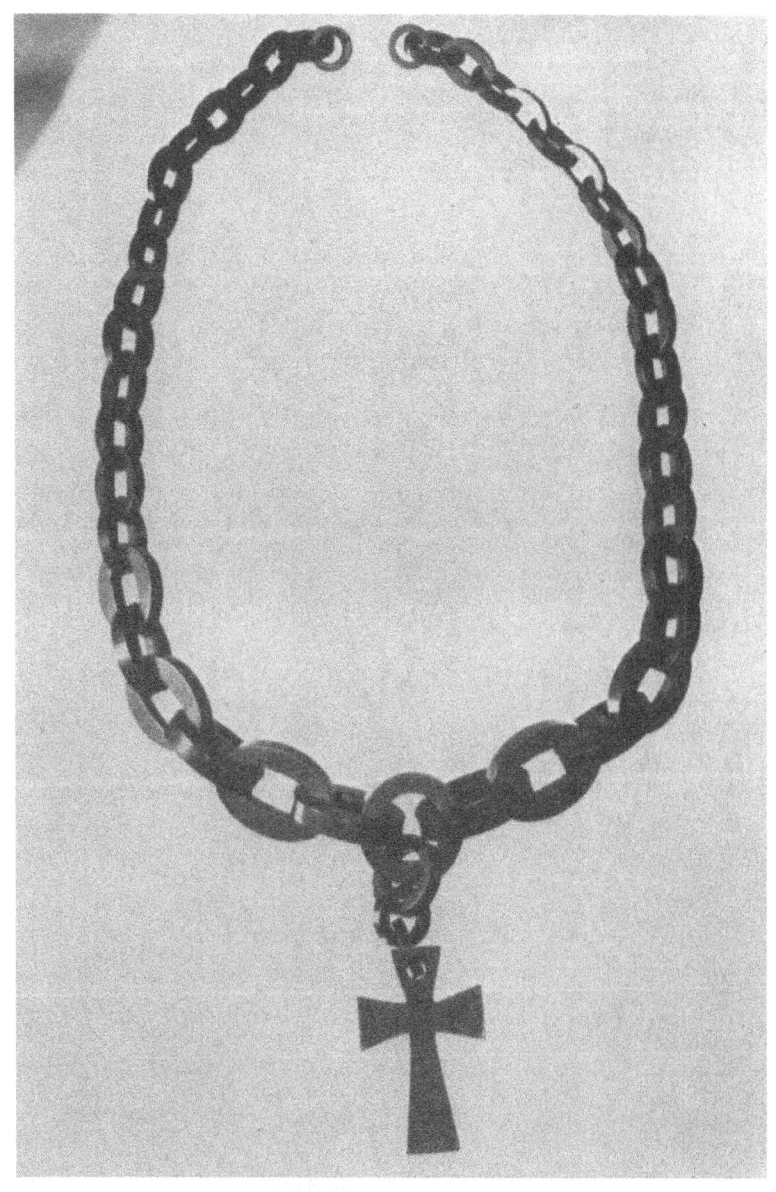

Apport received by Mrs M.E. Galvin of Wigan. It was presented to her by a materialised figure of a nun (see page 99) given through the mediumship of Isa A. Northage

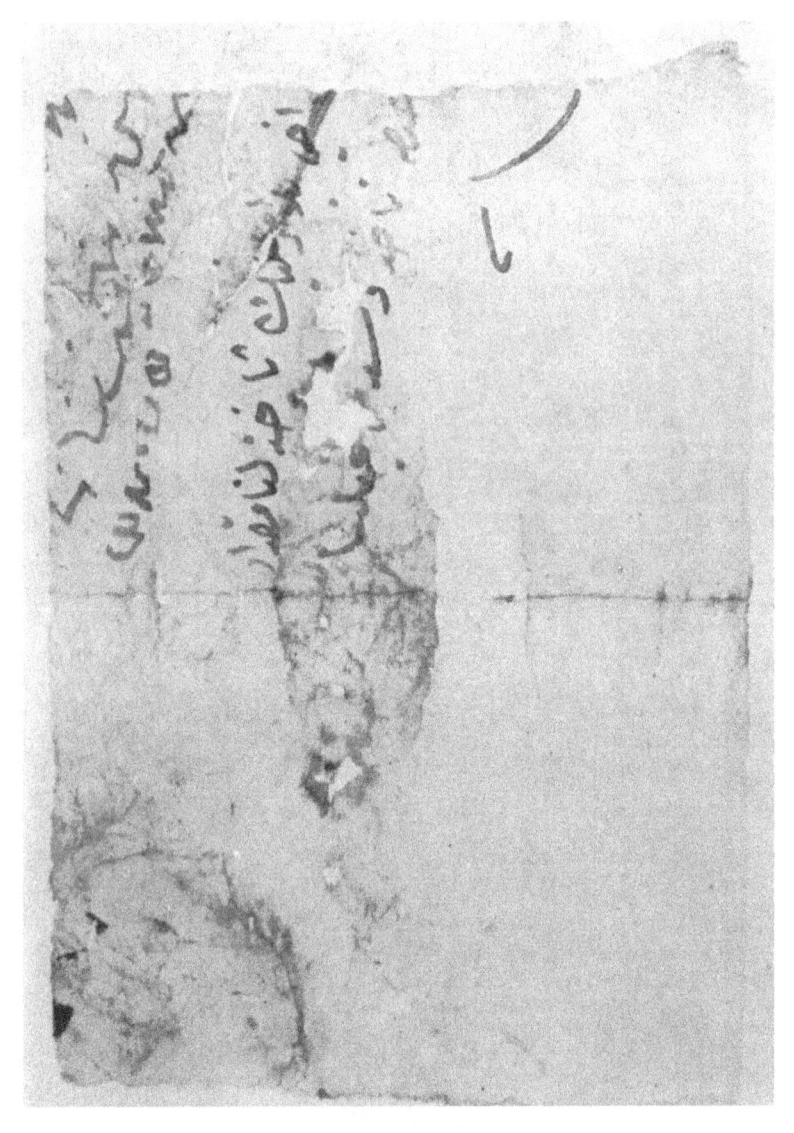

*This scrap of paper was found in the base of the Scribe's inkpot which was apported at the séance. (see p.208)
The inscription is Arabic.*

Apports (1936) brought by Mai-Feng-Shang from the Valley of Seven Altars. Weight 32lbs each.

In 1936, during a séance in which Isa A. Northage and a few friends were sitting, 'Sambo' decided to bring some apports. To do so, he had to have the help of another guide, Mai-Feng-Shang, the daughter of a Mandarin of the Valley of the Seven Altars, who had passed to the world of spirit 500-600 years ago. During the evening, permission was given from the spirit world to apport from China, two bronze vases, weighing 32 pounds each, and which had been entombombed 500-600 years ago. The same evening were also apported seven Chinese rings and one Egyptian ring, one Chinese incense burner, one vase inlaid with bands of mosaic work, and one ebony cross and chain beloging to a monk who passed into spirit, 1066. The rings were given to the sitters, the rest of the apports were kept in the home of Isa A. Northage.

1937.– Isa A. Northage, Audrey and Nina (daughters) and son (Bob) and friends sat for experimental purposes for receiving apports. Sambo (Chedioack), West African spirit guide, having received permission from friends in spirit, materialised carved wooden gods from his own country, carved stone gods from various places in Africa, a tray from Japan, bangles from India, and a prayer box (a monk's box, on which is carved 86 Monks and Monastery) from Tibet. It took 2 hours to complete this experiment, and the apports were received in the dim light of a 5watt white light. Each apport as it arrived was seen as a ball of white smoke descending from the roof.

207

Apports Received 1940/8.

Figure Christ and Lamb; St. Augustine Panel; Tibetan Cross; Cross, later fixed to Bow of 'S/S Master John'.
During the Second World War a private seance was held at Grimsby, at the home of Capt and Mrs Morck. In the course of the evening, a gold cross, beautifully inlaid with coloured enamels, was apported to Capt Morck. 'Sambo', who brought the apport, said it was brought specially to protect him and his crew, and to bring them safely through the war. On his return to his ship the captain had the cross fixed to his ship. After five years of war dangers captain and crew returned safe and well.

The Tibetan Cross with Chain *was apported for Mr Stocks at 'Pinewoods', 1948.*

Figure Of Christ. *– Apported through the medium Isa A. Northage at the home of Mr and Mrs Rose, Nuneaton, (1940).*

208

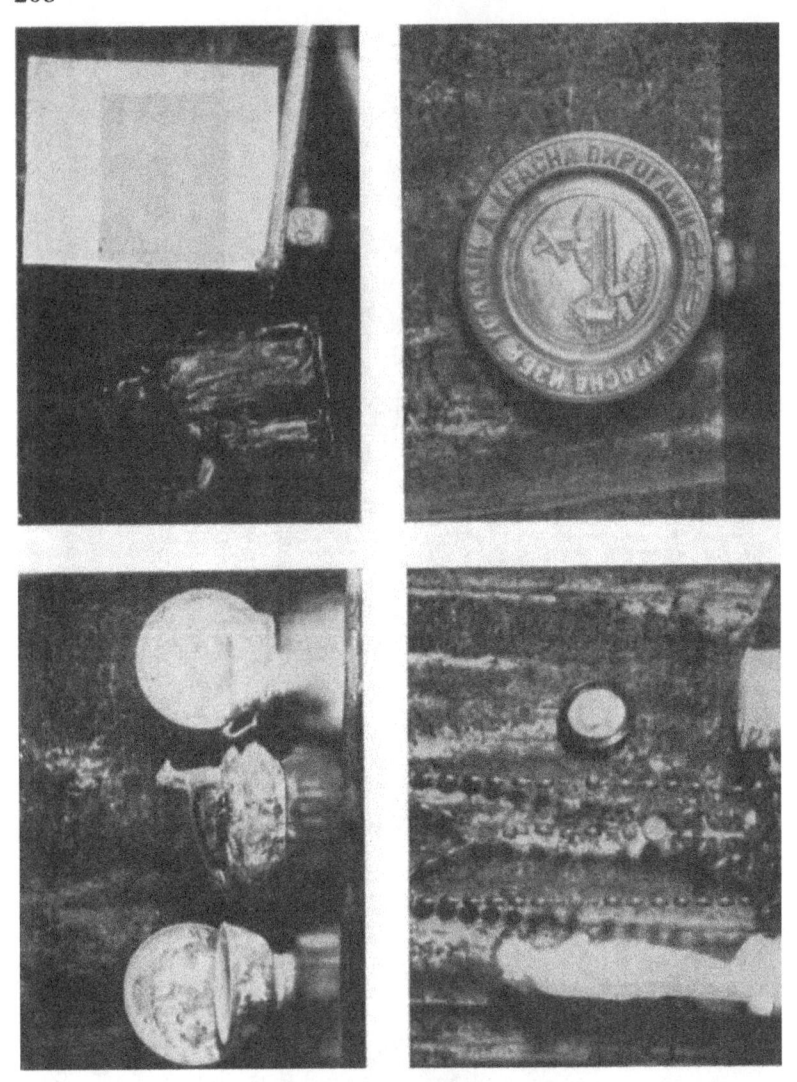

Apports received in 1941

Top Left: Scribe's pen case with Scarab Motif and fragment of Arabic script found in base (see p.204)

Top Right: Carved Russian Plate (Wood)

Bottom Left: Chinese Porcelain

Bottom Right: Ink and sponge in pot. (Translation of script: "My brother, we shall take with us plenty of corn which is needed..")

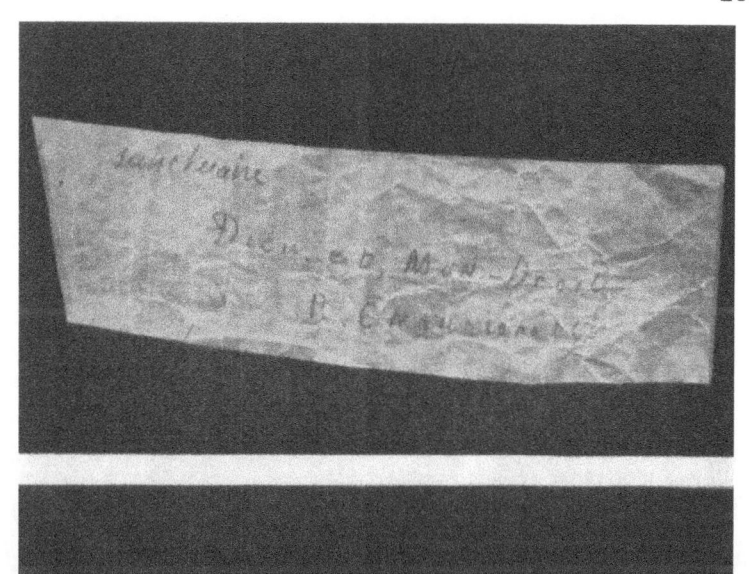

August 6th, 1941. – We were requested during a séance by General Victor De Cazale, Frenchman (in Spirit), to help his old comrades of his regiment, who had been taken prisoner when the Germans had entered France in 1941. On asking how we might help, he replied in French: "Put out five loaves in the centre of the séance room," adding that he and friends in Spirit would dematerialise the bread and apport it to these men in a prison camp (who had no food during the previous five days). The men were wounded, hungry and dirty. One of the sitters (a lady) left the séance room to purchase bread. The rest of the sitters (twelve in all) remained to continue the sitting. When the bread arrived it was placed as requested in the centre of the room, within three minutes it had all disappeared (dematerialised).

Above *– Photo of note of thanks apported from prison camp to us in the sanctuary. The note is from French and Belgian prisoners who shared the apported bread.*
Written in pencil on a scrap of paper.
Sanctuaire. Dieu, et Mon Droit (God and My Right). H. Chaunterell.
On the back of the paper is written – Des Amis du Sanctuaire (From the Friends of the Sanctuary.)

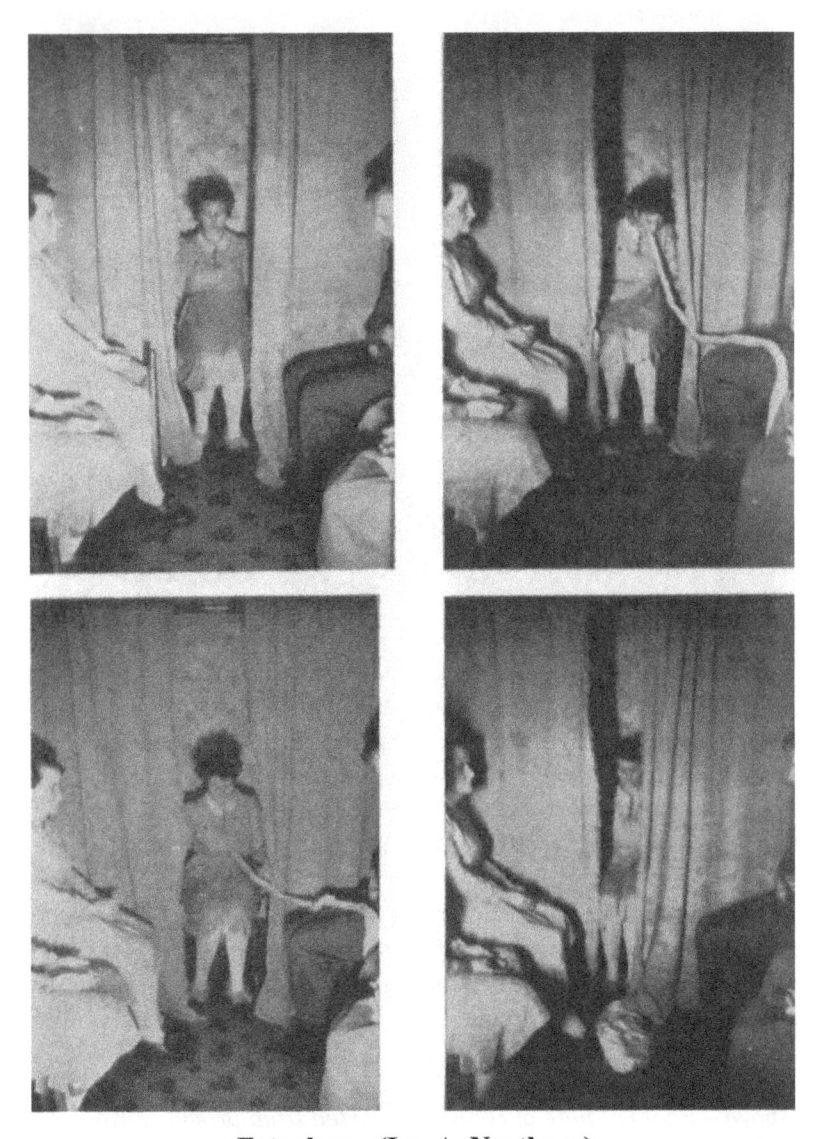

Ectoplasm (Isa. A. Northage)

Top Left: In trance.

Top Right: Ectoplasm from mouth.

Bottom Left: Ectoplasm from solar plexus.

Bottom Right: Mass of ectoplasm, on the floor, from which materialisation builds.

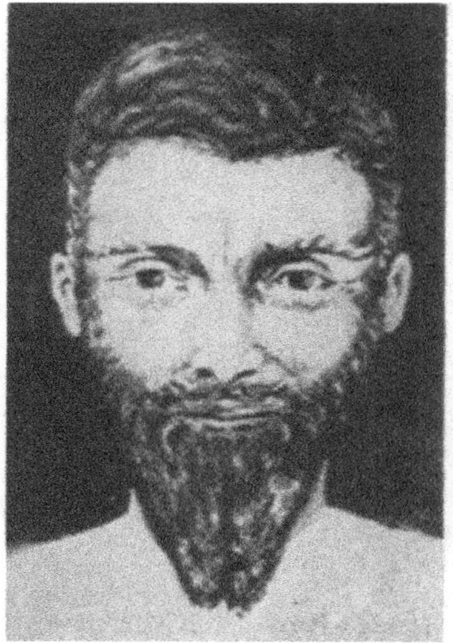

The Principal Spirit Helpers of Isa A. Northage

Dr. Reynolds   **Chedioack (Sambo)**   **Ellen Dawes**
(160: approx160: 27 years in Spirit respectively.)

Each stood for 20 minutes in 20watt white light to allow Mr Ives, of Northampton, to sketch them. Photo of Ellen Dawes was taken at the age of 18 years (1930). She passed to Spirit at the age of 19 years (1931).

A party of sailors materialised after being drowned when their ship was sunk. They appeared in uniform wet with sea water, and left the above cap badges behind as mementoes after they had dematerialised.

Apports

Apports are objects dematerialised and transported by spirit; these objects are again materialised when received by the medium.

Many of these apports have been placed in the tomb at the time of burial.

Nothing is ever apported without permission and agreement being given by the owners, be they in the flesh or spirit.

These apports are gifts and are not to be used for personal monetary gain.

Photograph with Spirit Extras (Faces).

Deciding to go for a short walk, Doctor Reynolds suggested we take a photo out of doors and he would try to impress himself on the plate.

The above is the result – Top left, Doctor Reynolds; top right, Sambo (Chedioack). Below: Ellen Dawes (between the faces of Mr. and Mrs. Northage).

Chapter Eight

Towards the Light

One of the purposes in writing this book recording the life of Isa A. Northage is to try to simplify this very complex subject: to offer comfort and hope to those who are trying to understand the purpose of life, such as I would have wished, many years ago in my early struggles to find truth.

So frequently does one, during those early years, choose books in which the early chapters offer promise of the very thing one is seeking, yet, there is always that 'elusive something'; that 'explanation' that seems impossible to find.

I venture to suggest this is a blessing in disguise, for if one does desire to progress, one will be looking for that 'something' until one is established in the next life.

However, for myself, I find it either colossal impertinence or splendid optimism to try and do those things so many have tried to do, and yet, I hope the experiences in this book will help others in their efforts.

The many direct questions by enquirers who are first drawn to Spiritualism, having experienced unusual happenings, or interested for the comfort it may offer, need careful thought.

We should seriously think before answering such seemingly simple questions, for, I believe, our reply will often, either set a soul in search of this truth, or regrettably, cause its dismissal as rubbish.

I can only claim a reasonable amount of common sense, which the years have taught me, and having seen life from many angles, I am forced to conclude that no person is really bad, and circumstances make or mar the individual.

The word 'Spiritualism', does I fear, seem hard to define. It has, like most other teachings, its various sects, some of which seem to lean towards the particular denomination to which they belonged before they became interested in Spiritualism and the most varied creeds and dogmas seem to creep in, thus destroying the truth we stand for. Others there are whose sole delight is in phenomena-hunting for the sake of entertainment. To them I can but say they need our sorrow and prayers for their wanton neglect of God's greatest blessing to mankind.

I believe that before one can make real headway, one must cast aside all one has previously been taught, however far advanced in years, and start with an open and unprejudiced mind, prepared to discard that which does not stand reasonable analysis, rejecting all that does not conform to your reason, or your better self, seeking guidance from the many sources available, and praying for understanding.

We are so often accused of denying the deity of Jesus, and this usually closes the door on further enquiry by the seeker. I can assure you that beyond any doubt we give far more credit and understanding to the life and purpose of this most blessed Soul than any other denomination, and further, we try to follow His teaching in word and deed.

The Holy Bible contains all that we practise and teach. This does not apply to the Book of Common Prayer, compiled by the Church Authorities.

I can never understand why a priest should at baptism announce that the tender little soul in his arms was born in sin; some even say that without this act of baptism, the child cannot enter the Kingdom of Heaven. This is an insult to God, Who gave the child life, an insult to the parents, indeed an accusation against the little one who is charged with carrying the sin a mythical Adam and Eve committed. According to this stupid teaching, should the little life draw to a close before being baptised, the child is forever lost. What a disgusting display by a religion that is a priestly monopoly controlled by fear; how very far from the teaching of Jesus!

When the life of a dear one has ended, one is informed that the body will remain in the tomb to await Resurrection Day, when the body will be raised and must face judgment. What a comfortless thought for those gathered around the grave! What a tragic close to a life of uncertainty as to its purpose while on earth! This travesty of truth, this disgusting misinterpretation of the Master's teaching is surely a reason for the lack of interest shown in the churches today and why they are losing their followers. Nothing can endure that is not based on truth, and people attending such places of worship find little comfort in times of need. These sorrowing souls were never told that the loved one whose body was in the grave, was alive and well; that he or she had discarded the body of flesh they used on earth, and now had a new one in keeping with their new conditions of life. Many orthodox clergy are indeed aware of this truth; many have, with us, witnessed the return of the so-called dead; some have even tried to comfort others by their experiences, but they are not permitted to teach such truth.

Statements I have made, and our work, have brought upon us many accusations of mental instability. I have been called a heretic by a priest of the church and I am sure we shall encounter these insults as long as we refuse to accept creed and dogma and the unquestioned authority of the priesthood. We believe man has within himself that which is necessary for progression, if he would follow his conscience – if he would do unto others as he would they should do unto him.

No man can say who or what God is. We only know God as absolute purity and love: such love is beyond our comprehension, and indeed, by the state of this world's affairs and mankind in general, we do not know much about love or its application.

Again, there are those who base their whole life and actions upon remote text; sects who claim the right to be called 'the chosen ones' and who ostracise all who do not follow their creed, believing that they alone shall inherit the Kingdom of Heaven, a heaven of their own creation. They are still concerned with an anthropomorphic theology, a God who is wrathful and jealous, and who has, in fact, every human failing. In this self-righteous attitude they are still Scribes and Pharisees, believing that all so-called miracles and wonderful events ceased at the close of the earth life of Jesus.

The Old Testament, a collection of some of the many religious writings written before the birth of Jesus, was spiritual guidance, given to man through man; its contradictions and errors are human errors, due to the imperfect amenuenses, and further, neither spiritual progress nor the continuity of life, as taught by Jesus, is mentioned. Jesus came to clear away the dross and empty formalism of the priestly teachings, to bring truth and spirituality into man's life, and to teach a gospel of humanity, and duty to God and mankind.

Because of this spiritual teaching to enlighten man, the priesthood hated and rejected Him, the truest, most god-like Soul who ever trod this earth.

No one can claim to know the whole truth; earth life is far too short to enable one to grasp more than the smallest fraction. No one can judge; each is his own judge, and no other punishment exists but one's own remorse and conscience. This can be a far greater hell than that understood by the religious teachers of today. It has been my privilege for many years to work and converse with spirit, to receive guidance and to assist materialised spirits to operate on suffering bodies, and I believe this could be the birthright of many, if the teaching of Jesus was practised. It does not come easily, as all worth-while things require the will and effort to accomplish; the greater the efforts, the greater the results.

Would that today, we had with us in the flesh such great souls as the Rev. Stainton Moses; R. J. Lees; Ernest Oaten, etc.; pioneers of priceless worth, authorities of the spirit, so that we might obtain from them the teachings they received first hand from their spirit guides. Today we are in need of such leadership to give to the world established truth, gleaned from first-hand experience, that all which does not express the beauty of the Master's teaching might be discarded. Earnest investigation would enable one to understand and to separate the good from the bad.

One great difficulty is to recommend a place of worship an investigator might attend; our churches are not always well sited. Either from lack of funds, or the stupendous difficulties of acquiring a favourable area, many small churches built by our pioneers could not expand, and many are in need of repair.

Our teaching is not fashionable with the established church; we have not the ordained ministers trained in the schools of theology, hence one of the reasons why we are accused of fraud and charlatanry.

We are familiar with those who promise to demonstrate survival and with those who attend the demonstration, who spend the whole evening trying to force a message from the demonstrator, to the detriment of all present; we are aware indeed of having among ourselves such undesirable parasites.

Investigation alone will not ensure a smooth course, and knowledge will not be acquired without great effort. There is much struggle and heartbreak to be met; the loss of friends, who cannot understand that one could dare to question an established religion and decide to find for oneself the possibility of truth in another's belief.

Wherever Spiritualism is practised or whatever phase is demonstrated, it is of the utmost importance that sincerity be the keynote. Nothing can bring ridicule upon Spiritualist exponents more than imposters; these are indeed the 'false witnesses' who destroy the possibility of further interest on the part of the enquirer.

Scientific minds everywhere have investigated our phenomena and verified the truth of our claims; that we do commune with souls that once lived on earth and that they return to help mankind. Yet, until legal recognition was granted some years ago, trouble makers had an open field to treat all followers of Spiritualism, almost as the church authorities treated those outside their own religion in the Middle Ages.

How terrible it is to think of the millions who have suffered torture and death in the name of religion!

Since the beginning of this century many have investigated Spiritualism, and not the least the orthodox Church. Many meetings were attended by these investigators, but the door has remained closed in spite of the many requests of Spiritualists for the publication of the findings.

There has never been a worthwhile cause that has not suffered abuse and ridicule, but what can be said about organised religion, whose leaders, when confronted with a teaching which threatens their authority and livelihood, refuse to make a public statement for or against?

The Spiritualist does not refer to a coloured man outside his own beliefs as a heathen, as does the orthodox church. We know that his colour, creed, or indeed his idol worship have not denied him access to the highest realms of the spirit world. His moral code, his concern for his dependants, and his worship of nature, could teach many so-called civilised people a beautiful code of life they could not equal. Is it surprising to know that there are countless highly developed souls, shining angels, who lived on earth thousands of years before the birth of Jesus, among whom are many coloured races, working with Jesus and other great servants of God, bringing comfort and help to all men? We teach that the angels who are nearest to us are almost always our own kith and kin; fathers, mothers, brothers and sisters, who have passed on ahead of us. Yet they are fully alive and helping us always, indeed as most of them would have done had they still been on earth. These are they of whom some churches say they are 'resting in peace', or 'awaiting Judgment Day', whatever that may mean. I can assure you, they, our dear ones, are living a full life and a busy one, in whatever they fitted themselves for when they were here. They have learned there is no death, no Judgment Day, no judge but oneself, no wings, and no harps; that the spirit is eternal. There is progress towards knowledge and the understanding of God's laws to advance or retard, and each has his own freewill.

I do not for one moment claim that we are perfect; I have sat in services that have been far from so. I have, I regret to say, witnessed, some of the most ridiculous impostures; the assuming of mediumship; the pouring forth of a lot of trash; and a claim to be controlled by souls who have been many years in spirit. Some souls would, to say the least, have preferred a thousand deaths, rather than give vent to such rubbish.

Further more the messages purporting to come from spirit would not have convinced the most gullible innocent present.

Again, there are those possessing gifts, whose arrogant poses and demands for answers to their questions, distress rather than aid the recipient, thus forcing him to seek elsewhere for comfort.

Many articles written on phenomena do not represent true spiritualist teaching, but are simply to increase sales.

There are very many sincere souls today, engaged in propagating true spiritualist teaching, who require protective powers to root out and destroy the parasites who are happy to profit from another's sorrow. It is comforting to know that the publishers of well-known psychic papers are, and have been, endeavouring to accomplish this difficult task for a long time. Those who try to do so need every possible help.

If, instead of the many awe-inspiring addresses given throughout the churches today, they could be tempered with love and tolerance as is the case in spirit teaching, there would not be churches enough to hold all the people.

One evening, after we had received diagnosis and instructions from Dr Reynolds, the discussion turned to the writing of this book, and with the various spirit friends present, it was agreed we obtain tape recordings, automatic writings, etc., that would perhaps be helpful and of interest to our readers. I was somewhat surprised when the Doctor suggested I should write my life story, saying also that my experiences and the materialisations I had so often witnessed would be of value.

It is to be hoped therefore, that it will encourage and perhaps guide those who may be in a like situation to mine during my search, and to assist them to appreciate the guidance and help I received from Isa A. Northage and her spirit guides.

My Story

I was born in Liverpool and educated at a church school until the age of fourteen. My parents were respected members of their churches. I, and the rest of our fairly large family were brought up in a happy home but with proper discipline. We attended church very regularly, and in due course were confirmed, and, as far as I was concerned, remained closely connected with all church activities, as a choir member, and later becoming a probationer in the cathedral choir, but when I was fourteen, our family doctor advised me to rest my throat until my voice 'broke'.

In 1911 I became apprentice to a branch of the engineering trade, but when I was seventeen, war came (1914), and I, being a member of the R.N.V.R. at once volunteered for active service. I was soon drafted to a field training centre, and in a very short time sent overseas to France and Belgium serving with the Royal Naval Brigade. We had some early setbacks, but eventually returned to England to be reorganised as the Royal Naval Division. I again volunteered, this time for marine service, and later joined the Dover Patrol. One of our many jobs was to board suspected ships and search them for any illegal traffic in passenger or cargo. This often meant rowing in a small cutter or whaleboat, and in the type of weather so often met around the Straits of Dover, this was not always pleasant going. After about two-and-a-half years of this work, I volunteered for the D.A.M.S. (armed merchant ships), and travelled to many parts of the world, receiving my discharge some eight months after the war but for the tragedy of war it was an excellent experience, and helped me to see the world in general.

After my discharge I returned to finish my apprenticeship at the age of about twenty-two. This was not too difficult owing to my father's foresight and co-operation; the training he gave me stood me in good stead in the later years. The tragic slump in the engineering trades in the early 1920s soon ended hopes of employment, and, having just married, I soon learned the meaning of unemployment. As months and years passed, hunger and hopelessness became my lot. As with many others, one was extremely fortunate to obtain an odd day's work now and then. The distressful 'means test' and periods of drawing the 'dole', and the added trouble of a very sick wife just seemed to make things impossible; it became a nightmare, wondering how to obtain the means of paying rent and getting a little food. It was long before I managed to find work and that only of a temporary kind, and a very long way from where we were then living, but we were glad of anything. As employment slowly began to improve, we – myself, wife, and now our child, travelled all over the country, ready to take any available work. The rough passage and lean years had turned our thoughts away from church or religion which had appeared of little use in time of need, nor could I find any satisfaction in what I had been taught (when I had attended church) about faith. To me this faith was all right in times of prosperity, but something was missing when needed for practical purposes.

So, as conditions improved, the aim in life seemed to be a day's work and an evening's enjoyment wherever they could be found, whether enjoyment or escapism I cannot say. About this time my wife received a letter from her mother stating she had attended a Spiritualist meeting and the 'medium' had told her I would meet with an accident in three weeks time. My views on Spiritualism were such that I at once wrote to express what I thought about the visit, Spiritualists, and such people, in very strong language and forbidding my mother-in-law ever to write about such rubbish again. Well, it happened just as foretold. Exactly three weeks later I was buried under several tons of pulp, receiving among other injuries, a fractured pelvis which entailed lying on a water bed for three months. I recollect some of my thoughts while in hospital, and the unusual experiences my mother and I had during my youth; these usually occurred when we were together doing household jobs. Sometimes a great crash would be heard coming from the china cupboard which we would open at once to see the damage, only to find nothing disturbed. Mother would always request me to note the time of the occurrence, telling me someone close to us had died at that moment, sure enough we would later find out this was quite true, to the very minute. At that time I took little notice; I did not think it in any way unusual. My mother was over eighty years old, when, during a conversation we were having on the new field of interest I had found (to which she listened far more intently than I realised at the time), she told me she had had many visions and experiences, but could never speak of them. It was not the kind of thing people would listen to, and, in fact, I was the only one to share her confidence regarding this subject. Three months after her passing, my mother returned to me, and said: "I used to listen to the things you told me when I lay in bed; I used to think very deeply about your views. I know now it is true." This was one of the most helpful and comforting supports I have received in this work.

After leaving the north, I and my family went to Wales. Here my wife again visited a Spiritualist meeting, and I took this unkindly, as before, forbidding her to attend such foolish gatherings, mixing with such crazy people.

Our next move was to the Midlands and I had more time for reflection on matters to which I had previously given much thought.

One evening, discussing Spiritualism, and the kind of people we thought were interested in it, having expressed myself without attending a meeting, my wife suggested that I went to one and see for myself. This was only fair, although I had no wish to know these people, and further had lost any interest I may once have had. I had at times attended an orthodox church, perhaps for memories' sake, or in the slim hope that the teaching might offer me something. The services seemed always the same, nothing solid or satisfying, always that same 'faith' in what was taught; not much about this world, and certainly nothing about the next.

However, after considerable persuasion, I decided to attend a local Spiritualist church, still full, I believed, of crude ideas, weird happenings, and credulous women. After walking up and down outside the church (to see the coast was clear) I slipped inside, keeping well at the rear, with one eye on the door. To my astonishment I witnessed a reverent service of devoted people, but was surprised to see a lady giving the address. All the prayers were spontaneous except the Lord's Prayer, and the change in the words, 'lead us not into temptation' to *'leave* us not, when in temptation', was really, I thought, better than expecting God to 'lead us into temptation'. As the address proceeded, I noticed a strange change take place in the speaker's face; whereas she appeared to be in her sixties her whole appearance changed to that of a young girl. Her features completely altered; I not only saw this, but even that her eyes were blue, and I was twenty feet away from her. At the close of the address she became as I saw her first. I did not know at this time that I was seeing with clairvoyant sight and was in fact, seeing the guide controlling her for the address. After the service the congregation was most friendly, and I was asked if I would care to hear a lecture the following Tuesday. I attended the lecture.

After a while we were informed that the speaker had not arrived, and one of those present suggested we sat and formed a 'circle'. A prayer was said and a hymn sung, usual, I was told, before any sitting as it was considered an act of devotion. The leader then stood and moved up and down in front of the sitters, gently, as I thought, talking to himself. After some of this, I became sure that he and the rest were plain crazy, and prepared to move towards the door, but before I knew anything more something happened to me. I became elated, a different person; oblivious of everything, sitters included. Soon I was myself again, feeling wonderful, at peace with everything, all fears and worries gone.

I learned later that I had experienced 'trance control'. Now for the first time, I was, from being antagonistic, becoming interested. I did try hard to get an explanation of these happenings, but could not find the help I thought I required. Some time later I was watching a demonstration of 'dowsing', that is water divining. Someone suggested I had a try at holding the rod, to see if it worked: I was most surprised to find it did on every occasion, and for some time after, I did this work for farmers, etc., and later had one or two articles published on the subject.

Still determined to investigate Spiritualism, my wife and I were invited to a healing service in a small house. Sitting close because of the limited space, as the service started I began to feel very drowsy, appearing to drop off to sleep every time the healer placed his hands upon a suffering person. In this condition I would see the spirit treating the patient, and as he finished he would throw me an illuminated ball with a comment such as 'a rotten apple', signifying the disease removed. I would put out my hands (as I thought) to catch this ball, and would at once awake to find I had not moved but still held my hymn book, then off I would go again in this strange sleep, as the next patient was treated.

I was aware of my good fortune in having so many remarkable experiences of something to which I had never given a thought, yet was disturbed as I could not get any advice.

I decided to practise at home at anything that might help me to develop. I tried psychometry, that is, holding or even looking at an article belonging to a person, and from this one is able to describe events, etc., concerning the owner's life. I would even see the owner build up if he or she were not present, and see various phases in their lives, and often this would enable me to help in their problems. Once in a frivolous mood, and treating it all as a game, suddenly I heard a voice say: "Don't play with them, let them stew in their own juice," and to impress me more, the words appeared alongside my head in golden letters. Somehow, I took very little notice of the warning, and suddenly became very ill, and saw the most revolting figure approaching me. At that moment my wife sharply called me to stop; I did, thanks to her. She told me afterwards that my whole appearance had changed and frightened her; 'like attracts like' was never more true. I had indeed learned my lesson, and never again did I attempt any investigation without prayer for help and guidance. I now realise these gifts are not for selfish use, but for helping others, and I have always emphasised this to people, in their development.

While determined to learn all I could I visited many churches seeking better understanding, but remained a member of the first church I had attended, and in time became secretary. As the days passed I saw a change taking place in my development. I would see many spirit friends about me, clearly noting their features and colouring.

Sometimes at my request for a particular spirit to return, the spirit would again confront me, usually showing me the eyes first, then the rest of the face, and when about to leave, giving me a gracious smile. These visits always left a peaceful and happy condition with me.

The church members very kindly did all they could to encourage me, in particular Mrs S. Moore, who was President. To her I owe so much, as she was ever ready to offer help and encouragement. Before long I read my first lesson, and later gave my first address.

The owners of the property we shared as a church decided they needed our part of the building to extend; they requested us to close the church, and we had to accede to their demand. This caused great sadness, chiefly among the older members who had met there for so many years, because of the great difficulty in trying to find another meeting place. Meetings were called, and at last it was decided we would build a church of our own. I made bold to undertake this task, and without the slightest hesitation, they offered me all their savings to do the best I could. I had no idea how to go about such matters, yet was determined to succeed somehow. I wanted to show my gratitude for their kindness to me. The first and most important step was taken by Miss E. Lees, the daughter of R. J. Lees, that great soul, who as a boy was medium to Queen Victoria, and who was instrumental in introducing John Brown as medium in his stead, as he had greater work to do for spirit. This lady who had given so much of her valuable time, was, with the help of her legal adviser, able to purchase a plot of land at a very reasonable price, and this became the site of the new church. Then with the help of four or five male members of the congregation, the foundations were soon laid. A sectional wooden building was purchased, erected, and furnished by the church members.

Our many difficulties were gradually overcome, and indeed, our thanks are due to the S.N.U. (Spiritualists' National Union) for their assistance in obtaining our building licence. In four months we had completed our task and were ready to open.

The new church was situated next to a Territorial training centre, and very soon the military authorities informed us of their intention to purchase our site for an extension to their premises. This really did distress our members, as they had given their all to create the new church. I at once decided to investigate the true position with the Commanding Officer who was stationed in a neighbouring town. Arriving at the military headquarters I could not gain entrance to his office and stood outside for some time. Then seeing two soldiers carrying a carpet towards the office, I followed them and was admitted. I am afraid the officer did not approve of my presence or my method, and very soon demanded my business.

I expressed the feelings of our members at the news we had received regarding the Army's intentions towards our church. The officer became impatient and informed me that the authorities could if they wished, purchase our site at a much smaller sum than we had paid; we parted, not the best of friends.

During my return journey I pondered on what seemed to me a very unfortunate position for our church, and was concerned as to how I could break the news to my fellow members.

I decided to write to the Home Secretary at once and in a few days received a most courteous reply, informing me that no action would be taken in the matter of our church or the site; everything would remain our property, and in our possession without further interference.

This situation happily settled, we prepared for the opening. The members had requested the services of Mrs I. A. Northage in performing the ceremony. I had heard of this lady's great work, but had never met her until the day of the opening; it was a very fortunate one for me indeed.

Mrs Northage travelled 120 miles to conduct this service and without any fee. The church was filled to capacity and an excellent service was held, many entire strangers received the most evidential messages, and it was very late when we closed the church. One of the members invited Mrs Northage to stay overnight at her house and she accepted, requesting I might be permitted to accompany her for a chat to finish the evening.

We had supper and sat talking; before very long the spirit people joined us in our conversation. It was the first time Mrs Northage and I had sat together and it would be impossible to express my gratitude and pleasure; my relatives, some of whom had been in spirit for many years, conversed with me just as though they were still in the flesh.

I knew that we should some day work together in this great service, for this had changed my life more than I could possibly realise. I knew that in some way I should help one who had laboured so much to bring truth and comfort to so many.

Within the next few days I had the remarkable experience of a panoramic view of my own life. I was sitting meditating upon spiritual matters, during the daytime, when a vision opened before me showing the years I had spent in ignorance, the darkened conditions my way of life had created for me, the many obstacles I would have to overcome if prepared to follow the teaching I was receiving, and in the distance, I could see the 'light' I might gain should I be prepared to overcome every difficulty. This was shown to me symbolically and in colours, first in dark blue and finally in brilliant light. The realities of such experiences so impress themselves upon the recipient that there can be no mistaking their significance and truth. It is quite impossible to explain it to another person; this somehow belongs to oneself, and one instinctively knows the meaning. Since I decided there was only this pathway to follow, I have met and am still meeting many difficult obstacles, but slowly and surely I am overcoming them, each time gathering a little more knowledge and light.

The church we had built was now functioning, and the members who had done so much towards its establishment were happy and continuing with services and meetings. I thought it better to continue my own development as there was no shortage of workers in the church and they were far more capable than I.

My wife and I were invited to attend a 'home circle', usually recognised as the best place for communicating with spirit. We were introduced to the sitters and made the acquaintance of one in particular, who was, apparently, considered well-versed in these matters and whose esoteric teaching was far beyond the ordinary. Indeed, his prayers and address were certainly distinctive and of an advanced nature. Sitting as we were, in darkness, the conditions perhaps lent themselves to an atmosphere of tension, but I had an uncontrollable urge to look in his direction during his discourse. I could not see him owing to the darkness, but when I looked towards him I saw a large head with an idiotic face, whose tongue was wagging from side to side, and at the same time I distinctly heard the words 'blabbering idiot'. Needless to say I was shocked and disgusted; however, we sat quiet until the close of the sitting.

Some days later the man concerned called at our home for a chat, and in a short time, seated himself at the piano and entertained us to some popular tunes. During an interlude I asked him why he said and did such things that he knew were false. He informed me that he was aware of what he did and that it was expected of him, otherwise he would not be invited. He was greatly shocked when I told him he neither believed nor cared what he said. I tried to warn him of the great risk he was taking in playing with such forces, but my words were ignored.

Again the symbolic vision was to prove true; we politely informed the people at whose home the 'circle' took place, that we would not attend again for various reasons, which at that time we felt we could not explain. This was taken very unkindly; we had apparently offended our hosts who had considered their 'circle' beyond reproach. Later we were treated with contempt and our friendship ceased from that day. We tried many times to reach a better understanding, but were rudely ignored.

My contact with the man, through whom we had left these people, was not finished. I began to have strange dreams in which I could see the course of his life; even the circumstances, time, and place of our next meeting would be shown and never fail to occur. His altered health, way of life, and our final meeting were shown me, and as each came true I shared sorrow for this unfortunate, and wondered at the revelation.

In time, a further series of experiences began to occur. I found that sometimes during conversations with people, their whole countenance would completely alter, revealing the character and very soul of that person. This was at times a little frightening; one would wonder what to do; yet I learned much, very much, that no earthly one could have taught me. I saw how one is seen in spirit life, the true character, in such a way that nothing can be hidden from God and one's fellows of the spirit world. Whenever possible I tried to help or encourage people towards a different outlook on life, but did not always get co-operation. I did not preach morals or try to impress with religious platitudes, but tried to change their attitude towards their fellow men, in the exercising of more tolerance and kindliness. This frequently brought good results, and often, at a sitting, gratitude was expressed for the change wrought. I am thankful that I have always delivered any messages received; the biggest difficulty being when they have concerned intimate matters between husband and wife; sometimes one was thanked, sometimes rebuffed.

There came the time when I received an invitation from Mrs Northage to visit her home and attend a séance; this was to be my first materialisation sitting. It was a memorable evening. I was to meet those spirit souls who were responsible for my varied experiences.

We were enjoying direct voice and trumpet voices, and at times there were three trumpets suspended in the air talking to three different people at the same time. I was looking at Mrs Northage, who was in deep trance, when my attention was drawn to a figure building up at my side. He was a Bedouin in flowing robes and headdress, but seen in profile. I mentally wished him to turn and face me; no sooner had I done this, than he did turn full face, his colour, beard, and features, standing out perfectly. Not quite sure what to say, I asked if he were my guide; he at once affirmed this, salaaming several times, and then gradually and very slowly dematerialised. We met many times afterwards, and he proved a very great help in my life. I also conversed with my father, who had been in spirit many years, and with several relatives. Next, a commanding voice addressed me in Egyptian. I could not understand, and at once Ellen Dawes, a young lady in spirit, who among her many duties acted as interpreter, translated. His name was Ali-Ben-Hassan. He said he had attached himself to me to help me when giving addresses. He and the Bedouin worked together. At a later sitting they both returned and requested me to meditate oftener, and become more amenable to spiritual influence. Hassan also said he was learning English, but found it very laborious. Before leaving, he called out: "Allah be praised!"

A grief stricken friend who had 'lost' a daughter some years ago, accompanied me to a séance; it was her first visit, and she had never heard much about spirit return. We had not sat long before a perfumed handkerchief was waved in front of her face, and while watching this, her daughter built up before her. It was a little too much for her, and she grasped my arm for comfort, as she cried: "It's G—!" Sambo, Mrs Northage's guide, came forward and spoke, saying: "When the white lady recovers, her daughter will again materialise." When all was calm again, the daughter came, and mother and child held a long conversation and embraced. I have spoken many times to this young girl since that meeting, and been privileged to receive and deliver messages for her. I have even received them while reading a newspaper during a train journey.

Although interested in ectoplasm (the substance used by spirit for materialisations, etc.) I had never handled it, but one evening at a sitting, the Chinese guide of a physical medium told me to examine the ectoplasm extruding from the mouth and nose of the medium. I gently gripped the flowing ectoplasm in my hands, rather fearing I might do some damage, but again the guide told me to handle it, to try its flexibility, etc. I found it of very strong texture and yet soft as the finest gossamer, and cool; I have since seen it made as strong as a steel bar. To see ectoplasm produced is not pleasant, and I have been informed by a spirit responsible for its production that it is necessary to 'freeze' (the best word to describe the process) the medium's being, otherwise the extraction of ectoplasm would be excruciatingly painful, as if countless needles were being drawn through the body. When necessary, the materialised figure can illuminate itself: usually the light seems to come from the palms of the hands, when held towards the body of the materialised figure.

Having by this time had many sittings, I was beginning to get a fair knowledge of phenomena, in fact to understand many things I had thought impossible: the kindly guidance and instructions the spirit visitants gave me, the purpose of their return to earth conditions, advice on diet and health, need for harmony and preparation for communication, a code of behaviour towards my fellow men, and duty to God and man.

In response to a request for help from some sick people we held a sitting for diagnosis from Dr Reynolds, and later, when everything was satisfactorily concluded, it was suggested by spirit that they should allow one or two friends to return and materialise. I was not aware at this time that it was the twenty-first anniversary of my daughter's passing into spirit. She passed at birth in a London hospital, where my wife had been taken for an urgent operation during my absence from home.

Had my daughter lived to be christened, I intended her name to be Jeanne (Jeannette). When Mrs Northage had passed into trance, in a few moments the figure of a young lady built up directly in front of me, calling: "Daddy, Daddy, it is I, Jeannette; remember the unlucky thirteenth. I shall be twenty-one in three weeks' time."

I stood and embraced our dear child. We talked and kissed, oblivious of everything. For ten minutes we stood thus; how could I explain these the most priceless moments of my life? If you, a parent, had as you thought, lost something that really made life worth while, how would you have felt in a like position?

I could now see the realities of my travels during sleep, in which I had visited my daughter in her spirit home and seen her grow up there. Her schooling and companions, all of these I had been shown in the sleep state.

Later, at another sitting, my daughter and I spoke of these experiences and they were verified: indeed it was but one of God's many blessings to us. The reference to the unlucky thirteenth, was Friday, the thirteenth of March, on which my child had passed to spirit.

Undeveloped Spirits

These poor souls, so often referred to as evil, by those who are ignorant, are dwellers in the lower spheres; places they have created for themselves, or built by their misdeeds on earth. They are sometimes brought to us to receive what help we might be able to give in prayer and contact. These souls are those who have seen the error of their ways and are struggling towards the light, the first step of progress. Many of the highly advanced spirit people are stationed at various points in the pathway of progression, and appear to the struggling souls as 'lights' towards which they may advance. When they reach the condition fitting them to go further forward they are passed by those 'lights' to the next 'light', and so on. It is a terribly hard fight, yet there is always help near for those who are sincere. When these souls appear in materialised form, they are in dark robes, and if very undeveloped, there is with them an odour of decay and a chilly feeling; the atmosphere becomes cold and unsettled in keeping with their spiritual condition. One cannot but pity them in their long and sorrowful strife, and do all in one's power to help. Throughout all this type of work, we are protected by our spirit guides, otherwise we could not stand the great strain. Such is the gratitude of these souls that when advanced to better conditions, they frequently return to offer their grateful thanks. This service we are honoured to perform, and it is one of the methods used by those blessed souls who themselves are 'angels of light'.

Trumpet For Direct Voice

When the trumpet is being used by the spirits to address people present it would appear to have an ectoplasmic mask in the wide end, for if it is watched closely (and one can obtain a side view against a red light or the luminous band on another trumpet which is often suspended in the air by another communicator), one can observe the pulsating of a web-like substance as the voice is speaking. Again in the red light when the curtains of the cabinet are closed around the medium, the trumpet may often be seen passing through the heavy velvet curtains (matter through matter). Great difficulty is experienced by the spirit using the trumpet if daylight penetrates the room; the light seems to have the effect of drawing the trumpet towards where the light enters. I have seen this happen, and heard the spirit explain: "I cannot hold the trumpet"; when the light is attended to they can carry on. When using the trumpet for the first time a spirit will find some difficulty, and often makes the request: "Speak to me," to whoever is addressed. When the sitter replies, the voice seems to add strength to the spirit who is then able to draw closer and speak more clearly and strongly. Another means of aiding the spirit to contact a sitter is to concentrate the thoughts on the person with whom the spirit wishes to speak. This, as explained by the guide, enables the spirit to travel along the thought beam and make contact. Sometimes sorrow is mixed with gladness, and it is indeed a heartbreaking experience to witness a soul returning to earth to make contact with a relative still in earth life to whom the spirit did wrong when on this side. To witness the distress, the effort to ask forgiveness for wrongs done, without which the soul cannot make progress in spirit, (and indeed none can progress until all such deeds are forgiven, hence the need to take care whilst we are still on earth), is tragic, and must be seen to be realised.

Distress

Distress and anxiety can often prevent phenomena. Both create vibrations which disturb the peace that is so necessary for the spirits to work properly. I have more than once sat next to a sitter, who on seeing the materialisation of a loved one for the first time, has broken down in the joy of reunion, and it has been necessary for the materialised figure to leave until the sitter has become calmer, and then rematerialise to show a perfect example of themselves as in earth life (but free of all suffering) and to converse with their loved one. Again, any demand for a particular spirit to return is never fulfilled; the condition created by a demanding sitter can destroy a whole sitting. People must realise that we cannot compel any souls to return. We sit and wait; the spirit in charge of the sitting will decide what takes place and who returns. So, as these souls return, they mingle with earth conditions, and we should sympathise with them, in having to return to this troublesome planet, and try to understand the difficulties involved in their efforts to make themselves known to their loved ones.

More Visitors

We sat one night to discuss arrangements with Dr Reynolds, and to obtain his approval regarding certain alterations to the church. Some additions were necessary to accommodate people after treatment, rooms for rest and refreshment, etc.; this meant removing a brick wall inside the church, and we were afraid that we might disturb the atmosphere already built up through our sittings and services; but everything was all right.

The Doctor now informed us that he wished to bring other spirit friends who were assisting the work. A few minutes later we were greeted by several monks, each speaking in Latin, Ellen Dawes (a spirit assistant to the Doctor) translating; then each monk approached the sitters, touching every one and giving a blessing. He who appeared to be the leader materialised and addressed us all, stating that he was formerly the Prior of the monastery (now the site of Newstead Abbey). The monastery had been destroyed by the Normans in 950 A.D.,* and many of the monks were murdered, but they managed to bury the monastery treasures which were still intact. He and his fellow monks had remained together throughout their spirit life, and they had each that evening chosen one sitter through whom he could work, and would remain with us all our earth life. He then gave his blessing and left us.

*The only priory known to have existed at Newstead was not founded until 1170 by Henry II and was closed at the Dissolution of the Monastries in 1539 when the inhabitants received pensions. (A.H.)

The next speaker was W. T. Stead who was drowned when the 'Titanic' was lost, followed by a Doctor Jim Bennett, of Glasgow University who stated he had passed into spirit soon after qualifying, having contracted T.B., caused by starvation during his studies.

I was then addressed by one who, after giving his full titles said: "That is only for evidence; these things do not matter now."

One night I was introduced to my 'doorkeeper', a North American Indian of the Cherokee tribe. His work was to care for me both physically and spiritually; he is responsible for those who wish to take charge of the body for controlled speaking, etc. He told me he was a scout with General Johnson at the time of the signing of the six nations agreement, about 1774. I then asked why he had attached himself to me, to which he replied that he came to help the white man and to show that love was stronger than hate. It had not been easy. During the fighting with the white man, his wives and children had been burnt to death in their wigwam by the white soldiers. He had been united with his dear ones for a long time now and his hate was forgotten in the service of the Great White Spirit.

Next to speak was a young lady who had returned to assist me in my healing work. She was attracted to me because she was a relative from seven generations ago and had passed into spirit through T.B., aged twenty-seven years. Her name was Murag.

I had received a request from Doctor to sit privately and Mrs Northage kindly gave her valuable time, though so fully occupied, for this special purpose. I had by this time practised healing in co-operation with Mrs Northage and her Doctor but often felt I was taking up too much of their time, when there were so many calls coming to her Sanctuary.

Of the many cases I was at this time treating, spinal ones were the most frequent. Mrs Northage, Dr Reynolds and I had been talking for some time about various people who were receiving treatment, and diagnosis was given when requested.

When cases had been completed and notes taken of the advice given, Dr Reynolds said to me: "I have heard your prayers and have decided to answer them," adding that for some time he had

had with him, a doctor desirous of having an instrument through whom he could return to heal the sick. He had watched me for a long while, and now believed I would be suitable. Doctor Reynolds then introduced us, stating that this was Dr Rennie, spinal specialist of Prince Albert and St. Ann's Hospitals, Sydney, N.S.W., Australia. This doctor then gave me many particulars of his hospital work when on earth. He had been eighty years in spirit and had brought one who would open my ears (clairaudience). This new spirit whose name was Sai-seek-eek-Koing ('Saiseek', I must call, should I need him at any time) then explained the work he would do with me and said that in earth life he had sung in opera with Sydney Grenville. We have since been very close companions, enjoying discussions on many subjects, particularly healing and diagnosis and the prospects of patients' recovery. If, as sometimes happens, the Doctor pronounces the case incurable, spirit helpers will make the passing easier.

In these helpful talks I seem to be treated as an equal; only the noblest souls could do this, knowing my many shortcomings. Like most beginners I was very enthusiastic in my early efforts at healing and after advising me to conserve my strength, the Doctor said: "Mac, you think we in spirit are wonderful; let me assure you, some cases can be cured, others cannot. When God has called we are powerless to intervene; they will die. You cannot cure a neurotic. We in spirit, have our limitations, as you in your earthly life. We help, inspire and impress you, and I will help you all I can. It is better to treat three people and cure them, than to treat twenty and have failures."

To me, this is sound common sense and I have always acted upon it.

Another spirit making contact with me one evening, spoke as follows: "I was a Presbyterian minister in Scotland during earth life. My name is George Robertson (or Robinson, I could not quite grasp the name). I found different teaching in the spirit world than I taught on earth and would like to speak again, through you, of this teaching. I have stood at your side many times when you were speaking, trying to get my voice to you."

The Doctor then warned us that he had overheard a conversation at a meeting at which it had been proposed that three of the people concerned should visit our church, pleading that they required healing. Their real purpose, however, was to gain entrance to a sitting in order to discover details of work we were not yet in a position to make public. We were given their names and addresses and told how they would be dressed. Knowing the day of their visit, we were able to prevent their entrance, but did not disclose the information we had received. This is one of the ways in which we are protected: nothing can escape the vigilance of spirit.

A Christmas Party

Each year we arrange a séance for a Christmas party, inviting about twelve people who have a close relative or child in spirit. The guests bring the toys they would have wished to give their loved ones had they still been in the flesh, and then spend some time arranging the toys on the tree in the centre of the Sanctuary and addressing the gift, sometimes adding a little message of love. It is also usual to hang extra gifts for little ones who are brought by the spirit children as their guests, generally coloured children.

We sit for about three hours on these occasions, from 8 pm. During the prayer and hymn, Mrs Northage goes into deep trance, remaining in this condition throughout the sitting. This being a materialisation sitting in red light, torches, plaques, and trumpets are placed ready for spirit use. Usually the first to appear are Dr Reynolds, Sambo, and Ellen Dawes. Doctor will supervise, Sambo take charge of Mrs Northage's body and Ellen will welcome sitters and advise. It is most delightful to witness the return of children from spirit, to spend an evening with their parents. They first greet them with a kiss and embrace, then walk to the tree and pick the gift bearing their name, returning to thank the donors. It is not uncommon to see two or three spirit children sitting on the floor playing with their trains and motor cars, winding them up and allowing the toys to run between themselves and their parents. When the tree seems stripped of most gifts, the children will stand around and shake it, as though making sure there is nothing left.

After a very joyous party and before leaving, the spirit children will request that their presents be given to a child friend or some child who they know is in need of a gift, and these requests are always carried out. Everything seems so natural that at times one can hardly realise that the little ones are not of this world. On these occasions it is not unusual for a child, who 'died' at birth, to return and greet his or her parents. The greeting and conversation are too intimate to be recorded, and the happiness of these reunited souls is abundant proof of God's love.

Many a tragic event, such as the loss of an only child, has been healed, happiness replacing sorrow when such parents have been so fully assured of the continuity of life, the continued progress of their dear ones; something that can never be taken from them and the knowledge that when their call comes, they will again be united for ever.

Curtains, Torches and Plaques

When it becomes necessary for the curtains around the cabinet to be closed in order to contain the ectoplasm in a confined area for some intricate experiment, the curtains are slowly drawn by the spirit. We do not touch anything unless requested; the torches are also manipulated by spirit unless they use their own powers of self-illumination, in which case the rays of light seem to rise from the palms of their hands. If, during the sitting, the Sanctuary becomes overheated, these same spirit people waft the heavy curtains for quite a time to create a cool breeze.

More than once, as the materialised form has stepped forward, the figure has trodden upon a plaque and completely crushed it, showing the density of the materialised matter. I have held a torch, giving a strong red light, within twelve inches of Mrs Northage's face during transfiguration, watched her own face disappear, and in its place a man's face proceed to build, a very aged one with beard and moustache, and quite toothless, whereas she herself has a full set of teeth. In this case I was permitted to look right into the mouth of the face that had built; the phenomena lasted for four minutes.

In order to test the 'power' accumulated, the medium is levitated in her chair to the ceiling and kept there for about four minutes before being gently lowered.

Place and Preparation for Sitting

The Sanctuary

A building nine feet by sixteen feet adjacent to the church, and generally containing eight chairs or according to the number of sitters. A small section is curtained off for use as a cabinet, the curtains being of heavy velvet material.

Lighting

A 60watt white light and a small 5watt bulb in centre of roof. White, green, and red torches are placed on the floor for the use of spirit communicators.

Plaques

Made of aluminium and covered with luminous paint they measure about nine inches by seven and have a small handle on the back; these are also for spirit use.

Trumpets

Conical, and of aluminium; usually three are in use at a time. They have a luminous band at the wide end to enable sitters to follow their movements, the wide end to magnify the spirit voices.

The Sitting

Is always opened with prayer and sometimes followed by a hymn. A sitting usually lasts about two to two-and-a-half hours and closes with prayer.

Weather Conditions

Heavy thunderstorms, lightning and fog have a disturbing effect on phenomena; in such conditions we are generally requested to close the sitting.

As far as I can ascertain, certain atmospheric conditions interfere with the vibrations.

Sitters

Sometimes people who have been granted a sitting bring friends with them to make a party. If all is not well, almost as soon as we have settled down, the spirit in charge of the séance will kindly request certain of those present to leave the room. When this request has been complied with we are permitted to carry on. The explanation given later is that these particular people were not in a proper condition to sit in a séance. Occasionally, in the middle of a sitting, the spirit doctors are called away and we are informed later in the evening on their return, that they were sent for to release some suffering soul from the body and sometimes they go to help in a serious illness. We have even been called upon to supply blood, as immediate donors, for an urgent blood transfusion. The blood is dematerialised and administered by the spirit doctor wherever the patient may be.

Floor Boards

During a sitting we were requested to examine the floor boards after the séance, as they were rotting, and this would interfere with the bringing of apports. Inspection of the floor later revealed rotting joists and boarding.

A.M.

A Glossary Of Terms

Apports – Objects brought by spirits.

Automatic Writing – Writing executed by a force controlling the writer's hand.

Clairaudience – Clear hearing; the faculty of hearing voices or sounds independent of the physical ear.

Clairvoyance – Clear seeing; a sensitive state of perception of many degrees of acuteness.

Clairvoyant – One endowed with the faculty of clairvoyance.

Control – The intelligence which uses the body of a medium, sensitive or automatist, to communicate messages, etc.

Dematerialise – The dissolving of a materialised form.

Direct Voice – The phenomenon of a voice being heard other than those physically present, generally that of a discarnate spirit.

Direct Writing – Writing executed by spirits without any human intervention.

Discarnate – Disembodied, opposed to incarnate, used to signify that part of man which survives bodily death.

Ectoplasm – Is the formation of divers objects, which in most cases seems to emerge from a human body, and take on the semblance of material realities, clothing, veils, and living bodies (Professor Richet). A section of ectoplasm was cut from the gown of a materialised figure and analysed in the bacteriological lab. at Warsaw, July, 1921. "The substance to be analysed is albuminoid matter accompanied by fatty matter and cells found in the human organism; starch and sugar are absent."

Etherealisation – A refined form of materialisation, in which the form, though visible, is not materially solid or opaque.

Extra – A term for the supernormal face or figure obtained on a photographic plate, etc.

Force – The energy which is cognizable to our senses through and by means of vibrations or waves which are included in the general term of motion.

Levitation – The lifting or movement of physical bodies without visible means or contact, in defiance of gravitation, and especially human beings.

Materialisation – The appearance of a spirit in tangible bodily form, differing from an apparition, which is supposed to be intangible.

Materialise – The act of a spirit clothing itself with matter. This word is so expressive that it has become of general use, with a wide range of meanings, and yet it conveys an entirely erroneous idea of the method by which spirits become visible to mortal sight.

Physical Medium – One in whose presence physical matter is acted on by forces outside the known laws of motion.

Psychic – One sensitive to psychic influence. A medium must be a psychic, but a psychic may not be a medium. A somnambulist, a mesmeric or hypnotic subject is a psychic, the word covering the whole field of sensitiveness, while a medium is one who has that degree of sensitiveness which can be directed by spiritual beings.

Psychic Medium – One receiving communications through the mind or spiritual sensitiveness.

Second Sight – Clairvoyance.

Sensitive – One capable of receiving impressions.

Soul – The celestial or spiritual body or soul is composed of attenuated matter, not cognizable by any of the physical senses. It is organised, and has as real an existence amidst spiritual things as it had in mortal life.

Spirit – A discarnate entity; the immortal part of man. The conscious intelligence originated in and sustained by the physical body, from which it is separated by death, to go forward in perfect and complete continuity of existence.

Spiritualism – The belief in the continuity of life after death and its continuous progress and the application of this belief to the right conduct of living. Modern Spiritualism stands for the supremacy of the Law in the realm of spirit as in the physical. The departed are near and communicate with their earth friends, not by permission but by law. It is the Science of Life and a religion which would build up the moral character on the foundations of knowledge, and is satisfied with the attainment of perfect excellence. It is therefore superior to all others.

Spiritualist – One who is satisfied of the truth of Spiritualism.

Telekinesis – The supernormal movement of physical objects, not due to any known force.

Trance – A sleep resembling death, into which certain persons fall; the medium may not be conscious in this state. Their spiritual perception or sensitiveness is quickened and they perceive thereby. The trance thus defined is similar to clairvoyance. This state is often induced by the control of the body by a discarnate spirit.

Transfiguration – Transformed, as when the medium takes on the appearance of a communicating spirit; the expression of the spirit when it transcends the body, as in clairvoyance, and sometimes at the moment of death.

Trumpet – A cone of metal or other material for magnifying the Direct voice.

Visions – A term of wide meanings. In the sense derived from the Scriptures, a revelation of supernatural appearances.

Some Examples of Spiritual Gifts

Clairaudience – The Lord God hath opened my ear and I was not rebellious. (Isaiah I: 4-5.)
Samuel heard the 'voice' when in the Temple, and was told 'in his ear' that Saul would visit him. (1 Sam IX:15)

Clairvoyance – And the Lord opened the eyes of the young man, and he saw; and behold the mountain was full of horses and chariots as of fire round about Elisha (2 Kings VI: 17.)
Jacob's vision of angels ascending and descending: Hagar and Elisha's servant had their 'eyes opened' (became clairvoyant).

Materialisation – In the same hour came forth a man's hand and wrote, over against the candlestick, upon the plaster of the wall and the King saw the part of the hand that wrote (Dan. V: 5).
Jacob wrestled with a man until daybreak – and Jacob called the place Peniel, for I have seen God (a Spirit) face to face (Gen. XXXII: 24-30).
Moses and Elias appeared and talked with Jesus (Math. XVII: 3).

Direct Voice.—Moses heard God speaking to him from the midst of the burning bush.(Ex.III:4)
Peter heard the 'voice': "Arise, Peter, kill and eat." (Acts X:13)
Paul heard the 'voice': "I am Jesus whom thou persecutest." (Acts IX:5)

Direct writing – There came forth the fingers of a man's hand and the King saw the part of the hand that wrote "Mene, Mene, Tekel, Upharsin."
The commandments were written by Spirit power upon tablets of stone (Ex. XXXII: 15-16).

Levitation – Philip was 'caught away' by the spirit of the Lord and found at Azotus (app. 30 miles). (Acts VIII: 39.)
Ezekiel was 'lifted up and taken' into the East gate of the Lord's House.

Inspirational Speaking – Take no thought beforehand what ye shall speak, neither do ye premeditate, but whatsoever shall be given you in that hour speak ye, for it is not ye that speak (Mark XIII: 11).

Trance – I was in a deep sleep on my face towards the ground, but He (the man Gabriel) touched me and set me upright.
Peter went up upon the house top, and fell into a trance (Acts X)
And it came to pass when I (Paul) was come again to Jerusalem, even while I prayed in the temple I was in a trance. (Acts XX)